THE DAILY BOOK OF

classical
music

THIS BOOK BELONGS TO:

_____

_____

_____

Walter Foster Publishing, Inc.
3 Wrigley, Suite A
Irvine, CA 92618
USA
www.walterfoster.com

ISBN-13: 978-1-60058-201-1
ISBN-10: 1-60058-201-X

Authors: Leslie Chew, Dwight DeReiter, Cathy Doheny, Colin Gilbert,
Katherine Federici Greenwood, Travers Huff, Susanna Loewy, Melissa Maples,
Jeff McQuilkin, and Scott Spiegelberg
Project Manager and Editor: Erika Kotite
Associate Publisher: Elizabeth T. Gilbert
Designer: Shelley Baugh
Production Artist: Debbie Aiken
Production Manager: Nicole Szawlowski
International Purchasing Coordinator: Lawrence Marquez
Copyeditor: Angela Brevidoro

Printed in China.

10 9 8 7 6 5 4 3 2 1

THE DAILY BOOK OF

classical

music

LESLIE CHEW

DWIGHT DEREITER

CATHY DOHENY

COLIN GILBERT

KATHERINE FEDERICI GREENWOOD

TRAVERS HUFF

SUSANNA LOEWY

MELISSA MAPLES

JEFF MCQUILKIN

SCOTT SPIEGELBERG

Introduction

I once heard that classical music was better for the heart than rock 'n' roll. It didn't make sense at the time—isn't it better to get the blood pumping with rock's insistent 4/4 beat than with the same beat played in a relatively gentle way by an orchestra string section? The answer is both nuanced and logical, just like the timeless music itself.

For centuries, classical music has evolved and undergone many variations. From the parallel voices of plainchant in monasteries, to the dance music of the Renaissance, finally sweeping into courts and concert halls as the glorious Baroque, masters both known and anonymous fused notes, instruments, voices, and beats to create extraordinary aural art. Classical music takes cues from math, science, and the human heart itself, emitting sounds that stimulate, soothe, and make us yearn for more.

Writing a book about classical music—something you must hear to appreciate—involves a strategy. A strategy built on knowledgeable authors who are both objective and passionate about their subject; a strategy of engagement that finds ways to describe the wonders of classical music historically, compositionally, and theoretically; and a strategy of persuasion, of musical suggestions and "homework" that give you, the reader, a heightened store of knowledge and appreciation for what you hear.

Organized into 10 categories, from Music Theory to Famous Operas, this book will open your eyes and your mind to the elements that make classical…well, the music that makes your heart sing.

Erika Kotite, *Editor*

CLASSICAL MUSIC PERIODS

 I must admit that as I sat down to write about the time periods through classical music history, I felt very overwhelmed. I mean, we're talking about *thousands* of years—how was I to do justice to the amazing musical transformations from the Medieval period to now? As I started, I wasn't exactly sure it was possible.

But, as I divided our recorded musical history into subcategories, everything suddenly became more manageable; I would even venture to call it *simple*. Each compositional venture eased into the next in a logical progression. I honestly didn't know this clear structure truly existed. This project has actually taught me a great deal.

So my hope is that the same will happen for you; that the summaries of each period of classical music will help to clarify the mysticism and confusion so many people feel when the topic of classical music is broached. The unknown can be scary, but as you'll see, the evolution of classical music will teach us a lot about ourselves—about musicians and audience members, of course, but also about our culture, society, and global community. —Susanna Loewy (SL)

COMPOSITIONAL FORMS

In discussions of compositional form, a common mistake is to assume that the end goal is to identify the form of a piece. But that is only the beginning of understanding a piece of music.

Think of it as similar to watching a sporting event. When I watch a basketball game, I start with a knowledge of the rules, but that is not the goal. I want to see how the two teams interact *within* those rules, producing both expected and unexpected plays.

Likewise when I encounter a new piece of music. I often do identify the form of the piece first, but that is so I can appreciate how the composer created a new work of art within an established framework. Were any conventions broken or any new forms created? Was the melody magnified or restrained by the form? How does the piece compare to other pieces in the same form by the same composer, of the same orchestration, or from the same time period? These are the questions that help us gain a deeper understanding of music, but we must start by learning the rules of the game.

I hope you enjoy delving through many of the compositional forms used in classical music, and are inspired to start asking deeper questions about the music you hear. —Scott Spiegelberg (SS)

GREAT COMPOSERS

Where does great music come from?

The ability to compose soul-stirring music is much more than simply having the skills to create chord progressions and melodies. Great music, as with any other art form, comes from within the artist. All the amazing musical works that have been passed down to us over the centuries began as seeds within the souls of the ones who wrote them—seeds watered not just by the composers' natural abilities, but also by their backgrounds, their life experiences, their joys, and their tragedies.

In researching the lives of just a few of the world's greatest composers for this project, I was amazed at how much better I could connect with their music. As a composer myself, I found myself relating with many of their stories and struggles; I saw a bit of myself within them. The process of writing about these remarkable men and women has had a deep impact on me personally, no doubt shaping my own story and the music I have yet to create.

As you learn just a little bit about these great composers and their unique stories, it is my hope that you too will find a deeper understanding and appreciation of the music that emanated from them. May their stories shape our stories, even as their music has enriched our lives. —Jeff McQuilkin (JJM)

CELEBRATED WORKS

 Narrowing down the entire canon of Western classical music to 37 "greatest hits" is no easy task. First, there's the question of what qualifies as a "work" (is Vivaldi's *Four Seasons* a single work, or four, or twelve, or one-third of his Opus 8?). Then, there's the question of what criteria qualify a work for inclusion (is Schumann's *Träumerei* really more exceptional than Beethoven's "Eroica" Symphony?).

The solutions to these conundrums were found in a balancing act between the forces of popularity, interest, influence, and beauty. There is something here for everyone, whether you are exploring the world of classical music for the first time or just seeking new bits of trivia to supplement your preexisting knowledge.

Each reading in Celebrated Works is accompanied by a recommended recording for the curious listener. The recordings chosen are widely acclaimed for their exceptional sound quality, caliber of performance, and faithfulness to the composers' vision. They provide an ideal starting point for newcomers and a promising option for those looking to hear new interpretations of their favorite works. —Colin Gilbert (CKG)

FAMOUS OPERAS

 It is often said that you either love opera or you hate it. To those who fall in the latter category, I would ask, "Do you hate a good story? How about beautiful music? Do you loathe watching skilled dancers and hearing accomplished musicians? And what about viewing a finely constructed piece of art?"

Like it or not, opera is everywhere—from television commercials to movies to Bugs Bunny. Even those who are not yet opera fans may find themselves humming Rossini's famous "Largo al factotum" or belting out Bizet's "Toreador Song" in the privacy of their very own shower. So within the context of Famous Operas, the occasional hummer and shower vocal artist are invited to delve a bit further and explore the masterpieces from which these far-reaching melodies were born.

For readers who are already opera lovers, Famous Operas provides some interesting snippets of information that serve to further deepen one's appreciation. In addition, this section is a valuable reference guide for opera patrons who need a quick synopsis or background refresher before heading out to a performance. Most of all, however, Famous Operas seeks to simplify a complex art form, making it more accessible to a larger population. After all, the puzzle of opera is incomplete without its most important piece: its audience. —Cathy Doheny (CCD)

BASIC INSTRUMENTS

 Musical instruments have been part of civilization for as long as there has been…well, music. Time after time over the millennia, men and women have picked up something and banged it or plucked it or blown into it or rubbed it and said, "Hmm, that sounds cool. Hey, listen to this…"

Following the trail and analyzing where and how an instrument of a certain time period came about is not always an easy task, especially when the footprints have faded away. Sometimes instruments are invented by a single person, but mostly they evolve over a long span of time. They often evolve differently in different regions at different times, but eventually knowledge is shared and they culminate into a standard—then everyone agrees to disagree about it and sets out to make their own new and improved version.

Enough cannot be said, though, about the time and effort and commitment that one must muster to master one of these contraptions. The many instruments involved in creating classical music are not easy to play. And they were frequently in their developmental infancy when brilliant composers were creating masterpieces.

They say music tames the savage beast. Whether you're a music admirer, an amateur musician, or a virtuoso, I hope you find some points of interest on these pages that put you on your path to tame, enlighten, and even inspire your inner animal. —Leslie Chew (LMC)

MUSIC THEORY

If we really want to heighten the sensuous pleasure of an art form, if we really want to boost the joy that touches us by knowing what we're looking at or listening to, then understanding *how* the art works is the most important thing. In art theory, it's all about perspective, form, and color. In music theory, we focus on how methods, concepts, and principles shape the way classical music is organized. We are examining the science of musical composition.[1]

In Music Theory, readings are presented so that you can see and conceptualize what's happening in an art designed for the ears.

Remember, this is meant to be an introduction, but we hope it sharpens your appetite. You'll be surprised how much is going on. Read on, and enjoy! —Travers Huff (TH)

VENUES OF THE WORLD

Because of the relative infancy of recorded sound, the history of classical music is very closely interwoven with the places in which it was performed. Classical music venues have a peculiar capacity to accumulate legend—ask any stage manager in the world to recount a few tales of past performances, and you'll be overwhelmed with the volume and color of response. Over the centuries these stories tend toward embellishment, exaggeration, and downright fabrication, but underneath it all is always a glimmer of truth that suggests these auditoriums are nothing short of magical.

Classical music venues are lovingly maintained and restored, with meticulous respect for their role in the context of both historical and modern live performances. Why would so much attention and scrutiny be given to concert halls and opera houses over other types of theaters? Perhaps it's because classical music, more than other performing arts, owes so much of its beauty to subtlety and nuance. The effective delivery of that nuance relies heavily on an appropriate channel through which an artist and an audience can connect, hampered neither by distraction nor interference.

Anyone fortunate enough to visit one of these 36 highlighted venues during a performance season will surely feel the palpable excitement of waiting for the musicians to take their places, and the certainty that the night will be an experience like none other. For the younger generation, this is often the gateway into a lifelong appreciation for classical music. For the rest of us, it is a celebration of our cultural heritage and a joyful way to fulfill our duty in carrying on the legacy of these great venues. — Melissa Maples (MM)

MUSEUMS & FESTIVALS

 It's not enough to only read about musicians, scores, and great works. To fully appreciate music it needs to be experienced live. I introduce you to communities of artists and listeners that materialize each year to collaborate in musical celebration. Included are the major festivals in Europe and noted events in North America, many with rich histories and traditions.

You will get a sense of the inspiration for the gatherings—whether born out of the rubble of World War II or a renewed interest in early music—and of the atmosphere—whether concerts take place in remote grottos accessible only by boat, by candlelight under the stars, or in historic architectural treasures.

Dotting Europe, where the classical composers were born and created their masterpieces, are preserved homes of the masters that are now museums open to the public. By describing what visitors learn and see as they wander through the houses—instruments and furniture, original scores, and correspondence—I offer a glimpse into the composers' lives and times. Join us on an armchair tour of festivals and museums, and vow to someday visit the sites in person. —Kathy F. Greenwood (KFG)

POP CULTURE MEDLEY

 For many people, classical music and opera are areas in which they believe they have no interest. Many are intimidated, thinking that they are just for a higher social class. But sometimes it only takes hearing the right piece of music at the right time or being exposed to it in an unusual or unconventional way to finally open the door.

Our lives are flooded by popular culture: television shows, movies, music, celebrity gossip, news broadcasts, magazines, novels, and art, all created to appeal and ultimately sell to the largest number of people. So when an artist decides to use classical music or opera in his or her pop, film, or commercial work, the possibility of a connection being made to thousands of people at one time is great.

In the Pop Culture Medley category, I'll mention many uses of classical music (particularly audio recordings) in pop culture that have had profound effects on many lives. I'll explore the influence of classical music in this regard as well. Some of my favorite examples may be new discoveries for you. —Dwight DeReiter (DD)

Medieval Music (400–1400)

WHERE IT ALL BEGAN

Medieval music is music written in Europe in the Middle Ages—a time period that started with the fall of the Roman Empire and ended in the middle of the 15th century.

Because the creation of lasting manuscripts in the Middle Ages was quite an expensive endeavor (including the need for rare parchment and the use of scribes), there are very few surviving scores left from the Medieval time period, and the scores that do exist are from wealthy families and organizations—consequently not at all indicative of the common music of the day.

Medieval music, for example, can be classified into the sacred and the secular. However, since the majority of the studied scores are of the sacred variety, there isn't much solid, accurate information about secular music.

Another hindrance of musicologists' study of Medieval music is the rudimentary nature of the notation system of the times. Much of the music made was communicated through oral tradition, and when music was written, it certainly wasn't with our exacting musical language. Instead, vague approximations of harmonic lines were outlined, and rhythms were merely suggested.

Unlike the notation, though, the instruments of Medieval music were strikingly similar to our modern versions. Both string and wooden wind instruments were used; pictures even suggest a comparable bow usage.

Medieval music is quite beautiful; it may sound a bit repetitive at times, but if you allow the plainsong chanting to wash over you, listening to it can be a wonderfully meditative experience. —SL

LISTENING HOMEWORK

Hildegard von Bingen's Ordo Virtutum

Philippe de Vitry Motets

Guilliuame de Machaut Messe de Nostre Dame

Binary Form
WE KNOW WHAT WE WANT

Most musical forms result from two conflicting desires: the desire for something familiar, and the desire for something new. The binary form is the most basic example of this.

A simple binary form is in two parts—A and B—roughly equal in duration, and distinguished by different melodies. These parts are divided by clear cadences, and quite often each part is repeated, becoming a two-reprise form. Thus we end up with AABB, repeating A material to give us something familiar before moving to a new B section. The repetitions provide boundaries for the sections and give us the opportunity to hear and remember the melody.

Bach's famous *Air on the G String* demonstrates how the B melody of the Air can be related to the A melody, with some similar rhythms and contours, but it also creates the feeling of something new by starting on a lower pitch and using different chords.

We like familiar things so much that a common variant of the binary form is the rounded binary form: ABA. The music is still in two sections, but the second section finishes with a return to the starting A melody, usually shortened. With the typical repeats, this becomes AA BABA. The theme from the third movement of Mozart's Piano Sonata K. 284 shows how A can change when it returns. A modulates to a new key, but the return of A in the second section is altered to stay in the original key. —SS

Ludwig van Beethoven (1770–1827)

THE MUSIC INSIDE HIS HEAD

Ludwig van Beethoven's life and work straddled the classic and Romantic periods, and thus he is claimed by both. While many composers came from strongly musical families, Beethoven stood out from his kinfolk. There were musicians in his line—his father first taught him piano and violin—but none in his family before or since took any interest in composing.[1] Nevertheless, from an early age Ludwig showed such genius that he was fancied to be the "new Mozart."[2]

Taught by Haydn and Salieri in the classical style, Beethoven took a more emotional turn than his predecessors. Noticing (with panic) that his hearing was failing, Beethoven entered a period of fierce creativity, composing some of his most famous works. By 1818 he could no longer communicate except by writing; yet amazingly he continued to produce some of his most profound pieces while completely deaf—most notably his Symphony No. 9.

It is suggested that in his early years Beethoven wrote for his audience, but in his latter years—alone in his deafness—he apparently wrote for himself.[3] His last pieces were so advanced and progressive that audiences of his day could not comprehend them. When Beethoven's outer world fell silent, he could no longer draw influence from the music surrounding him. All that was left was the music inside his head.

—JJM

Symphony No. 5 in C minor

BY LUDWIG VAN BEETHOVEN, 1808

In the entire history of music on planet Earth, there might not be any composition more renowned than the tour de force that is Beethoven's Fifth Symphony. A commanding exhibition of power, majesty, accessibility, and sophistication, it towers as a testament to the magnificent possibilities of structured sound. Having said that, by no means is there universal consent that the work is even Beethoven's finest accomplishment, but such is the subjective nature of musical interpretation, and such is the genius of Beethoven.

Of course, the symphony's sinister *da-da-da-DUM* opening motif (which has been imaginatively compared to fate knocking on the door) has taken on a life of its own, but it functions as much more than a catchy hook. Not only in the frenzied first movement but throughout the entire symphony that authoritative rhythmic phrase makes a series of dramatic reappearances that serve to unify it. In the thrilling final movement, after 30 minutes of C minor turbulence, a long and satisfying sequence of C major chords brings a relieving sense of stability that the piece seems to frantically seek from the start. —CKG

RECOMMENDED RECORDING

Beethoven: Symphonies Nos. 5 & 7; Carlos Kleiber (conductor); Wiener Philharmoniker; Deutsche Grammophon; 1995

Dido and Aeneas

HENRY PURCELL (1659-1695)

"Remember me, but ah, forget my fate." This haunting line from Dido's lament, "When I Am Laid in Earth," exemplifies for many listeners the exquisite example of Baroque opera that is *Dido and Aeneas,* the tragedy in three acts by English composer Henry Purcell that premiered in 1689. Librettist Nahum Tate loosely based the story on Virgil's *Aeneid,* a love story involving Dido, Queen of Carthage, and Aeneas, who is shipwrecked at Carthage. When witches remind Aeneas that he is destined to found Rome, he leaves Dido, and the heartbroken Dido kills herself.

"With drooping wings ye cupids come and scatter roses on her tomb. Keep here your watch, and never part." These words from the imploring chorus, set to descending minor scales typical of the Baroque era, bring the opera to a close.

With a duration of approximately one hour and a cast of only four primary singers, several minor roles, a soprano/alto/tenor/bass (SATB) chorus and a few dancers, this opera is often performed by college music departments or smaller regional opera companies.

Dido and Aeneas offers audiences a moving drama accompanied by a score of musical innovations. These include Purcell's use in three arias of *ground bass,* a musical technique in which the bass line repeats throughout the composition. Purcell adds interest to this technique by having the vocal line overlap and harmonize with the bass line. To complement Tate's poetic libretto throughout the opera, Purcell uses word painting, a device that relies on *melisma,* a technique in which one syllable is stretched over many different notes to more fully express the meaning of words. —CCD

The Orchestra

MAKING BEAUTIFUL MUSIC TOGETHER

Little compares to the majestic sound of a 120-piece symphonic orchestra. Under the guidance of a great composer, the orchestra is an instrument that can tell a wonderful tale and take the listener on an incredible journey. Using lush strings and dancing woodwinds contrasted with powerful brass and percussion, the range of expression appears boundless.

Spawning from 17th-century Baroque violin bands, the evolution of the orchestra is tied to many composers over the eras. Jean-Baptiste Lully and Arcangelo Corelli were paramount in organizing larger assemblages and bringing the element of discipline that led to the creation of the orchestral ensemble.

"Muvesz" Symphonic Orchestra performs at MUPA in Budapest, Hungary.

The classical orchestra established itself largely on the works of Haydn, Mozart, and Beethoven. Consisting fundamentally of violins, violas, cellos, and double basses along with pairs of oboes, horns, and bassoons, this small, agile orchestra also accompanied most Italian opera.

The romantic era witnessed the orchestra's increase in popularity and size as Beethoven and Wagner strengthened their brass sections and a baton conductor became common.

At the turn of the 20th century, composers Strauss, Mahler, Elgar, and Ravel helped form the modern orchestra with bigger brass sections and quadruple woodwinds, while the advent of motion pictures helped to create the film orchestra most familiar to listeners today.

The symphonic orchestra is a living, breathing acoustic wonder, rich in complex overtones that can only be fully realized while sharing the air with it.
—LMC

Music Theory

FULL OF SOUND AND THEORY

Music is arguably the most emotionally moving of all the arts. But the theory and analysis of its structure is surprisingly mathematical, rational, and logical, both with regard to the mathematics and physics of sound, or acoustics, and with regard to the architecture of music itself, which is just one part of the world of sound. Thus a full appreciation of music demands the engagement of both the cognitive and affective parts of the mind.

Music theory shows you the structure of music—how it is built. Music theory trains the parts of the mind that process music to become closer in sophisticated discernment to those parts that process the visual arts. It's a way to raise awareness of music. Most people today miss out on the details of the music they're hearing because they have no knowledge of what's going on. And with classical music it's especially necessary to know what's happening so you can relax and enjoy it.

We will use many musical examples in Western music notation. In a music theory class, you use these examples as ear training to hear what the examples mean in terms of sound. The instructor would play them for you. Since you are reading a book, your best bet for learning music theory is to refer to the piano and music staff keyboard chart, find middle C, and orient yourself and your ears to the pitches of the notes from there. —TH

Arena di Verona

THE GODFATHER OF AMPHITHEATERS

Some classical music venues are prized for their superior acoustics, and others for their history. The Arena di Verona is exceptional in that it has copious amounts of both. A Roman structure dating from AD 30, the Arena was first used in typical Roman fashion as a venue for athletic tournaments, bazaar-style markets, and even gladiator contests. In those days, the amphitheater had a seating capacity of more than 30,000, about twice what it seats today.

In 1117, an earthquake destroyed a large part of the theater, and for several centuries there were no significant attempts to reclaim the building for performances. It was only in the mid-19th century that the Veronese people began to show an interest in using the arena again—this time for opera.

The annual summer opera season started in earnest in 1913, and today is one of the most well-attended opera festivals in the world. Despite the enormity of the seating area and the intentional lack of artificial sound amplification, even patrons at the very back of the arena can hear the singers clearly (though seeing them is sometimes a challenge). Through the wonders of the theater's perfect natural acoustics, visitors have been treated to the talents of such major singers as Maria Callas, Giuseppe Di Stefano, and Renata Tebaldi. These days the Arena di Verona hosts four productions each summer, all with world-class performers, and tickets for performances often sell out many months in advance. —MM

Mozarthaus Vienna

AT HOME WITH MOZART

Mozart moved around a lot. The longest he lived in any one place in Vienna was two and a half years from 1784 to 1787. Today that flat, located at Domgasse 5, the only apartment of his that has survived, is a museum called Mozarthaus Vienna. The spacious home where he created some of his best-known compositions, including the popular opera *The Marriage of Figaro,* has been open to the public in various arrangements for more than 60 years, but reopened in its current state after a significant refurbishment in 2006.

Visitors step into his world and get a sense of the man, his musical oeuvre, and the Vienna of Mozart's time—the late Baroque era—when he was a celebrated composer at a high point of his creativity.

Exterior view of Mozarthaus Vienna.
© Mozarthaus Vienna/David Peters.

On the third floor, museumgoers learn about Mozart's relationship to the Freemasons and his passion for gambling, fashion, and women. One installation provides a bird's-eye view of Mozart's Vienna—a magnifying glass moves over a map of the city, stopping in places where he lived. On the second floor there's a multimedia installation of *The Magic Flute* consisting of an abridged version of the opera and a four-minute potpourri of its most famous arias. The first floor—his flat, designed by the Wien Museum—is focused on the time that Mozart lived there.

The composer flourished in Vienna, reflected in the famous quotation: "I assure you that this is a magnificent place—and the best place in the world for my profession."[1] —KFG

Beethoven and *Rosemary's Baby*

THE DEVIL'S IN THE DAKOTA

Who would have guessed that one of Beethoven's most well-known piano pieces can be heard in a film about the birth of Satan's child? "Für Elise," a short and light piano composition written in 1810 for a woman the composer loved, is heard wafting through the walls of New York City's Dakota apartment building in Roman Polanski's 1968 horror masterpiece, *Rosemary's Baby.*

Newlyweds Rosemary and Guy Woodhouse decide that they need a bigger living space because they want to have a baby. They take an apartment at the Dakota, Manhattan's oldest, and decidedly gothic, apartment building. This unfortunate decision leads to the ultimate horror as their new neighbors reveal themselves to be worshippers and disciples of the devil.

While the couple is being shown the apartment, after they have moved in, and during the various stages of Rosemary's pregnancy and their strange new social life, we hear a neighbor practicing scales and playing Beethoven's "Für Elise" on a piano. The piece no longer sounds like a beautiful tribute; instead the famous melody sounds eerie and foreboding. It's an unexpected and brilliant use of the music. —DD

FUN FACT

"Für Elise" can be heard in many feature films, including Fearless, Patch Adams, *and* Immortal Beloved. *Perhaps most will remember the cartoon character Schroeder in Charles Schultz's wonderful series,* Charlie Brown and the Peanuts Gang, *playing the piece on his small toy piano.*

Early Medieval (BEFORE 1150)

MORE THAN MEETS THE EAR

Regardless of their religious beliefs or denomination, most people will agree that the music in church/synagogue services is gorgeous.

You might be surprised to know that liturgical chanting didn't originate within the confines of religion. Early Medieval music is considered the first traceable influence on the Judeo/Christian musical tradition.

As if that weren't enough, Early Medieval musical time period influenced more than sacred music. The development of organum (two voices singing different notes) marked the beginnings of our modern system of harmony and counterpoint.

And if you need any more proof of the importance of Early Medieval music, here's a giant piece: *Opera* also originated around this time! Called "liturgical dramas," these traveling productions included acting, instrumental music, speaking, and singing. Seems pretty much like our modern-day opera, right?

The last important influence of this time period was the introduction of *Goliards*. Goliards were scholars that wrote Latin poetry (mostly of the secular variety) and set the poems to music. Most of these settings have been lost, but the poetry survives, and it has been the basis of many future musical offerings.

Although Early Medieval music tends to sound completely prehistoric and overly simplistic, you'd be very well served to instead think of it as the drawing board for the entirety of our Western musical tradition. —SL

LISTENING HOMEWORK

Hildegard von Bingen's Symphonia armoniae celestium revelationum
Perotin's iderunt omnes
Leotin's Magnus Liber

Ternary

TO RETURN, ONE MUST FIRST LEAVE

Hearing the return to a familiar theme is a very satisfying experience, but hearing the constant repetition of a theme can be quite boring, especially when there are no lyrics. The simplest way to return to a familiar theme is to divide the music into three parts: ABA. The B section is a new theme, which is followed by a return to the first theme.

We have seen this pattern before in the rounded binary form (see page 9). What distinguishes the ternary form is the independence of the three sections. The B section is usually in a new key, and often has a different feel due to a change in loudness, texture, or tempo.

Norwegian composer Edvard Grieg wrote a beautiful collection of piano works called *Lyric Pieces*, including "Hjemve" ("Homesickness"). This piece starts with a haunting melody in E minor. After a sustained cadence, the mode shifts suddenly to E major, with a fast and lively melody that reminds us of the happy times we had at home. This is the B section, which is independent because of its new theme, new mode, longer duration, and clear cadence in its tonic key at the end. Alas, we are still homesick, so the haunting theme returns as the second A. This second A is identical to the opening, but it feels different thanks to the contrast with B. —SS

Johannes Brahms (1833–1897)

LOOKING BOTH WAYS

Johannes Brahms, one of the great composers of the Romantic period, often looked more to the past than the future for his inspiration, living in an ironic tension between innovation and tradition. Eschewing the unbridled emotionalism and lack of structure of many of his contemporaries, Brahms's style might best be described as "controlled Romanticism," infusing rich textures into the more standard classical forms.

Methodical and deliberate by nature, as a child Brahms reportedly invented his own form of music notation so he could write down the melodies in his head.[1] As a composer, he chose to write small-scale chamber works and songs until he felt ready to attempt larger compositions. He did not write a full symphony until his early 40s,[2] by which time his reputation was already well established.

As a young adult, Brahms met the Schumanns, Robert and Clara, with whom he maintained a lifelong connection. Kindred spirits, the Schumanns and Brahms were critical of the unstructured styles of Wagner, Liszt, and others in their vein of composition. Brahms was likely also in love with Clara Schumann, though even after Robert's death the two maintained only a deep friendship.

Something in Brahms's solid, conservative style resonated with the public, for his works became increasingly popular. His choral piece *German Requiem* is considered one of the most significant works of his time, and a testament to Brahms's own faith. He is remembered today as one of the "three Bs" of classical music: Bach, Beethoven, and Brahms. —JJM

Eine Kleine Nachtmusik

BY WOLFGANG AMADEUS MOZART, 1787

Like the *da-da-da-DUM* that kicks off Beethoven's Fifth Symphony, the first few bars of Mozart's Serenade No. 13 in G major are instantly recognizable, even to the person with little or no interest in classical music. The serenade's familiar title, *Eine Kleine Nachtmusik,* aptly describes the work, literally defining it as "a little night music." Classy and light, the piece is perfectly suited for an elegant cocktail party under the stars.

The serenade was composed while Mozart was simultaneously working on the opera *Don Giovanni.* It's divided into four movements—sonata, romanza, menuetto, and rondo—although Mozart's records mention another menuetto that may have been lost. The opening movement contains the work's most famous motif, which is developed and recapitulated in classic sonata form. That is not to say that the remaining movements are in any way inferior; as a whole, the composition is concise, cohesive, and irresistibly tuneful.

Analogous to the Top 40 hits blasted in clubs and cars today, *Eine Kleine Nachtmusik* would have been considered party music in Mozart's time. He wrote pieces like this not to challenge or impress but simply to entertain. Nevertheless, it showcases the composer's unrivaled melodic sense and mastery of form. —CKG

RECOMMENDED RECORDING

Mozart: **The Great Serenades;** *Neville Marriner; Academy of St. Martin-in-the-Fields; Philips; 2000*

Le nozze di Figaro (The Marriage of Figaro)

WOLFGANG AMADEUS MOZART (1756–1791)

From the pubescent Cherubino's endearing search for the meaning of love in his Act Two arias, "Voi che sapete" ("You who know"), to the forlorn Countess's aria of Act Three, "Dove sono i bei momenti ("Where are the beautiful moments?"), *Le nozze di Figaro (The Marriage of Figaro)* satisfies an opera lover's every craving in only four acts. Written by Wolfgang Amadeus Mozart, this opera buffa, or comic opera, premiered in 1786 in Vienna and is considered by many to be Mozart's most ingenious opera.

Ailyn Perez as Countess Almaviva.
Photo courtesy Opera Carolina
(Charlotte, North Carolina),
www.operacarolina.org.

Librettist Lorenzo da Ponte based the story on Pierre Beaumarchais's controversial 1784 play by the same name, which was censored for many years due to its satire of aristocracy. *The Marriage of Figaro* is a continuation of Beaumarchais's *The Barber of Seville,* later the basis for an opera by Gioachino Rossini.

The storyline involves the complicated and often comic interactions between the Count and Countess Almaviva and Figaro; the count's valet; the valet's fiancée, Susanna; the countess's chambermaid; and Cherubino, a lovesick teenage boy infatuated with the countess. Comic misunderstandings, along with the deeper universal issues of infidelity and the challenge of maintaining a marriage, are highlighted by the Count's pursuit of Susanna, Cherubino's awkward lust for the countess, and the countess's realization that her marriage may be ending.

Usually performed in its original language of Italian, *Le nozze di Figaro* is loved for its many popular melodies and is one of the most performed operas in North America today. —CCD

The String Section

LOTS OF STRINGS ATTACHED

Joy, sadness, foreboding, and elation are just a few of the feelings conveyed by this multiplayer instrument. In an intimate setting, a string quartet of two violins, a viola, and a cello creates a light sound, spotlighting delicate four-part discourse, whereas a string orchestra (typically featuring 12 to 21 players) can fill a larger hall with a grand sound.

The largest incarnation, usually comprised of 60 players in five separate sub-sections, is the string section of the symphony orchestra. The most common configuration is 16 first violins, 14 second violins, 12 violas, 10 cellos and 8 double basses arranged in a semicircle, with the first violins to the conductor's left, the second violins to the left center, the violas to the right center, and the cellos and basses to the right. It was common in the 19th century for compos-ers to have the second violins trade places with the cellos and basses, putting the violin sections on opposite sides. Tchaikovsky beautifully exemplifies this in his Symphony No. 6 by alternating notes in the melody between the first and second violins.

Whether you listen to works written by Haydn for the string quartet, one of Mendelssohn's spirited string symphonies, a boastful Beethoven symphony, or watch a scary movie, it's clear to see how the range of expression and ability of this assemblage to influence the emotional state of a listener has made the string section paramount for so many composers. —LMC

Ear Training and Sound Recognition

SOUNDS LIKE...

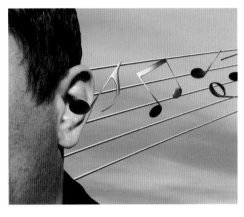

You easily recognize many sounds by their timbre, or tone color: a police siren, a ringing phone, a human voice, etc.

If you want to stop looking at something, you do just that. But if you want to stop *hearing* something, it's a little tougher. You have to use earplugs, go in the next room, or just try to mentally "tune it out."

In fact, in our noisy contemporary world, we're better at "tuning out" than "tuning in." Why? It's because sound is transitory. It's often just easier to let it go than to hang on to it, unless you know it specifically pertains to you. And you're always subject to "noise pollution." Noise is chaotic, disorganized sound.

Unless a specific sound "pokes its head up" above the surface of the disorganized, ambient, encircling noise, like a prairie dog above the ground, the chances are good that you won't consciously hear it. Unless...unless....

Unless it's organized in a certain way! That's what lets you hear it above the noise. And that's what can make music beautiful.

Most people don't have trained ears, except for tuning out extraneous sounds. Instead, we have trained eyes that can easily ascertain the shape, color, dimension, and distance of what we see. To understand musical form, you need to train your ears as well as your eyes. In fact, in music courses, ear training— training your ear to recognize chords, pitches, rhythms, modulations, etc.—is part of music theory. —TH

Carnegie Hall

NEW YORK'S FINEST

In the late 19th century, at a time when America was starting to define its cultural identity, American symphonic music struggled to find a place to call home. A chance friendship was about to change all that: Walter Damrosch, a young American conductor on a mission to build a symphonic concert hall in New York, befriended steel tycoon Andrew Carnegie during a sea voyage to Scotland. The two hit it off, and by the end of the summer Damrosch had convinced Carnegie to fund the venture. In 1890 the first stone was laid, and just over a year later Carnegie Hall opened to the public with a concert featuring Tchaikovsky himself as conductor. The ticket price for opening night? One dollar.

Carnegie Hall soon became much more than just a venue for symphonic music. The building's multiple performance areas and superior acoustics attracted not only the finest soloists and ensembles in the classical arena, but also world-class musicians in every genre. Despite its artistic significance, however, Carnegie Hall suffered financially for many years, and it was scheduled to be demolished in 1960.

Fortunately, an effort headed by Isaac Stern to save Carnegie Hall ultimately resulted in the city of New York purchasing the building. In the decades that followed, not only was Carnegie Hall restored to its former glory both structurally and artistically, but its name has since become synonymous with the mastery of music.

So how do you get to Carnegie Hall? Everyone knows the answer to that: practice! —MM

The International Chopin Festival

EUROPE'S OLDEST PIANO FESTIVAL

In the summer of 1826 a teenage Frédéric Chopin, who would become Poland's greatest pianist and composer, traveled from Warsaw to the springs in Duszniki Zdrój in search of the supposedly healing "Silesian waters" in the town's spa. Suffering from what is believed to have been an ailment affecting his upper respiratory system, he drank water from the spring and took walks into the mountains around the spa.[1]

During his stay, Chopin gave charity concerts for several local orphans whose father had died in an accident at the Mendelssohns' iron foundry.

To honor Chopin's stay and his concerts in Duszniki Zdrój, the International Chopin Festival was founded in August 1946, marking the 120th anniversary of his visit. During the nine-day event, concerts and recitals feature the world's best pianists and winners of Chopin contests; among those who have performed are Edward Auer, Fu Tsong, and Piotr Paleczny (also the festival's artistic director).[2]

Musicians perform in Chopin's manor, located within the beautiful Spa Park and close to the Stolowe Mountains National Park that surrounds the town. —KFG

Claire Huangci performs at the International Chopin Festival in Chopin's manor.
Photo by Marek Grotowski © 2009.

Khachaturian's Adagio in
2001: A Space Odyssey

THE COLD, LONELY, INFINITE EXPANSE OF SPACE

As a preteen back in 1969, I went to see Stanley Kubrick and Arthur C. Clarke's film *2001: A Space Odyssey.* I was transfixed, transported to another place and wondering about a hundred things I had never thought of before. Even though I wanted to really know about and understand everything I was seeing, I didn't. Much of the film and story's meaning went over my head. However, I had a most amazing experience understanding it all in other ways.

Kubrick decided to use classical music as the film's score. Beautiful and dramatic standard repertoire combined with complicated modern music created by some of the great classical composers drove the film to the extreme. From the glorious *Blue Danube* by Johann Strauss II to the very exotic and strange modern sound designs by composer Gyorgy Ligeti, I was connected to the film in a completely emotional way. Kubrick's use of Richard Strauss's *Also sprach Zarathustra* has become legendary. Many believe the work was written specifically for the film.

The most profound and emotional moment of the film is when we see spaceship *Discovery One* heading out into space on its Jupiter Mission. Kubrick gently and perfectly places a wonderful recording of Aram Khachaturian's Adagio (from his larger work *The Gayne Ballet,* performed by Gennadi Rozhdestvensky conducting the Leningrad Philharmonic Orchestra) over the amazing footage.

This marriage of visual art and classical music makes you understand and feel what the cold, lonely, infinite expanse of space must be like. —DD

High Medieval (1150–1300)

POETRY IN MOTION

We recently discussed the goliards of the Early Medieval time period. Just to review: The goliards were scholars who wrote secular Latin poems and chants. We don't have much left in terms of surviving scores, but we do have their poetry, and this poetry later became the basis of a great deal of music.

If you ever had any reason to doubt this, here's proof. In the years following the Early Medieval period, called the High Medieval time period, the most important musical development was the emergence of troubadours and trouveres.

These two groups were very similar to the goliards. Both created popular and secular songs and poems—they were professional musicians and poets and were, more often than not, accompanied by instrumental musicians. They sang about love, war, and chivalry. Each group used differing ancient forms of the French language and traveled to Portugal, Spain, northern Italy, and northern France, creating a path of significant musical influence wherever they went.

Never to be outdone by their Western counterparts, the Germanic tradition also had its own version of the goliards. Known as the "minnesingers," they also mainly developed in the late High Medieval period. Though there isn't much accurate information available about them, their importance in regard to both musical past and future is clear.

The High Medieval time period created music of development—concepts that began in the Early Medieval era were developed and brought into the musical mainstream as part of a worldwide expansion of Western music. —SL

LISTENING HOMEWORK

Music by: **Denis of Portugal**

Raimon Jordan

Guilhen Magret

Wolfran von Eschenbach

Inner Forms 1: Motive

WOULD YOU REPEAT THAT?

While most compositional forms regard the entire piece or movement, there are forms that exist within a larger framework. These inner forms guide our ears through long pieces, just as paragraphs and chapters guide us through a novel.

The most basic structural idea, our musical atom, is the *motive*. The motive can be of any length, but is usually 2–5 note lengths. The key is that this musical idea is repeated, either exactly or modified in some way, later in the piece.

The opening of Beethoven's Fifth Symphony is an excellent example. That combination of three repeated eighth notes followed by a longer note a third below, often called the "fate motive" is repeated at a variety of different transpositions (shifting all the pitches equally).

The key identifying features of the motive (also spelled motif) can be melodic, harmonic, or rhythmic. The motive in Beethoven's Fifth Symphony starts out as a melodic motive, but right before the first big pause, Beethoven repeats the rhythms of the motive while changing the melodic idea. This provides more variety while still maintaining that sense of familiarity. —SS

> ### Fun Fact
>
> *Motives can be associated with extra-musical ideas, such as a person, a place, or a plot point. Richard Wagner used these associated motives, called* Leitmotifs, *to highlight dramatic elements of his operas. Bach would encode his own name as a motive: B (Bb in German)–A–C–H (B natural in German), as did many other composers.*

Felix Mendelssohn-Bartholdy (1809–1847)

A SHORT, BRIGHT LIGHT

Refined, structured, reminiscent of the classical and Baroque periods, the music of Felix Mendelssohn stands in contrast to the unfettered Romanticism of his day. While his contemporaries wrote music devoid of rules and lived lives of excess, Mendelssohn emulated Bach, practiced restraint, and loved one woman passionately.

Mendelssohn grew up in an educated, Jewish-turned-Christian family (hence the surname Bartholdy). A child prodigy, he began composing prolifically from the age of 11. He was influenced by Bach and Mozart, the writings of Shakespeare (from which came *A Midsummer Night's Dream*), and the poetry of Goethe. His Octet for Strings in E flat major, Op. 20 was the first piece of its kind, interweaving two string quartets together—written when he was 16.[1] He went on to write symphonies, operas, and many other vocal and instrumental works. In 1829, in a personal high point, Mendelssohn conducted Bach's *St. Matthew's Passion,* its first public performance in 100 years.

Mendelssohn's life was tragically cut short when he died of a stroke at age 38 after losing his parents and sister. Even so, Mendelssohn's short, bright light illuminated the music world for many generations since. —JJM

FUN FACT

Felix Mendelssohn was not the only prodigy in the family. His older sister Fanny was an equally gifted composer and performer; however, it was not considered appropriate at that time for a woman to have a public career.[2] Mendelssohn remained very close to his sister until her death.

Air on the G String

BY JOHANN SEBASTIAN BACH, CA. 1720

Some things just never get old, no matter how familiar they become. Like the sweet smell of a rose or the cozy warmth of a fire on a winter's day, the gentle elegance of Bach's *Air on the G String* (1717–1723) is always a welcome treat. With stately Baroque charm, the ubiquitous Air manages in five short minutes to calm nerves and promote reflection. Don't be deceived into thinking that the work is unsophisticated, though. Bach is unsurpassed in his ability to weave complex melodies together into a harmonious whole that flows as effortlessly as breathing.

The work was conceived as the second movement from Bach's Orchestral Suite No. 3 in D, where it is simply called "air." It didn't come to be known as *Air on the G String* until the late 19th century when the great German violinist August Wilhelmj arranged it for piano and violin. Wilhelmj adjusted the piece's key in such a way that the entire melody could be played on the one violin string tuned to G.[1] Regardless of how it's played, however, the winsome humility of this composition continues to elicit universal affection. —CKG

RECOMMENDED RECORDING

J. S. Bach: The Complete Orchestral Suites; *Boston Baroque;*
Martin Pearlman; Telarc; 2004

Don Giovanni

WOLFGANG AMADEUS MOZART (1756-1791)

"Là ci darem la mano, là mi dirai di sì." ("There we will join hands; there you will say "yes" to me.") Don Giovanni sings these seductive words in an Act One duet as he attempts to lure the peasant Zerlina away from her wedding to Masetto. The young Zerlina is just about to succumb to his advances when Donna Elvira, one of Giovanni's many former conquests, appears to warn her of his true nature.

This famous scene from Wolfgang Amadeus Mozart's *Don Giovanni,* an opera in two acts, could have been written for the latest hit television show. Yet the clever nature of the Italian libretto, written by Lorenzo Da Ponte, coupled with the brilliance of Mozart's musical score elevate this common dramatic scenario above a passing source of entertainment to a timeless and essential work of art.

Better known by the name Don Juan, the title character is the stereotypical womanizer, making sport of one broken heart after another until he is confronted by the ghost of a man he killed, the Commendatore. As the father of Donna Anna, one of Giovanni's victims, the Commendatore, now in the eerie form of a statue, offers the villain one final opportunity

Kristopher Irmiter as Don Giovanni and Myron Myers as Commendatore. Photo courtesy Opera Carolina (Charlotte, North Carolina, www.operacarolina.org).

to repent for his sins. When Giovanni refuses to change, the statue sinks into the earth, dragging Giovanni into the depths of hell.

"Questo è il fin," sings the final chorus. "Such is the end of the evildoer: The death of a sinner always reflects his life." —CCD

The Violin

A 450-YEAR-OLD LOVE AFFAIR

This small wooden instrument with four strings, tuned in fifths, and played with a bow has become the quintessential classical music instrument. Composers often assign the melody of their pieces to violins, as their ability to evoke a wide range of emotions is unsurpassed.

The mysterious origin of the violin may be traced back to Asia and its plucked ancestors, while the bow and its accompaniment spread across the world through Nordic tribes. The European roots of this fine apparatus run back to the 9th century with design development reaching a peak in Italy in the mid- to late-1500s. Another 100 years of fine-tuning brought us the instrument we now know and love, and by the early 1700s Antonio Stradivari and Guarneri del Gesù had created masterpieces that are still sought after today.

During the late 18th century, accomplished violinists like Vivaldi, Corelli, Locatelli, and Paganini were creating their own compositions. Giuseppe Tartini wrote nearly 150 concertos and 100 sonatas for the violin. His most famous, "The Devil's Trill," is believed to be one of the most difficult pieces ever written for the instrument.

The violin has found its way into our hearts. Whether you're watching your favorite romantic movie, listening to Vivaldi's *Four Seasons,* or learning Bach's Double Violin Concerto in D minor, you're sure to be moved by the sound of this masterpiece. —LMC

What Is Musical Form?

TIME AND PATTERN ARE ESSENTIAL

How can music have a form? We can't see it. But musical sound *does* have a form. If it didn't, it wouldn't be music.

Its form is based on the rhythmic principle of repetition in time. Without the element of time, music as we know it could not exist. The pleasure we take from life is determined by how we spend the repeated patterns of time, the cycles of day and night. And in the same way, much of the enjoyment we get when we listen to music is from the repeated patterns of the tunes, melodies, rhythms, and pure sounds in time that we hear, again and again.

Music, like movies or the theatre, is a performance art that utilizes the human concept of time. In fact, music depends on time for its expression, so it has to be considered in a different mindset than the visual arts, such as sculpture and still pictures. In the visual arts, you can choose to look at a painting for as long as you wish. When you leave the painting or statue and come back, it will look the same. In contrast, for maximum enjoyment and participation in the musical experience, you let yourself move along in time with the music or the movie as you follow it with your mind. You have to be willing to let the music itself move along. —TH

> *Something to think about: Music moves. When you stop listening to music and walk away, it's guaranteed that you'll be hearing a different part of it when you come back.*

Royal Albert Hall

BRILLIANT SET OF PIPES

It's a quirky building for sure, but the distinctive dome of the Royal Albert Hall in London is known and loved by classical music fans around the globe. Since 1871, the venue dedicated as a memorial to Queen Victoria's husband has entertained audiences with performances rich in the classical repertoire, as well as rock concerts and charity events. The highlight of Royal Albert Hall's performance calendar, however, is the Proms festival, the largest annual classical music festival in the world.

The crowning jewel of the Royal Albert Hall is its pipe organ. The aptly named "Grand Organ" boasts nearly 10,000 pipes, and was the largest pipe organ in the world when it was completed in 1871. It has a history as rich as the Royal Albert Hall itself, and continual restoration projects have kept this magnificent instrument going for well over a century.

Though the Royal Albert Hall has always been popular with musicians and audiences, its acoustics have often left something to be desired in the eyes of its critics. The highly recognizable elliptical shape is unfortunately also responsible for a distracting echo inside the performance space. Sir Thomas Beecham, the orchestral conductor known for his sense of humor, half-joked that the Royal Albert Hall was "the only place a modern composer could hear his music twice." The addition of acoustic diffusers has enhanced the sound quality to a great degree, and these days the Royal Albert Hall is one of the finest-sounding venues in Europe. —MM

Get in Line...Early

BAYREUTH FESTIVAL AND RICHARD WAGNER MUSEUM

It's tough to score a ticket to the annual monthlong Bayreuth Festival, the brainchild of composer Richard Wagner. The event started in 1876 with the premiere of his four-opera cycle, *Ring des Nibelungen,* in the opera house he designed. Some opera-lovers linger several years on a wait list.

Wagner came to the small Bavarian city of Bayreuth, Germany, in 1872 to fulfill a lifelong dream: to build a new kind of opera house away from the cities that would serve as a home for his works. Located up a hill north of the town center in a bucolic setting, Festspielhaus is devoted exclusively to staging Wagner's operas. A fan of Wagner, Hitler came to Bayreuth so often in the 1920s and '30s that the festival became associated with the Nazi regime, and it was discontinued for several years after the end of the war.

Even if you can't secure a festival ticket, you can get a Wagner fix at Wahnfried, the villa where he lived from 1874 until his death in 1883. The house remained in his family until 1966 and was turned into a museum in 1976. Due to bombing during World War II, only the front of the house is original.

The museum's collection, which the *Times* called "wonderfully eccentric," includes thousands of handwritten documents and original letters, autographed scores, pianos, a death mask, and the couch he died on in Venice. Outside in the garden is Wagner's grave, wrote the *Times,* "under an unmarked stone slab next to the marked tombstone of his dog, Russ."[1] —KFG

Beethoven's "Ode to Joy" in *Help*

TIGERS HAVE TASTE

In the dreamlike storyline of the movie *Help,* Raja the man-eating Bengal tiger is taken from the London Zoo and led to the basement of a local pub where the Beatles are enjoying an afternoon pint. Clang, the leader of an obscure Asian religious cult, thought that this plan would finally remove Ringo from this life after many previous failed attempts. Little did he know that Raja was a gift to the London Zoo from the Berlin Zoo and was raised on the classics.

An inspector from Scotland Yard on the scene tells Ringo and everyone else in the pub that Raja's favorite piece of music is "Ode To Joy" from Beethoven's Ninth Symphony. When everyone starts to sing, the big cat becomes happy and docile, and Ringo is saved. The power of the music tames the wild animal.

Though the story is a bit trite and fluffy, the film itself was an important vehicle for the Beatles' music. It also turned out to be a key forerunner to the music videos that singers, rock bands, and other recording artists would produce with lavish budgets in the 1980s and '90s. Beethoven's big choral and orchestral song does nothing to help improve the humor, drama, or tension in the story, but it does add a great deal to the overall celebratory spirit of the film. —DD

Late Medieval (1300–1400)

WHEN POETRY AND MUSIC CAME TOGETHER

So much of the time, music periods are loosely defined subdivisions figured out by a music historian hundreds of years later. With the Late Medieval period, though, the division is a firm line drawn by the publication of the *Roman de Fauvel* in 1310, a compilation of important musical and literature works to date.

With this publication came a new era, the Late Medieval period, or the time of *Ars Nova*. Ars Nova literally translates to "new art" or "new technique," and appropriately refers to an era of new beginnings.

The dominant musical form of Ars Nova was the *chanson*. Chansons were composed in a group of predetermined forms according to the poetry to which they were set, and were entitled rondeau, ballade, and virelai. It should definitely be said that these chanson sets were precursors to our beloved Bach cello suites and violin partitas.

Once again, the Ars Nova movement was based in France, but of course there were other musical genres around the West. In Italy the corresponding movement was called the Trecento, while in Germany it was Gesslerlieder; there were small differences between the movements (including the preferred intervals and harmonies), but all in all, the idea of a new beginning, along with a new way of approaching music, prevailed through all Europe. —SL

LISTENING HOMEWORK

Check out the Roman de Fauvel—*along with the collection of music and poetry, it even includes some ancient religious and political anecdotes!*

Minuet and Trio

ONE, TWO, THREE, ONE, TWO, THREE...

The minuet epitomizes the elegant ballroom dance, with men in tails and women in silk gowns stepping to a triple meter. This dance originated in the French town of Poitou in the 1650s, and it was quickly included in Baroque dance suites. Starting in 1700, minuets were paired together. The first minuet was followed by the second minuet, and then the first minuet returned. If you think this looks suspiciously like a ternary form—ABA—you are correct.

Poitou-Charentes on an old map of France, where the minuet originated.

The second minuet became known as the trio, usually written in a contrasting key or texture. Both the minuet and trio are in binary form, often rounded binary. This is called a "compound ternary form," where each of the three sections has their own complete compositional structure.

The minuet and trio are found as the third movement of most symphonies from 1730 to 1800, a nod to the previous Baroque suites. In fact, the minuet was the only Baroque dance that was not abandoned in the Classical era, unlike the gavotte, sarabande, galliard, passepied, and bourrée. Classical composers regarded the minuet and trio as an opportunity to create elegant melodic frameworks that contrasted with the more complex sonata or rondo forms of the other movements. The minuet lost favor in the Romantic era and was resurrected only in the 20th century to evoke the older Classical style within a more modern context. —SS

LISTENING HOMEWORK

Boccherini String Quintet No. 5 in E major

Sergei Rachmaninov (1873–1943)

MUSIC FROM HIS DEPTHS

Russian composer Sergei Rachmaninov is considered by many to be the last great composer of the Romantic period. Heavily influenced by predecessors like Tchaikovsky, his compositions blended haunting themes with strong, rhythmic accompaniments. Rejecting the experimental styles of his contemporaries,[1] he adhered to the "old school" practice of crafting beautiful melodies, many of which are still recognized today.

No stranger to hardship, Rachmaninov saw his father gamble away the family fortune before abandoning the family. As a young man he suffered a nervous breakdown, recovering only through hypnotic therapy. During the Russian Revolution of 1917, he was forced to leave his homeland with his wife and children and start over in the United States.[2]

Almost on cue, however, some of Rachmaninov's greatest works emerged on the heels of some of his worst moments. In particular, three of Rachmaninov's most notable works mark different seasons in his life. His Prelude in C sharp minor was written when he was still a student of 19. Piano Concerto No. 2, which contains possibly his best-loved melodies, was written as he recovered from his nervous breakdown. And *Rhapsody on a Theme of Paganini* was written in America, ending a long dry spell after his exile from Russia.

In addition to composing, Rachmaninov was a famed concert pianist, traveling extensively to play his own compositions. —JJM

FUN FACT

Rachmaninov is possibly the only romantic composer for whom we have actual recordings of him playing his pieces.

Adagio for Strings

BY SAMUEL BARBER, 1936

Sometimes the simplest expression is the most poignant, as in the case of Barber's haunting masterpiece the *Adagio for Strings*. Clocking in at about eight minutes, the austere work offers a visceral kind of satisfaction as it traces the arcing trajectory of a classic narrative plot. Graceful interplay between violin, viola, cello, and bass creates bittersweet undulations and cycles that build to a cathartic climax (about two-thirds of the way through) before dissolving into calm resolution. An overall feeling of sadness pervades the composition, yet intermittent glimpses of hope prevent it from being overwhelmingly depressing.

When he was just 26 years old, the young composer from Pennsylvania first created the *Adagio's* somber theme as part of his first string quartet's second movement. Later, recognizing its potential to stand alone as a complete work, Barber expanded the arrangement for a larger string orchestra. The familiar, finalized version was premiered in 1938 by the famous Italian conductor Arturo Toscanini and the NBC Symphony Orchestra.[1]

Since then, *Adagio for Strings* has garnered universal affection and become a timeless symbol of melancholy beauty. It was the 20th century's most performed piece of American concert music.[2] Today, as a staple among cleverly named classical compilations, its legacy is alive and well. —CKG

RECOMMENDED RECORDING

**Thomas Schippers Conducts Barber, Menotti,
Berg & D'Indy;** *New York Philharmonic; Sony; 1997*

Cosi fan Tutte

WOLFGANG AMADEUS MOZART (1756–1791)

Cosi fan Tutte or *The School for Lovers* is, in this case, not a place but an opera where the audience is the class and composer Wolfgang Amadeus Mozart and Italian librettist Lorenzo Da Ponte are the teachers. The lessons in this curriculum are the stories of two couples, Dorabella and her beloved Ferrando, and Fiordiligi and her fiancé, Guglielmo.

Through a series of slapstick, somber, and ultimately profound scenes that explore the issues of trust and acceptance within relationships, audiences today learn the same lesson those at the opera's premiere in 1790 took to heart: each partner in a relationship is human.

Coerced by the cynical old philosopher Don Alfonso, Ferrando and Guglielmo devise a scheme to test the fidelity of their fiancées. Though fiercely loyal at first, the women are eventually tempted to stray, as the men who know them best employ those things they are certain will lead to their downfall. Ironically, by scheming to test their fiancées' loyalty, the men deceive the women, proving that they themselves are not trustworthy.

Though classified as an *opera buffa,* the Italian form of comic opera, Mozart delivers a message of profundity to listeners through pieces like Fiordiligi's Act Two aria, "Per pietà, ben mio, perdona" ("Please, my beloved, forgive"). The composer demonstrates the ups and downs of relationships through his frequent use of octave intervals within the vocal line. This musical symbolism is exemplified in Fiordiligi's famous Act One aria, "Come scoglio" ("Like a rock"). —CCD

Photo © Carol Rosegg; courtesy New York City Opera.

The Viola

KISSING COUSIN TO THE VIOLIN

Closely related to the violin, the viola's sonorous timber and larger size distinguish this midsized member of the family. Reflective of its French name *l'alto,* the viola speaks in a range similar to the alto singer in a choir. Its lower, richer sound favors a supportive role in the ensemble, while its thicker strings and heavier bow make it less suited for fast melody performance. The viola is often underappreciated, but the sound of a string section would not be the same without the beautiful harmony of this instrument in the middle.

The viola and violin were not simply invented but rather developed in Italy in the early 1500s. Finding their origins in the viola da braccio, the term "viola" was generally used to mean any stringed instrument during that time period. Since the word "violin" is a derivative of viola, many violists believe themselves to be the leaders of the band, historically.

Famous violists include J. S. Bach, Mozart, Schubert, Dvořák, Paganini, Primrose, and John Cale of the Velvet Underground. To quote C. P. E. Bach from a letter regarding his father Johann, "As the greatest expert and judge of harmony, he liked best to play the viola…" It is also said that Mozart preferred to play the viola when he performed and that Paganini fell in love with a viola made by Stradivarius. Literature written for this instrument is diminutive compared to that of the violin and cello, but Mendelssohn's Viola Sonata in C minor and Bartók's Viola Concerto are beautiful examples of this Cinderella's ability. —LMC

How We Perceive Musical Form

THE SHAPE OF SOUND

Musical form is largely unconscious. If music is playing and we're doing something else besides listening, it's automatically in the background; we just keep talking to the person next to us or go on reading a book. But musical form is powerful. Even if we're only listening with "half a mind," when a familiar part of the music comes along, it will nudge the brain and we'll start to listen more closely or tap our feet. Why? It's because a part of the *form* of the music, such as a familiar tune or rhythm has captured our ears. These are just little glimpses of *part* of a sonata or a symphony that come into focus, leaving the rest fuzzy and out of focus. They are sound *contours,* or *patterns.*

In Leonardo da Vinci's *Mona Lisa,* if you could only see her smile, just her lips and mouth, it wouldn't mean much, would it? But add the context—the shape of her face and hair, the expression in her eyes, her manner of dress, the position of her hands, and the mysterious landscape in which she sits—and the whole painting arrests your gaze and your psyche. That's what makes art.

A beautiful symphony does the same thing. Classical music is filled with echoes and contrasts which, heard in context, create the unique sound that is a composition. —TH

La Fenice

FORGED BY FIRE

O pera lovers are accustomed to drama onstage, but some venues take on a dramatic life of their own. The Teatro La Fenice in Venice has more than earned its name "The Phoenix," having risen from the ashes of devastating fires on not one but two separate occasions. Its turbulent history has not, however, stopped a torrent of famous composers from staging operas there, often cast with some of the finest singers in the world.

Right from the beginning of its story in 1792, La Fenice comfortably secured its place in the history of classical music. Rossini, Meyerbeer, Donizetti, Bellini, and Verdi all premiered operas there; modern composers such as Stravinsky and Britten wrote commissioned pieces for contemporary music festivals hosted in the venue. Through more than two centuries of alternating triumph and disaster, a steady stream of famous performers and conductors has graced the various incarnations of the theater, and though fires and wars have sometimes put a stop to the performance calendar, La Fenice always seems to come back stronger than before.

The most recent reconstruction of the theater began after La Fenice was burned to the ground in 1996 by arsonists. After a five-year period of stagnation, many believed that the rebuilding project had stalled irrevocably, and that the venue was lost forever. Nonetheless, in 2001 the construction teams finally got the ball rolling, and in December 2003 Venice's famous Phoenix rose to its former glory once again. —MM

Teatro La Fenice. Photo © Michele Crosera.

Moab Music Festival, Utah

MUSIC IN CONCERT WITH LANDSCAPE

A string quartet performs the work of a master while sitting in folding chairs on a canyon floor. Stunning red rock shapes carved by years of river currents serve as a concert hall. Such chamber music concerts in grottos along the Colorado River are signature events at the Moab Music Festival in Moab, Utah.

Moab Music Festival concert in a grotto along the Colorado River. Photo by Neal Herbert.

The festival's motto, "Music in concert with the landscape," infuses every performance at the open-air venues in this former frontier mining town. On Festival musical walks, audience members are shuttled to a "secret location" for a moderate hike to a natural concert hall. On a four-day musical raft trip, they traverse Canyonlands National Park by boat and enjoy intimate concerts in the evenings.

Classical chamber music by masters such as Bach and Mozart is the mainstay of the festival, held during late August/early September, but the repertoire also includes traditional folk music, jazz, Latin music, and compositions of living composers.

Founded in 1992 by pianist Michael Barrett and his wife, violist and festival Artistic Director Leslie Tomkins, the festival has an informal feel. And you don't need to be a classical music connoisseur to revel in the experience. "Although I don't know Tchaikovsky from Brahms," wrote Julie Dugdale, a first-time festivalgoer, "the beauty of this festival is that I don't have to. It's about what you feel when the music starts, not about what you know."[1] —KFG

Benjamin and *The Man Who Knew Too Much*

STORM CLOUDS ARE BREWING

Legendary filmmaker Alfred Hitchcock often hired Bernard Herrmann to compose and conduct the orchestral scores for his films. *The Man Who Knew Too Much*, starring Doris Day and Jimmy Stewart, is one of them. However, the story's climactic point involves a piece of classical music called *Storm Cloud Cantata* by Australian composer Arthur Benjamin.

Dr. Ben McKenna and his wife, Josephine, take their young son on a trip to Morocco. Upon entering North Africa, they witness the murder of a French businessman. The dying man whispers information about a murderous plot that will unfold in London to Dr. McKenna.

Mrs. McKenna wants to take no part other than to report what they know to the authorities, until she discovers that their young son has been kidnapped in order to keep them silent. The story then takes us to London, where ultimately their son is located after the plans to murder a visiting diplomat during a concert at the Royal Albert Hall are discovered.

This concert, which features Benjamin's *Storm Cloud Cantata*, is where a gunshot is to be fired simultaneously with the big cymbal crash near the conclusion of the piece—but Mrs. McKenna manages to foil the assassin's plan. —DD

Fun Fact

The audience can catch a rare glimpse of film composer Bernard Herrmann on screen conducting the London Symphony Orchestra and Covent Garden Chorus during the concert scenes.

Renaissance (1400–1600)

MUSICAL PROGRESS IN THREE PARTS

When it comes to music, the Renaissance really consists of three different time periods: early, middle, and late. Because so much happened in those 200 years, with developments in all aspects of music, we'll start by examining the period as a whole, followed by notations, instruments, and then the time periods on pages 58, 68, and 78.

Some important characteristics emerged with Renaissance music. First, polyphony (see page 224) increased, and the interval of the third became more common—it was used as a smooth and consonant chord tone. This usage opened the way for other, more dissonant, intervals. Also, increasing vocal range allowed smoothness between the voices since there wasn't as much vocal overlapping.

Both sacred and secular music were written in great earnest. The mass, the motet, and the madrigal spirituale were common liturgical forms. Frottolas, chansons, and madrigals were written within the secular genre. Mixed forms (such as the motet-chanson) also surfaced, so clearly composers were interested in creating new, groundbreaking works. —SL

Inner Forms 2: The Sentence

A STUDY IN COMPLEXITY

Arnold Schoenberg, the famous 20th-century composer, noticed that Beethoven often used motives in a particular way. He would compose a one-measure motive, then transpose that motive up or down by an interval for the second measure, followed by two additional measures of a new or related musical idea. Schoenberg called this inner form a *Satz* (or sentence).

But Beethoven is not the only composer who used this inner form. The opening theme to Mozart's Piano Sonata No. 11 in A major is in a sentence form, with the opening measure, a, shifted down by a second, a′, and followed by two more measures to complete the idea, b. It is typical to use letters as labels to indicate repeating ideas, with apostrophes (called primes) included after letters for ideas that have been modified. Thus the shifting of the opening measure down by a second is a modification. Demonstrating how rich classical music can be, this simple four-measure phrase, seen in the illustration, also contains a nested sentence.

The last two measures can also be heard as a sentence, c – c′ – d. The last movement of Mozart's Sonata No. 11, his famous "Turkish Rondo," also starts with a sentence, but this time the motive is shifted upward by a third.

You can identify sentence forms for yourself by listening for repeated motives followed by something twice as long. They are quite common at the beginning of a piece or movement. —SS

Richard Wagner (1813–1883)

LOVE HIM OR HATE HIM

Richard Wagner (pronounced "VAHG-ner"), a German composer in the heart of the Romantic period, was no stranger to controversy. Impulsive and headstrong, his life was marked by unpaid debt, scandalous affairs, and backlash over his provocative opinions. Wagner loathed the artistry of the French,[1] was anti-Semitic,[2] and was even forced into exile from his homeland for his radical political involvements. With Wagner, there was no middle ground: people loved him or hated him.

Wagner's music was equally controversial. His formal musical education was comparatively limited, possibly enabling him to dispense with convention more easily. Opera being his medium of choice, he wrote 13 in all, his earlier works following traditional forms, his latter works progressively defying them. He wrote his own *libretti* (lyrics), and wrote his music not as accompaniment to, but as an incarnation of the story line. True to Romantic style, Wagner's music was more about feeling than form, each sound a representation of something else. His operas were expansive and highly complex, often lasting hours on end. His masterwork, the mythological *Der Ring des Nibelungen,* was a four-opera cycle that took more than 26 years to write (and 16 hours to perform)—one of the most ambitious artworks ever attempted.[3]

In a lifetime as complex and colorful as his music, Wagner completely reshaped the musical landscape of his day. His impact on music is probably more profound than that of any other composer. —JJM

The Four Seasons

BY ANTONIO VIVALDI, 1725

During the early 18th century, it was typical for Baroque composers to compile instrumental concerti into groups of 6 or 12 and release them under a single title. One such group of 12, conceived by the great Italian maestro Vivaldi, was given a name that translates to *The Trial of Harmony and Invention,* and the first four concerti in that group of 12 combine to form the immensely popular work known as *The Four Seasons.*

As you would expect, the four concerti are named "Spring," "Summer," "Autumn," and "Winter," and Vivaldi adeptly infuses the three movements in each concerto with the spirit of the season. It's no small feat that the music reflects the intangible moods of the passing months while faithfully adhering to the genre's form. What is even more remarkable, though, is that Vivaldi wrote poetic sonnets to accompany each concerto. In a striking example of early program music, he directly relates each movement to vivid illustrative scenes. Thunderstorms, festive dances, and chattering teeth are just a few of the ideas expressed by this highly accessible music. Try listening to *The Four Seasons* with the sonnets in hand for a fresh take on this classic work. —CKG

RECOMMENDED RECORDING

Vivaldi: **The Four Seasons;** *Joseph Silverstein; Boston Symphony Orchestra;*
Seiji Ozawa (conductor); Telarc; 1990

Die Zauberflöte (The Magic Flute)

WOLFGANG AMADEUS MOZART (1756–1791)

The handsome prince, Tamino, plays a magic golden flute to ward off danger while the feather-clad bird catcher by his side, Papageno, merrily totes a magic set of bells. These are our guides through the fantastical world that composer Wolfgang Amadeus Mozart and librettist Emanuel Schikaneder created in *Die Zauberflöte (The Magic Flute),* an opera masterpiece in two acts. Composed in 1791, it was Mozart's final opera and may very well represent a culmination of his less obvious achievements in prior works.

Die Zauberflöte is an all-inclusive union of contradictions where evil and good coexist, and comedic and tragic elements make for the most rewarding theatrical experience. This concept of contradictions may be most evident when observing the basic style of the opera. Written as a *singspiel,* this type of opera includes both singing and spoken dialogue rather than the traditional aria and recitative form.

In addition, vocal pieces within the opera vary greatly in complexity depending upon the character. For Papageno, Mozart wrote simple folk melodies, such as the entrance aria "Der Vogelfänger bin ich ja" ("A Birdcatcher I am indeed"). However, within the same opera he gave the Queen of the Night the famous piece "Der Hölle Rache kocht in meinem Herzen" ("Hell's vengeance boils in my heart"), a coloratura soprano aria requiring extensive training and advanced vocal technique.

The theme of allowing opposites to coexist and even complement one another has made *Die Zauberflöte* one of the most beloved operas in history. —CCD

The Cello

GIVING VOICE TO THE MUSIC

Coming into form in the 17th century, this versatile performer is, among many things, the bass instrument in a string quartet, a solo instrument in chamber music, and the tenor voice in the string section of an orchestra. The cello is played while seated and held between the musician's legs, using an endpin extending from the bottom to hold it up off the floor. A descendent of the viola de gamba and known as the "violoncello" until the 20th century, the cello reached peak popularity in the 18th century and continued to be a favorite solo instrument for composers and audiences throughout the 19th.

Karl Davidov, called the "Czar of Cellists" by Tchaikovsky, is considered one of the most important cellists of the 19th century. During his lifetime he inherited a cello made by the legendary Stradivarius that has famously become known as the "Davidov." Owned and played for a time by the English cellist Jacqueline du Pré, it is currently used by Grammy award-winning cellist Yo-Yo Ma. Both artists have made exquisite recordings using this near priceless piece of history performing the music of Bach, Boccherini, and Elgar. —LMC

FUN FACT

Featuring a sound reminiscent of the human voice and a range of more than three octaves, the cello is often considered the most expressive instrument in the orchestra. Antonio Vivaldi was so moved, he wrote over 20 solo concertos for the cello, and the virtuoso cellist Luigi Boccherini scored over 100 string quintets, pioneering the use of two cellos.

Music as Organized Sound
AS OPPOSED TO DISORGANIZED NOISE

In everyday life, in a car or on the street, you are subject to two kinds of sounds: nonpitched sounds and pitched sounds. Nonpitched sounds can be scientifically (acoustically) classified as "white noise," containing all the vibrations of the frequency spectrum. White noise sounds like the whoosh of the wind or the distant rumble of city traffic. You can imitate it by blowing air through your lips.

A car horn is a pitched sound. And if you whistle by blowing the air through your lips, you get a pitched sound. Make the sound "Whew!"—you control the pitch by the position of your tongue.

A visual analogy is watching a color wheel. When it's spinning, you see only a neutral color. All the colors blend together like the rumble of city traffic or the wind. But when the wheel is stopped, you can easily see the colors, the red, the blue, and the yellow.

You can also think of it as singing (pitched) and speaking (nonpitched). Speaking is not exactly nonpitched, but the voice doesn't stay with any one pitched frequency as long as singing does.

All the other frequencies are filtered out of pitched sounds, and we're left with one pitch, one purely refined tone, with its series of overtones. The overtones let us tell the difference between a singing voice and a bassoon, or a flute from a violin. —TH

Sydney Opera House
WORTH THE STRUGGLE

Ask any 10 people to name a famous building in Australia, and at least nine of them will cite the Sydney Opera House. Its distinctive look is instantly recognizable, and its place of pride in the Sydney Harbor frames it as the jewel of Australian venues.

Today it may seem odd that anyone could have opposed the construction of such a magnificent performance complex, but any structure as innovative and unusual as the Sydney Opera House is bound to attract controversy. Even before construction began, the building was fraught with budgeting and political complications, and due to rumblings of public uncertainty about the unconventional design, construction teams were pressured to begin laying the foundation before the design was even finalized. The resulting chaos led to misunderstandings, major delays, and a project that ran 1,400 percent over its original budget. As construction slowly progressed against all odds, tempers flared and figurative lines were crossed, eventually causing Jorn Utzon, the architect who created the design, to resign from the project amidst a cloud of financial and political scandal.

More than a decade behind schedule, the Sydney Opera House opened in 1973, an architectural victory in spite of overwhelming challenges. Since then, the Australian public has largely moved past the pain, as the internationally renowned concert hall and performance venue continues to outshine the shadow cast over it during its rocky establishment. —MM

London Handel Festival

HANDEL COMES HOME

Baroque composer George Frideric Handel adopted London as his home for 50 years, and London adopted the master, says London Handel Festival Musical Director Laurence Cummings. Festival artists see it as their duty to honor Handel's music in the spaces he inhabited by re-creating the high drama and "tapestry of human emotion"—from intense passion and joy to misery, persecution, and redemption—evident in his operas and oratorios.[1] The festival's home is St. George's, Hanover Square, where Handel himself worshipped.

Founded in 1978, the festival runs from late February through early April. It has contributed to a Handel revival in the United Kingdom and specializes in performing little-heard works.

Each year the London Handel Orchestra, made up of some of the city's finest Baroque players, performs. The annual Handel Singing Competition, inaugurated in 2002 at the festival, has helped launch many a career.

In addition to listening to operas, recitals, concerts, and master classes at venues including St. George's, the Foundling Museum, the Royal College of Music, and Handel's former house, festivalgoers can attend talks about Handel's works and take walks through London on which they learn about Handel's life and visit historic sites. —KFG

Performance of Handel's opera Poro *at the Royal College of Music Britten Theatre, London Handel Festival. Photo © 2007 Chris Christoudoulou.*

Gustav Mahler and *Death in Venice*

LIKE THE MUSIC? GET THE BOOK

German author Thomas Mann was inspired to write his novella *Death in Venice* (completed in 1912) after seeing composer Gustav Mahler break down in tears while aboard a train leaving Venice. The composer had an often painful preoccupation with death, and it is reflected in his heavy and heartfelt music. In the late 1950s and '60s, Mahler's music became very well known around the world following many concerts and recordings. Mann's novella and Mahler's music propelled Italian film producer and director Luchino Visconti to create his own version of the tragic story. In 1971 he released his film of the same name.

Visconti stayed very true to the original story and characters, changing only main character Gustav von Aschenbach's profession from author to composer. The ailing older gentleman visits a beach resort near Venice and encounters a young Polish boy named Tadzio whose beauty and innocence reawaken his emotions and memories. Venice was then in the midst of a cholera epidemic, but rather than leaving the city and dangers there, Aschenbach decides to stay, enchanted by the young boy. While watching Tadzio on the beach, Aschenbach dies suddenly from complications of the dreaded disease.

Mahler's famous "Adagietto" from his Fifth Symphony both opens and closes the film. It's a hauntingly beautiful melody orchestrated for strings and harp, fitting perfectly with the death scene on the beach. This is perhaps Mahler's best-known work. It leaves the listener with unresolved feelings of longing and sadness. —DD

Renaissance—Notation (1400–1600)

THEY DID IT THEIR WAY

As the Renaissance began, music was notated in a manner familiar to us modern-day musicians and music-lovers.

"Great!" you're thinking. "I could pick up a motet score from 1400 and sing it with my choir!"

Well, not quite. Unfortunately, the meaning of the notes was slightly different.

Nowadays, a young music student will first learn that a quarter note has one beat, a half note has two beats, and a whole note has four beats.

Back in 1400 though, what we would now know as a whole note (called a "semi-breve" then) was the equivalent of one beat. A "double whole note" (breve) was the standard unit of measure, and the smaller semi-breves could subdivide the breves in groups of two or three (like our eighth notes or triplets). Then those semi-breves could in turn be divided into smaller groups of either two or three "minims."

Lastly, scores in general were very rare. Musicians simply read off of their own parts. (You have to wonder what the conductors did.) —SL

FUN FACT

Noteheads were not filled in during the Renaissance (music in the Medieval time period used filled-in noteheads). There is speculation that this "white mensural notation" was brought on by the increased use of paper (instead of vellum), which was fragile in that time and wouldn't have stood up to the scratching required to fill in the noteheads.

Da Capo Aria

AN OPPORTUNITY TO SHOW OFF

The da capo aria is a type of ternary form (ABA) that was used quite often in the Baroque period. It got its name from the Italian term *da capo* (from the head). Either *da capo* or *D.C.* would be written at the end of the B section in the musical score, indicating that the performers should return to the top (the head) of the score. The performers would then perform to the end of the A section, marked with the term *fine* (ending).

This form was used in arias (songs within operas) as a means of allowing the singer to show off. When the A section was performed the second time, the singer would add embellishments. Fancy runs, large leaps, very high notes, and big crescendos would be added to show the performer's virtuosic skills. Sometimes the orchestra would perform a theme at the beginning and/or ending of the A section.

A particularly popular form of the da capo aria combines a solo trumpet with the vocalist. The trumpeter either precedes or succeeds the singer in playing parts of the melody, allowing the two to compete. The famous castrato Farinelli "won" such a competition when he was only 17, swelling and trilling longer than his brass-playing foe could, and all on one breath! —SS

LISTENING HOMEWORK

Handel, "The Trumpet Shall Sound" and "Rejoice Greatly" from the Messiah;
"Let the Bright Seraphim" from Sampson

Arnold Schoenberg (1874–1951)

COMING FULL CIRCLE

Arnold Schoenberg is considered one of the most influential (and contro-versial) 20th-century composers. He is best remembered for creating a new system of tonality, but his body of music actually represented a journey that touched on many forms and eventually came full circle.

As a composer, Schoenberg was almost completely self-taught. His early works such as *Verklarte Nacht* echoed the late German Romanticism of his day; from there he gravitated toward musical expressionism, echoing the distorted im-agery of expressionist art just as Debussy had done with impressionism. His pivotal work *Pierrot lunaire* (1912) represented a complete deconstruction of the conventional tonal system, eventually evoking a consistent stream of complaints from his detractors.

As if in response to this forsaking of traditional tonality, Schoenberg began de-veloping a new compositional technique called the 12-tone system, in which all 12 notes of the chromatic scale are constructed in a preset order, and the entire piece is based on variations of this series. This new form was embraced by Sch-oenberg's protégés Anton Webern and Alban Berg, and even other composers such as Stravinsky and Copland explored it. Yet his 12-tone method represents only a season in Schoenberg's musical evolution.[1] His later compositions sur-prisingly came back to a more traditional tonality.

Schoenberg never considered himself a revolutionary. His musical explora-tions took him full circle, but the path he walked changed the face of music forever. —JJM

Clair de Lune

BY CLAUDE DEBUSSY, 1890

The melancholy moonlight, sweet and lone,
That makes to dream the birds upon the tree,
And in their polished basins of white stone
The fountains tall to sob with ecstasy.[1]

The excerpt above is a translated stanza from the French poem *Clair de Lune*, written in the 19th century by Paul Verlaine. Around the same time, French composer Claude Debussy wrote a lovely piece for piano, likewise called "Clair de Lune." It is highly unlikely that the two compositions are unrelated, especially in light of Debussy's known admiration for the poet. In fact, Debussy's *Suite Bergamasque* itself, which contains "Clair de Lune" as its third movement, is seemingly named after a theme in Verlaine's *Clair de Lune*.[2]

Literally meaning "moonlight," the piece is appropriately ethereal in mood, its first few chords evoking the stark beauty of a landscape bathed in celestial glow. In its relation to ideas beyond the music itself, "Clair de Lune" is another example of Romantic program music. Furthermore, its impressionistic texture—poetic in its own right—is quintessentially Debussy. —CKG

RECOMMENDED RECORDING

Debussy: **Children's Corner, Estampes, Suite Bergamasque;**
Pascal Rogé; Onyx Classics (UK); 2007

Il Barbiere di Siviglia (The Barber of Seville)

GIOACHINO ROSSINI (1792–1868)

"Figaro, Figaro, Figaro!" The public has come to associate opera with this line from Figaro's Act One aria, "Largo al factotum," found in Gioachino Rossini's opera *Il barbiere di Siviglia*. From classic cartoons like *Bugs Bunny* to mainstream television shows *Seinfeld* and *The Simpsons*, Rossini's immortal opera carries the banner of remembrance for an art form that often gets lost in the shuffle of modern-day life. A pioneer from the beginning, *Barbiere* was the first opera to be performed in the United States, where, in 1825, it brought to New York the musical genre Italians had already enjoyed for more than 200 years.

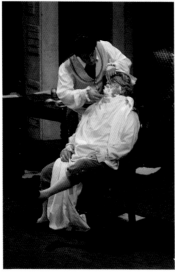

Ryan Taylor as Figaro and Peter Strummer as Doctor Bartolo. Photo courtesy Opera Carolina (Charlotte, North Carolina, www.operacarolina.org).

Il barbiere di Siviglia, ossia L'inutile precauzione (The Barber of Seville, or The Useless Precaution) was based on the first play from the "Figaro trilogy" by Pierre Beaumarchais. Ironically, the second play from the trilogy was used by Mozart when he composed *Le Nozze di Figaro* 30 years prior to that. Librettist Cesare Sterbini collaborated with Rossini to create the opera buffa, or Italian comic opera, in two acts, and *barbiere* premiered in Rome in 1816. Legend has it that Rossini worked quickly to compose this opera, completing it in less than three weeks.

The plot revolves around Count Almaviva's plan to win Rosina's hand in marriage while avoiding her overprotective guardian, Doctor Bartolo. Audiences will recognize Rosina's famous Act One coloratura cavatina, "Una voce poco fa" ("A voice just for now"), in which she vows to let no one interfere in her quest for love. —CCD

The Double Bass

HIGHLIGHTING THE LOWDOWN

Over the centuries makers have experimented with numerous styles and tunings of a larger violin and viola da gamba to add lower bass tones to the sound of a string section. Originally made with as many as six strings, composers such as Mozart found favor with a five-string version, while the three-string bass began to gain popularity in the late 1700s. It wasn't until the 20th century that the four-string double bass, tuned in fifths, established a permanent place in the orchestra…as well as in the Rock and Roll Hall of Fame.

Attributed to their masters Domenico Dragonetti and Giovanni Bottesini, two completely different bowing techniques are used today. Dragonetti developed the powerful underhand technique using a German bow, and Bottesini was the first to perfect a gentler approach with the French violin-style bow. As part of the orchestral string section, the bass commonly will play from the same music as the cello, doubling an octave lower.

The double bass is a true standout—it is as tall as an average man—but the marvel of this *lusus naturae* is easy to find in compositions such as Bottesini's Concerto No. 2 in B minor, Dvořák's lively string quintet, Opus 77, and the haunting "Romance" movement of Prokofiev's suite from the movie *Lieutenant Kijé*. Composers Schoenberg, Strauss, and Stravinsky use the double bass masterfully in much of their works, while Mahler's First Symphony, Rossini's string sonatas, and Stravinsky's *Pulcinella* have handsomely exposed passages. —LMC

Music Notation

JUST THE BASICS

Notation is the visual representation of the musical patterns that will be sung and played. *Notes* and *rests* are the visual signs we use to write music on the staff.

Below is the staff on which music is notated for a melodic instrument or voice. There are no notes for sounds here. It's just a framework. Each bar contains a black "whole rest" hanging from the second line down to indicate four beats of silence.

Why does music need to be written down? Couldn't you just put it on a sound recording without going to the trouble to *see* the musical thought on the paper in front of you? The answer is control. With notation, a composer no longer has to rely on improvising (composing and playing simultaneously). Written music gives the composer control over the final product from its inception. Sinuous curves and powerful rhythms can be calculated for maximum effect ahead of time and revised after a performance. Thus, creating a work of art is more likely because composers can concentrate *exclusively* on the pure music itself—as pure as thought—before it is manifested as sound. Here, imagination is the key to good classical music.

Instruments and the human voice, which can only play or sing one note at a time, are written on a staff of five lines and four spaces. Instruments that can play many notes at once, such as an organ, harp, or piano, are written on the "grand staff," which is two staves (the plural of staff) hooked together. —TH

Treble Clef
Beats: 1   2   3   4   THE BASIC STAFF

Time Signature

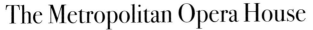

The Metropolitan Opera House

YOU HAVE ARRIVED

The famous and beautiful Metropolitan Opera House in Lincoln Center, New York City, is a relative latecomer to the party of internationally known venues. That on its own is not so strange, except that the Metropolitan Opera Company itself had already been performing for the better part of a century before the current opera house was constructed.

The Lincoln Center location was a replacement venue for the Met's original building, which had fantastic acoustics but a stage that was inadequate for major performances. That building was demolished in 1967, the year after the opera company moved its headquarters to Lincoln Center.

The current Met has one of the most majestic façades of any venue in the United States, and the opulence continues inside, as well. The art of Chagall graces the lobby area, and everything from the auditorium decor to the mechanisms controlling the stage exudes elegance in both construction and presentation. Even the gold damask stage curtain, which has the distinction of being the largest tabbed curtain in the world, is a testament to the superior artistry and craftsmanship that the Met is known for.

Seeing a performance at the Met is a privilege, as the likes of Pavarotti and Domingo made their names there, and the standard of quality for performances remains as high as ever. More than a century of Metropolitan Opera company history has given this relatively new venue a sense of artistic and emotional depth that only adds to its physical magnificence. —MM

Verbier Festival

NEWCOMER FESTIVAL TAKES OFF

Inspired by the Aspen and Marlboro music festivals in the United States, the relatively young Verbier Festival in Switzerland quickly has grown into one of the most important classical music festivals in Europe. The brainchild of founder and Executive Director Martin T:son Engstroem, the event brings together young artists and master musicians in a mountain ski resort in the Swiss Alps. When Engstroem thinks back to the first concert in July 1994, he has said, "The first words that come to mind are: anguish and frenetic activity! We really had no idea what we had let ourselves in for."[1]

Some 40,000 people attend the two-week event and enjoy repeat performances from noted musicians, many of whom come back year after year, such as cellist Mischa Maisky and violist Yuri Bashmet, as well as the Verbier Festival Orchestra and Verbier Festival Chamber Orchestra. Concerts are held in a tent erected every year that seats 1,700, as well as in a church and other small venues.

The exquisite sounds aren't relegated to those venues; since the creation of the Verbier Festival Fest'Off in 1999, artists spread out to the resort and surrounding villages. From sunrise until late at night, festivalgoers can feast on a host of free musical events, from jazz quartets playing in bars and cafes against the backdrop of the Alps to street artists in the center of town and cultural rambles through alpine meadows. —KFG

Outdoors at the Verbier Festival. Photo by Aline Paley.

Classical Music Television Broadcasts

SOMETHING FOR THE ENTIRE FAMILY

The New York Philharmonic and the Boston Pops delivered wonderful television shows that educated and entertained. The shows focused on the symphony orchestra, soloists, the works of the great classical composers, and in the case of the Boston Pops, light classics or popular music arranged for and played by the orchestra.

The New York Philharmonic began what they called "Young People's Concerts" in the mid-1950s with live performances on broadcast television of works ranging from Holst's *The Planets* to Beethoven's symphonies as well as modern works by the likes of Shostakovich, Hindemith, Ives, and Copland. When Leonard Bernstein became resident conductor of the New York Philharmonic in 1958, he made this series the centerpiece of his work with the orchestra. He created, conducted, scripted, and hosted 53 programs before his departure in 1972. The series was so popular that it was translated into many different languages for international broadcast.

The Boston Pops' weekly PBS television show entitled *Evening at Pops* ran from 1970 to 2005. The three principal conductors for this show were Arthur Fiedler, film composer John Williams, and Keith Lockhart. Each show featured performances of light classics, movie/television music, and many other types of music arranged for the symphony orchestra. The Pops often performed along with pop and jazz singers and instrumentalists. *Evening at Pops* became the longest-running show in the history of PBS. —DD

Renaissance—Instruments (1400-1600)

MEET THE PLAYERS

Renaissance instruments were categorized into some familiar families: woodwinds, brass, stings, and percussion.

Meet the Woodwinds

Examples include the shawn, reedpipe, hornpipe, bagpipe/bladderpipe, panpipe, and recorder. In the woodwind instruments of the Renaissance, holes were simply drilled into the wood at a place easy for hand placement, without regard to pitch irregularities, so players had to compensate on their own.

Meet the Brass

Examples include the slide trumpet, cornett, trumpet, and sackbut. Brass instruments in the 1400s were actually very similar to their modern counterparts. They were (and still are!) quite difficult for the novice to play. The slide trumpet and sackbut both refer to different sizes of our modern-day trombone.

Meet the Strings

String instruments have certainly undergone many changes since the 15th century. There was a viol, which is the predecessor to our modern-day violin, viola, and cello. Then there was a lyre, which looked like a harp but was played with a bow. A hurdy-gurdy (see page 73) was basically a mechanized violin. Lutes and harpsichords: Do you know what current instruments they influenced?

Meet the Percussion

Percussion was much simpler than it is today, only including the triangle, tambourine, and an assortment of drums. One instrument that has all but disappeared is the Jew's harp, played by plucking at a steel instrument while making different vowels with the mouth. It was actually banned several times for being a type of Siren's call—apparently women couldn't resist a man playing it! —SL

Inner Forms 3: Subphrase and Phrase
LEARNING MUSICAL GRAMMAR

In discussing compositional forms, we are talking about three main ideas: melodic (themes), harmonic (chords), and key area (C major, D minor, and so on). These are not separate, since melodies imply harmonies and key areas are chord progressions writ large. This interconnectedness becomes quite obvious when considering the smallest complete musical form: the phrase.

When the melody comes to a clear stopping point, accompanied by the harmonies coming to a clear stopping point, this is a complete idea. This stopping point is called the "cadence," usually compared to punctuation marks in written language. Just as punctuation can be strong (exclamation mark), normal (period), or weak (comma or question mark), musical cadences also have different levels of finality based on the final note of the melody and the chords used in the harmony.

The strongest cadence is the perfect authentic cadence, which ends with the melody on the tonic note and the last two chords as root position dominant and tonic chords (V and I; see pages 154 and 164). Strong cadences are usually saved for the ends of sections and pieces, whereas weaker cadences are used at the beginning and middle to keep the action going forward.

Sometimes the melody will come to a pause—called a "caesura"—but the harmonies have not followed a typical progression for a cadence. These smaller sections are called subphrases, often setting apart motives or creating a sentence within a single phrase. —SS

Wolfgang Amadeus Mozart (1756–1791)

CHILD STAR

Few would dispute that Wolfgang Amadeus Mozart was a musical genius, an icon of the Classical period. What many might not realize is that most of Mozart's success occurred in his early years as a child prodigy. His adulthood was plagued with financial difficulty, a lack of steady work, and even a measure of unpopularity with his music.[1]

Born to a musical family in Salzburg, Austria, Mozart showed great talent at an early age, playing piano proficiently by age three and composing by age five. By his early teens, Mozart was composing symphonies and operas with a maturity rivaling composers many years older.[2] His father, a noted musician himself, took Mozart (along with his sister, also quite talented) and traveled abroad on tour for years on end, allowing his children's remarkable gifts to bring money into the family coffers. Mozart was a "child star" of his day.

However, all child stars grow up, and as Mozart matured, he found less of a market for his immense talent. He lacked the administrative skills or patience for any permanent official musical position, yet he had trouble getting regular commissions because his music was considered too complex, especially in his later years.

A sickly man to begin with, the child star Mozart died tragically young and deeply in debt. He was buried in a commoner's grave, his genius widely recognized but underappreciated. Today, however, he is commonly revered as one of the most gifted musicians in history. —JJM

Piano Concerto No. 2 in C minor

BY SERGEI RACHMANINOFF, 1900

The story of this gorgeous piece of music is almost as moving as the work itself. In 1897, a few years before he composed the Piano Concerto No. 2, Rachmaninov was devastated when the premiere of his Symphony No. 1 ended in catastrophe. A drunken conductor butchered the piece, critics mocked it mercilessly, and the emotionally battered composer suffered a nervous breakdown that prevented him from composing for the next three years. Eventually, with the help of a psychotherapist named Nikolai Dahl, Rachmaninov regained the confidence to compose, and he began work on his second piano concerto. The work was a triumph, the premiere a success, and, as a token of his gratitude, Rachmaninov dedicated the work to Dr. Dahl.[1]

The concerto is characteristically Russian, reminiscent of Tchaikovsky in its imposing grandeur, and it is a tremendous technical challenge for the pianist. But it is the work's beauty that accounts for its lasting popularity. Each of the three movements overflows with lyrical melodies and crescendos that swell into dramatic climaxes. In fact, the themes are so drenched with romance that some listeners deride the piece as excessively sentimental. Most, however, are happy to let its cinematic passion sweep them away. —CKG

RECOMMENDED RECORDING

The Originals; Rachmaninov: Piano Concerto No. 2; Tchaikovsky: Piano Concerto No. 1; Sviatoslav Richter; Deutsche Grammophon; 1996

La Cenerentola (Cinderella)

GIOACHINO ROSSINI (1792–1868)

What happens when a fairy tale has no magic? Does the heroine still find love and live happily ever after?

Gioachino Rossini and librettist Jacopo Ferretti attempt to answer these questions in *La Cenerentola (Cinderella),* a two-act operatic *dramma giocoso,* a comic opera that also contains serious themes. Although based on Charles Perrault's classic fairy tale *Cendrillon,* Rossini's Italian comic drama relies on reason rather than magic. An interesting commentary on societal and class issues for audiences even today, the opera transforms an otherwise sweet story for children into a relevant piece for all ages.

To accomplish this, Rossini and Ferretti transpose several key elements of the original story. They give the title character the name Angelina, referencing her angelic qualities and innate goodness. The evil stepmother is replaced by a stepfather, Don Magnifico, and the Fairy Godmother is forfeited in favor of Alidoro, a philosopher. In the end, Angelina is united with her Prince Charming, Prince Ramiro, using a bracelet, not a glass slipper. While the couple does indeed find love, it is based on true elements of human nature and not fairy tale magic.

Completed by 25-year-old Rossini in three weeks, *Cenerentola* premiered in Rome in 1817 and soon became as popular as *Il barbiere di Siviglia.* Both operas include heroine roles written for *coloratura contralto,* a rare type of female voice that sings most comfortably in the range between tenor and soprano, yet still maintains enough flexibility to perform extensive ornamentation of a melody, employing fast cadenzas, trills, and *melismas,* which are single syllables sung over many different notes. —CCD

From left to right: Matt Lau as Don Magnifico, Christopher Feigum as Alidoro, Kirstin Chavez as Angelina, Paul Austin Kelly as Don Ramiro, Marianne Bindig as Thisbe, Daniel Belcher as Dandini, and Jeanine Thames as Croinda. Photo by John Fitzgerald; courtesy Kentucky Opera.

The Hurdy-Gurdy

FUNNY NAME, STORIED PAST

Unique, misunderstood, and often confused with a barrel organ, the hurdy-gurdy is a marvelous example of mechanical and musical ingenuity. Pictorial evidence of this stringed instrument dating back to the 12th century shows a violin-shaped instrument (called an "organistrum") being played by two people.

To produce its sound, one player turned a crank that spun a rosined wheel rubbing against the strings, while the other musician played melodies on a keyboard. Wooden wedges called "tangents" were connected to the keyboard and pressed against the melody strings to alter their pitch.

This mechanized marvel also incorporated an additional set of drone strings whose notes remained unchanged by the keyboard. Each string produced a constant tone, similar to that of a bagpipe, while the wheel was in motion.

By the 13th century, a smaller, single-player hurdy-gurdy, known as the "symphonia," was introduced. This minstrel's instrument was a favorite in palaces, churches, and village squares as the accompaniment for dance, song, and celebrations.

Photo by Michiel Kamermans.

In the early 1700s, French maker Henri Bâton improved the sound and appearance, enabling the hurdy-gurdy to be used for chamber music, but by the turn of the century its high-class status waned. Giving way to newer bowed instruments, it found favor with street musicians and as a regional folk instrument.

In addition to recordings by Michelle Fromenteau featuring music from the Middle Ages, Vivaldi, and Leopold Mozart, you can hear Sting play the hurdy-gurdy while accompanying Alison Krauss on "You Will Be My Ain True Love" from the *Cold Mountain* soundtrack. —LMC

Building Blocks

NOTATIONAL ILLUSTRATIONS OF ORGANIZED SOUND

The examples in the Music Theory sections of this book can be played, but they're not real music. They just depict the building blocks of music and a very few ways those blocks can be stacked and lined up.

Let's look at the basic staff example again:

The treble clef is the first symbol on the left-hand side of the staff. It used to be called the "G clef, and the final curl pointed to the second line from the bottom, indicating that anytime the composer wanted to hear the pitch "G" he or she would write it on that line. It's repeated on every staff.

The five horizontal lines and the spaces between them indicate the pitch (the relative highness or lowness) of the sounds when notes are written on them, from the highest line or space to the lowest. (Please be patient, we'll get to that soon; but you can see the pitches on the big chart.)

The next symbol is a fraction, 4/4, called the time signature, or meter signature. The top number, or numerator, shows that there are four beats to each measure. The bottom number, or denominator, shows that a quarter (1/4) note gets one beat.

Pitch is read up and down, and rhythm and meter (time) are read left to right.
—TH

Massey Hall

IF MASSEY BUILDS IT...

Great classical music venues are often made possible by the generosity of wealthy patrons, and the city of Toronto was fortunate that Hart Massey, a late 19th-century entrepreneur, had a taste for both the arts and philanthropy. Massey financed the construction of the concert hall in the hopes that it would encourage a stronger and more vibrant arts scene to develop in Toronto. His plan worked exceedingly well, and Massey Hall has become a venue that is important not just in Canada, but in an international context, as well.

In 1894, the hall opened with an ambitious performance of Handel's *Messiah.* As it was the only dedicated concert hall in Canada at the time, Massey Hall quickly became the go-to place for the world's most respected performers. Presenting orchestral and choral music was the main function of the hall in its early days, but as time progressed, Massey Hall became increasingly multi-purpose, hosting dignitaries and even athletes as well as musicians. Winston Churchill delivered a speech there in 1900, the tenor Enrico Caruso made his Canadian debut there in 1908, and boxer Jack Dempsey put on a demonstration match there in 1919. Massey Hall even helped launch careers; pianist Glenn Gould gave his very first concert there in 1946, when he was just 13 years old. These days, Massey Hall is as well known for jazz and pop music as it is for classical, but the caliber of musicians it attracts has kept its reputation strong. —MM

Aspen Music Festival and School

ALL OF NATURE'S A STAGE

Julliard touring pianist Conrad Tao, who has participated in the Aspen Music Festival and School for a number of years, has said Aspen—at an altitude of 7,900 feet and surrounded by seven peaks all over 14,000 feet—reminds him of "the essence of music." He keeps coming back, he told *The Aspen Daily News,* because "it allows me to rejuvenate myself. Besides, it should be illegal to be in Manhattan in August."[1]

More than 625 students and 150 artist-faculty members perform at the eight-week summer festival of more than 350 events, including orchestral concerts, chamber music, opera, contemporary music, master classes, and children's programs.

Student playing in flowers up in the mountains. Photo by Alex Irwin.

For audience members too, the atmosphere nurtures the soul. All attire—whether an elegant cocktail dress or boots and shorts—is acceptable at all venues, including the Benedict Music Tent, the restored 1889 Victorian Wheeler Opera House, or the Harris Concert Hall, which the *Denver Post* called "the Carnegie of the Rockies."[2]

This summer event grew out of the 1949 Goethe Bicentennial Convocation and Music Festival held in the dusty, nearly abandoned ex-mining town of Aspen to celebrate the 200th birthday of the German poet and dramatist Johann Wolfgang von Goethe. It was meant to be a healing gesture in the wake of the world wars.

Even in its earliest days, the mood was casual and the music came first: In 1951, composer Igor Stravinsky conducted a concert in jeans and tennis shoes because his luggage was lost. —KFG

Raging Bull and "Intermezzo" from *Cavalleria Rusticana*

MASCAGNI'S ORCHESTRAL CONTRAST

D irector Martin Scorcese's brilliant 1980 movie *Raging Bull* is based on the professional and personal life story of boxing champ Jake LaMotta. Scorcese's direction of Academy Award–winning actor Robert De Niro, his use of black and white film, and his exciting vision of shooting fight scenes from within the boxing ring (as opposed to the view normally seen from the audience's perspective) are key elements to the intriguing magic he achieved. Perhaps some of the most overlooked magical ingredients are Italian composer Pietro Mascagni's orchestral pieces from three of his operas used as themes and underscoring.

During the film's opening titles and credits, the audience hears Mascagni's elegant and delicate "Intermezzo" from the composer's most successful opera, *Cavalleria Rusticana*. This almost becomes the theme of the film and the main character, Jake LaMotta. This gorgeous piece is heard briefly and during the closing credits. Also heard in the film is "Barcarolle" from Mascagni's opera *Silvano*, used as underscoring to a scrapbook montage of clips and stills of personal LaMotta family gatherings. The third piece heard is the "Intermezzo" from *Guglielmo Ratcliff* (one of Mascagni's lesser-known operas).

All three orchestral pieces have a slow to moderate tempo, feature a strong, beautiful, and melancholy melody, and create a profound contrast with the often brutal professional and domestic violence. The music helps give the audience an understanding of the delicate balance between love and jealousy, compassion and violent temper that seem to drive the legendary boxer. —DD

Renaissance–Time Periods (1400-1600)

EVERYBODY DANCE NOW

With a grasp of Renaissance notation and instrument usage, let's see how the music progressed through its 200-year time span.

Early Renaissance (1400-1460)
This music was all about simplification. The ideal was a completely flowing work that increased energy toward a final climactic cadence.

Middle Renaissance (1460-1530)
The invention of the printing press largely influenced the music of the turn of the century. With the possibility of mass production came the ability to write for more instruments, as well as wider distribution. More people listening to new music led to the rise of an educated, bourgeois class. The music itself, while still carrying on the ideal of clarity and smoothness, became slightly more complicated with the addition of voices and instruments.

Late Renaissance (1530-1600)
Just as history swings on a pendulum in a repetition of sorts, music follows much the same concept. As the turn of the 17th century rapidly approached, the move toward simplification gave way to the Baroque—ornaments and chromaticism were introduced, and extreme emotion reinserted itself into the music.

With all this, you can no doubt picture a scene at a Renaissance dinner party perfectly, with musicians, hurdy-gurdies, Jew's harps, and swooning wenches. —SL

LISTENING HOMEWORK

Guillaume Dufay's motets (Early Renaissance)
Josquin des Prez's masses (Middle Renaissance)
Giovanni Pierluigi da Palestrina's Missa Papae Marcelli
(**Pope Marcellus Mass**) *(late Renaissance)*

Suite

BAROQUE DEEJAYS...

In the Baroque era, composers began collecting various dances into a suite for instruments. The number of movements varied greatly—anywhere from 3 to 24. The dances were usually short binary forms, though minuets, gavottes, and bourrées were often paired to create compound ternary forms. The most typical dances were the allemande, courante, sarabande, gigue, bourrée, gavotte, minuet, galliard, and passepied.

Bach often started his solo suites—composed for harpsichord, flute, cello, violin, and lute—with a prelude, and many of his suites followed the same pattern of dances: prelude, allemande, courante, sarabande, optional, and gigue, where the optional spot could be pairs of bourrées, minuets, or gavottes. The dances are almost always in the same key, unlike other multimovement works such as the symphony or sonata. Besides solo suites, there are orchestral suites and some chamber suites.

In the 19th century, composers began taking excerpts from ballets or operas and creating suites for orchestra based on them. These suites were used to make more money from works that had already done well financially. Famous examples include Tchaikovsky's *Nutcracker Suite, Sleeping Beauty Suite,* and *Romeo and Juliet Suite;* Stravinsky's *The Firebird Suite;* and Bizet's *Carmen Suite* and *L'Arlesienne Suite.* These suites have no particular form, often flowing from one excerpt to the next without pause, though sometimes there are clear movements. —SS

Claude Debussy (1862–1918)

BREAKING ALL THE RULES

French composer Claude Debussy has long been linked to what is called musical impressionism, largely because his music seems to reflect mood rather than imagery, similar to impressionist painters like Monet. However, Debussy resisted being tagged with the impressionist label.[1] In fact, he didn't seem to want to be constrained by any rule or label at all.

As a student, Debussy constantly frustrated his teachers by deliberately violating the textbook patterns of "acceptable" compositional style. But somehow, in pressing these boundaries, Debussy pushed beyond proper technique and unlocked harmonies and melodies that were controversial and beautiful all at once. One of Debussy's professors once told him, "I am not saying that what you do isn't beautiful, but it's theoretically absurd." Debussy's response: "There is no theory. You have merely to listen. Pleasure is the law."[2] In effect, this statement captures the heart of his entire approach; his music is unconstrained by tradition, yet it emanates a subtle sensuality. It is the music of pleasure.

Debussy composed pieces in nearly all musical forms; his most memorable works include the orchestral piece *Prelude to the Afternoon of a Faun* and the widely recognized "Clair de Lune" for solo piano. At heart, Debussy was a rebel who broke the rules to find beauty—and in so doing, he reinvented the language of music. —JJM

Rhapsody in Blue

BY GEORGE GERSHWIN, 1924

In 1923, a well-known bandleader named Paul Whiteman asked Gershwin to write a concerto for Whiteman's jazz orchestra. Gershwin casually agreed to the idea and resumed his other projects. A short time later, the composer was quite shocked to read an announcement from Whiteman in the newspaper saying the concerto would be premiered in six weeks at a New York event called "An Experiment in Modern Music." Amazingly, Gershwin finished the work in under a month, and his arranger, Frede Grofe, prepared it for the band in time for the program. *Rhapsody in Blue* was an overwhelming success at its premiere and has since become one of the major icons of American music.

With more time to refine the piece after the premiere, Gershwin completed the solo piano part and Grofe arranged the melody for larger orchestras.[1] The full version for piano and orchestra that is most commonly heard today is more than just a combination of jazz and classical music. Gershwin's genius is manifest in the way he unifies the genres in such a way that they become inseparable. The final product, filled with the thrilling spirit of Manhattan's hustle and bustle in the Roaring Twenties, still sounds fresh today. —CKG

RECOMMENDED RECORDING

Gershwin: Rhapsody in Blue / *An American in Paris; Leonard Bernstein (piano and conductor); Columbia Symphony Orchestra; Sony Classical; 1987*

La Sonnambula (The Sleepwalker)

VINCENZO BELLINI (1801–1835)

*B*el canto (beautiful singing), an Italian operatic technique that emphasizes purity and evenness of tone production while requiring an agile and precise vocal technique, is perfectly exemplified in Vincenzo Bellini's seventh opera, *La Sonnambula (The Sleepwalker)*. Bellini collaborated with Italian librettist Felice Romani in 1831 to write this two-act *semiseria,* an opera containing both comic and tragic elements in a pastoral setting.

The story, based on a ballet-pantomime by French dramatist Eugène Scribe, revolves around Amina, a former orphan and adoptee who is plagued by chronic sleepwalking. Her engagement to Elvino is sabotaged by what appears to be her infidelity during one of her sleepwalking episodes. He refuses to believe her innocence until he witnesses Amina walking in her sleep across a dangerously unstable mill bridge. Amina awakens in Elvino's arms, and the story ends happily.

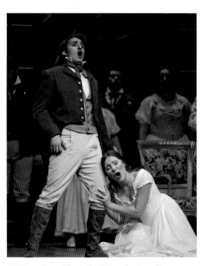

Michigan Opera Theatre's 2008 production of La Sonnambula *directed by Renata Scotto. Charles Castronovo as Elvino, Ekaterina Siurina as Amina. Photo by John Grigaitis; courtesy Michigan Opera Theatre (www.michiganopera.org).*

As audiences might expect, Bellini lavished the bulk of the bel canto jewels upon the title character, Amina. Her joyful Act I cavatina, "Sovra il sen la man mi posa" ("Put your hand on my bosom") is a florid characterization of her innocence and zest for love and life. With staccato writing utilized throughout, paired with treacherous chromatics sustained in the upper register, this piece contrasts well with her final sleepwalking aria, "Ah, non credea mirarti" ("Ah, I didn't believe I would see you"). Relying on an endless current of melody, this haunting piece requires a supreme amount of breath control from any soprano who dares to attempt it. —CCD

The Woodwind Section

A LARGE FAMILY WITH DISTINCTIVE VOICES

From the agility of the flute to the vocal quality of the oboe to the rich tones of the clarinet and bassoon, the instruments of the woodwind section combine to form the most versatile section in the orchestra. It is a favorite of composers to draw upon for poignant solos and melody lines.

During Bach's lifetime the section would have consisted of recorders, oboes, and bassoons, all wood instruments. By the time Mozart finished composing, the metal transverse flute and the newly invented clarinet had become part of the section.

Mozart is thought of as a link between early string-oriented symphonies and the big, lush Beethoven orchestra. His ability to weave each instrument's idiosyncrasies and distinctive tonal qualities together in his later symphonies shed new light on their use in the orchestra.

The double woodwinds, typical of Beethoven and Schubert, consist of two flutes, two oboes, two clarinets, and two bassoons. The triple section utilizes two flutes, one piccolo, two oboes, one English horn, two clarinets, one bass clarinet, two bassoons, and one contra bassoon. The quadruple section, as used by Strauss and Mahler, adds another flute, piccolo, oboe, and bassoon.

Apart from the orchestra, the octet, made up of two oboes, two clarinets, two horns, and two bassoons, is a perfect way to enjoy the allure of the winds.
—LMC

A French horn, clarinet, bassoon, and oboe are all part of the woodwind section.

Notation of Rhythm and Meter

FASTER AND FASTER

In the staff below, you can see some examples of note duration in 4/4 time, with a whole note, half notes, and quarter, eighth, sixteenth, and thirty-second notes. They can also be written in groups of three called "triplets." However, music's basic pulse is more often in groups of two.

Each note is twice as fast as the one preceding it, chopping up the whole note into exponentially smaller and smaller pieces. Each time a visual element is added to a note, it halves the value, as you can see, with the stem added to the whole to make halves, blacking-in for a quarter, and bars for eighths, sixteenths, and thirty-seconds.

We can get one whole note into the first 4/4 measure, two half notes into the second measure, four quarters into the next measure, and so on, proportionately. Notes mean sound. Each note has its time-equivalent rest. A rest signifies a period of silence. —TH

NOTE DURATIONS WITH PULSE BEATS PER BAR

Vienna State Opera House

A SYMBOL OF PERSEVERANCE

Vienna was once the epicenter of the classical music world, and it remains one of the most important cities for music performance. It makes sense, then, that quite a few of the world's most important music halls reside in the Austrian capital. In a city that has been marked by political upheaval and ravaged by the destruction of war, the Vienna State Opera house stands as a testament to the strength and determination of the Austrian people, as well as their commitment to the reputation of their musical heritage.

The Vienna State Opera house is such a magnificent structure that it is difficult to believe how unpopular it was when it was built and how much trauma surrounded its construction. In fact, due to the untimely deaths of both the architects, neither of them even saw the completion of the building, and when it did open for its inaugural season in 1869, public response was scathing at best. Trouble for the opera house continued when it was inadvertently set on fire near the end of World War II, destroying the entire auditorium. The opera company went through a nomadic period for the next decade as reconstruction efforts suffered numerous delays.

Despite its tumultuous past, the Vienna State Opera house boasts an impressive roster of artists and conductors both past and present, including Gustav Mahler and Herbert von Karajan. Today it is one of the most active opera houses in the world, producing as many as 200 performances per year. —MM

Vienna State Opera House. Photo courtesy Frank Wouters.

Boston Early Music Festival

JUST LIKE OLD TIMES

Some opera houses stage modern takes on operas written long ago; actors wear jeans and sets are spare.

The Boston Early Music Festival will have none of that.

Working in the tradition of historically re-creating early music by performing with appropriate instruments and performance styles, the Boston Early Music Festival (BEMF) prides itself on "unearthing musical gems from the distant past and presenting their first modern performances."[1]

The biennial festival—held for a week in June every other year—aims to fulfill what music critic Andrew Porter described in 1981: "Music sounds best the way its composer wrote it, and by 'best' I mean most expressive, most beautiful, most enjoyable. … Music can only be made accurately, truly, fully, on the instruments and by the techniques for which it was composed." [2]

Founded in 1980, the BEMF has been called "the world's leading festival of early music."[3] Each festival features multiple performances of a fully staged Baroque opera; a series of concerts by early music soloists and ensembles; an exhibition of instrument makers; and professional symposia.

Inspired by the biennial festivals, BEMF started an annual concert and chamber opera series in Boston and New York that highlights smaller-scale Baroque operas. —KFG

Amanda Forsythe and Holger Falk in a performance of the Monteverdi opera L'incoronazione di Poppea (The Coronation of Poppea). *Photo by Frank Siteman © 2009.*

Strauss and *2001: A Space Odyssey*
WHO SAYS SPACECRAFTS CAN'T DANCE?

Johann Strauss II composed the world's best-known and loved waltz, *Blue Danube* (or *On the Beautiful Blue Danube*), in 1866. The gentle waltz time structure, majestic melody, and glorious orchestration are some of what make this work a perennial favorite.

Blue Danube is one the most used pieces of classical music in films and television shows, as well as in television and radio commercials. Films in which it is heard include *Heaven's Gate, Titanic, The Age of Innocence, Strictly Ballroom, The End of the Affair,* and even *Austin Powers.*

In Stanley Kubrick's masterpiece *2001: A Space Odyssey,* we hear the waltz played three different times throughout the film. It's a most unlikely use considering that an original score was composed for the film before the director changed his mind and used only classical music as the score. During the lengthy scene where the Pan Am space plane travels from Earth and docks with a space station, the waltz plays out in its entirety.

Even though the space plane glides horizontally across the screen and the space station rotates, both with no rhythmic motion at all, the ¾ time signature seems to drive the motion. The same is true when we see the spacecraft traveling from the station to Clavius Base on the Moon…machines waltzing in space. The waltz is then heard during the rolling of end credits one final time. —DD

Baroque Music (1600–1750)

A TREE BEARING MUCH FRUIT

As you'll see with much of music history etymology, we often steal terms from the art and architecture worlds. The term "Baroque" actually means "misshapen pear," and the first popular usage referred to the style of architecture popular in the 1600s.

As with any term applied *ex post facto* (the term became part of the vernacular between 1920–1940), there is of course argument about how comparable art really was with the music of the time. However, one thing is for sure: both loved ornamentation! Trills and turns in music were the aural equivalent of columns and gilded ceilings.

Regardless of word usage, though, Baroque music gave birth to many forms that we still use today. The concerto and the *symphonia* (a short symphony) developed the orchestral repertoire, and the sonata, cantata, and oratorio increased the music for solo instruments and voice. Furthermore, opera came into its present-day form during the Baroque period. Lastly, the usage of the "ground bass," or repeated bass line, became standard.

Influential composers of the Baroque were far too numerous to even begin to name, but the three most popular were our beloved Vivaldi, Handel, and J. S. Bach.

Classical music as we know it was easing into existence. —SL

Theme and Variations

THIS MELODY HAS LOTS OF POTENTIAL

Composers enjoy showing off their technical skills by taking a single theme and spinning it into many variations. The theme is presented first unadorned, though sometimes an introduction will set the stage. Then the whole theme is varied in some way. Composers may change the mode from major to minor or add elaborate ornamentations like trills and fast scales. A *figure* (a particular rhythmic and melodic pattern) may be used throughout the variation (see the example by Brahms), or the melody may be passed between several different instruments in the orchestra or different hands in the piano. The goal is to make each variation sound different, yet always evocative of the style of the theme. The number of variations can range from 3 to 30, and there can be small transitions between each variation, but always with a clear cadence at the end.

The theme and variations started in the Baroque era, but became very popular in the Classical and Romantic periods. The most popular instrumentation was for solo piano, such as Bach's *Goldberg* Variations or Beethoven's *Diabelli* Variations, but there were many sets of variations composed for orchestra, like Brahms's *Variations on a Theme by Haydn*. Tchaikovsky's *Variations on a Roccoco Theme* for solo cello and orchestra is a lovely example; a beautiful arrangement for flugelhorn and orchestra is performed by Sergei Nakariakov. —SS

Frédéric Chopin (1810–1849)

ROMANCING THE IVORIES

For many, Polish pianist and composer Frédéric Chopin symbolizes the very heart of the Romantic era. His pieces took liberties with structure, form, and rhythm while expressing deep passion, and his playing technique was known to be both flawless and incomparable. He also held a widely known rivalry-friendship with Franz Liszt. It is said that during a party Liszt played one of Chopin's pieces, taking the liberty of improvising on it. Chopin, who was present, was annoyed.

"If you do me the honor to play my composition," he said, "please play what is written, or else favor me with something else. Only Chopin has the right to change Chopin."[1]

Despite this rivalry, the two shared a mutual admiration. Chopin once wrote, "I should like to rob him [Liszt] of the way he plays my études."[2] After Chopin's death of tuberculosis at age 39, Liszt even wrote a biography for him.

Chopin is also remembered for his nationalism, for weaving Polish traditional dance into his music, and for his frail health. But his chief legacy is his unique style of piano composition, instantly recognizable but never duplicated. —JJM

Nocturne No. 2 in E flat major

BY FRÉDÉRIC CHOPIN, 1830-1832

Throughout his stellar yet too short career, French composer Frédéric Chopin wrote a total of 21 nocturnes, and it was clearly one of his preferred forms. The nocturne's style, which is defined by arpeggiated bass lines and florid melodies on solo piano, was developed by an Irish composer of the Romantic era named John Field, but the form was really perfected by Chopin.[1] Tinged with sweet sadness, Chopin's nocturnes create an affecting mood that invites deep reflection.

Nocturne No. 2 is the most familiar of Chopin's nocturnes and perhaps of his entire life's work. While some of his later nocturnes were more technically elaborate or mysterious in atmosphere, this one is a favorite because of its simple elegance. The melody is direct but, like all of Chopin's nocturnes, disarms the listener with its fragility. The major key gives it a relatively light feel, but a deeper yearning lies just under the surface, lending the nocturne the same bittersweet quality that pervades many of Chopin's compositions. Fittingly, this piece and its nocturnal counterparts are especially stirring in the stillness and darkness of night. —CKG

RECOMMENDED RECORDING

Chopin: The Nocturnes; *Maria Joao Pires; Deutsche Grammophon; 1996*

Norma

VINCENZO BELLINI (1801–1835)

"Casta Diva" ("Pure Goddess") has become known as the quintessential bel canto piece, yet too few classical music lovers are familiar with the opera from which this prayer for peace was born. Vincenzo Bellini's two-act tragedy *Norma* was his eighth opera and sixth collaboration with Italian librettist Felice Romani.

Based on Alexandre Souemet's play *Norma, ossia L'infanticidio (Norma, or The Infanticide)*, the story revolves around the Druid high priestess Norma and the father of her two children, Pollione, the Roman proconsul. Pollione has fallen in love with Adalgisa, a younger priestess, and wants to leave Rome with her. Adalgisa, who loves her superior Norma too much to betray her, refuses. When Norma discovers that Pollione was planning to leave her, she considers murdering her children, but then decides to give them to Adalgisa to care for. Adalgisa promises to convince Pollione to return to Norma, but is unable to.

Michigan Opera Theatre's 2005 production of Norma. *Ewa Podles as Norma. Photo by John Grigaitis; courtesy Michigan Opera Theatre (www.michiganopera.org).*

Norma is enraged and enlists the help of the Druids, who proclaim war against the Romans. The Druids capture Pollione and intend to sacrifice him. After Pollione reveals that he is the father of her children, Norma decides to relinquish their care to him and take his place in the sacrifice. Pollione is so moved that he remembers his love for Norma and joins her in death.

In addition to "Casta Diva," many operagoers will also recognize the Act II duet, "Mira, o Norma," in which Norma and Adalgisa's vows of friendship are mirrored in identical melodic lines harmonized in thirds. —CCD

The Flute

WIND IN, MELODY OUT

Having ancient origins, the flute is possibly mankind's earliest-known instrument. Over the centuries, this edge-blown aerophone has been constructed in a variety of sizes, styles, and tunings from elements including wood, ebony, ivory, ceramic, nickel, silver, gold, and platinum.

Like the whistle, sound is produced by a stream of air blown across a hole in a tube or vessel. Flutes are generally divided into two classifications depending on whether they're end-blown, as with the recorder, or side-blown, as found on the transverse or German flute.

The simple flute found in European courts of the Renaissance period underwent a transformation at the turn of the 17th century, and the Baroque *traverso* emerged. The popularity of the transverse flute was established in the 18th century, supported by method books and essays by Jacques Martin Hotteterre and Johann Quantz and solo compositions by J. S. Bach and Mozart.

In the mid-1800s, Theobald Boehm invented a mechanical key system to replace the fingertips and cover the holes, which dramatically changed the instrument's sound and performance.

The modern flute generally provides the light and airy upper voice in the woodwind section of the symphony orchestra, where in addition to the C flute, a concert flautist may be required to play the smaller piccolo as well as the larger alto or bass flutes. Works by Schumann, Tchaikovsky,

Brahms, and Mahler, along with Debussy's orchestral tone poem *Prélude à l'après-midi d'un faune* are elegant examples of its alluring sound. —LMC

Tempo and Italian Terminology

IT JUST SOUNDS BETTER

Both technical and expressive terms in written music are in the Italian language. Historically, we believe it comes from the Italian Renaissance period. Most Western countries agreed that Italian was more fluid, and therefore better at conveying emotion than the more stolid Anglo-Germanic-Scandinavian languages.

Apparently the Italians did not dispute this.

The Italian term "tempo" indicates the rate of speed at which a piece of music, or a section of a piece, is played or sung. This is not the same as rhythm or meter. It's just how fast or slow a song (or a symphonic movement) goes.

Sonatas usually have three movements, indicated by Italian tempo markings, such as *adagio* (slowly) or *allegro* (fast). Often it's a fast movement, then a slow movement, and then a fast movement again. Once more, music is movement.

Tempo indications in the music can also be metronomically precise, such as MM = 136. This indicates the exact number of beats per minute, but is devoid of the emotional implications of *adagio,* which can connote "dark" or "sad," or *allegro,* which can imply "joyful," so sometimes composers use both. Often these Italian names are used as titles for movements.

Tempos can be rigid and steady, as in pop, rock or jazz, or they can be flexible, almost conversational in nature, changing virtually from bar to bar (*rubato*).

In English language musical usage, *bar* and *measure* are interchangeable, both meaning the metrical space from barline to barline. —TH

Symphony Hall, Boston
REMARKABLY WELL PRESERVED

In Europe, a concert hall built in 1900 would be considered fairly new. In the much younger context of North America, however, buildings from 1900 are historic treasures, especially when the venue in question is the architecturally handsome and acoustically spectacular Symphony Hall in Boston. Constructed at the turn of the 20th century, Symphony Hall is a testament to how great American venues can be, and indeed it is one of the most respected concert halls in the world.

Everything in Symphony Hall is superlative, from its resident orchestra, The Boston Pops, right down to its impressive 4,800-pipe organ. The auditorium seats about 2,500 people, and ticket holders have the comfort of enjoying the original leather seats from 1900. But the most talked about feature is the sound of the hall, the acoustics that no other American venue can quite match. In fact, the acoustics are so important to the reputation of Symphony Hall that when it came time to replace the floor in 2006, a team was brought in to make sure that the original materials and methods were used to assemble it. This meant that even the nails had to be constructed and hammered in by hand in order to ensure no change to the hall's sound.

It was a lot of trouble to go through, certainly, but for the sake of preserving the integrity of what is arguably the finest venue in the United States, it seems a small price to pay. —MM

Boston Symphony Hall. Photo courtesy Richard Moffitt.

Music Still Floats Through the Halls

MENDELSSOHN HOUSE AND FESTIVAL IN LEIPZIG

Soon after Felix Mendelssohn moved into Goldschmidtstrasse 12—just a three-minute walk from the famous Gewandhaus concert hall where he served as music director—his house became a gathering place for artists. One guest, the musician Louis Spohr, called an evening spent at the Mendelssohn's house "splendid…The host himself, with great style, played an extraordinarily grave and rather unusual piece of his own composition."[1]

Born in Hamburg and brought up in Berlin, Mendelssohn, a composer, conductor, and pianist, was closely linked later in his life to Leipzig; he served as conductor of the Gewandhaus Orchestra and founded the first German music conservatory in the city.

Carefully restored and furnished in the late Biedermeier style, his former home, where he lived from 1845 until his early death at age 38 in November 1847, was turned into a museum. The only one of Mendelssohn's residences that can still be visited, the Mendelssohn house provides visitors a rare glimpse into his life and work. Among the collection are letters, sheet music, watercolors painted by Mendelssohn, and original furniture.

The rooms still echo with his music, as his former music salon is used as a venue for morning concerts. The house also serves as a site for concerts during the annual two-week Mendelssohn Festival, launched in 1997, which pays tribute to the composer with orchestral concerts, choral works, chamber music, and scholarly symposia. Other festival venues include the Gewandhaus, the Schumann-Haus, and the Grassi Museum of Musical Instruments. —KFG

Interior of Mendelssohn Museum; the music salon. Photo by Benjamin Ealovega.

Puccini's "O mio babbino caro" and *A Room With a View*

ARIAS OF ADVENTURE

In 1985, an aria from Giacomo Puccini's lesser-known opera *Gianni Schicchi* (*Il Trittico* Act III) entitled "O mio babbino caro" was suddenly heard by thousands of movie fans at the very beginning of Ismail Merchant and James Ivory's adaptation of E. M. Forster's wonderfully romantic story *A Room with a View*. The melody of the aria became the theme of the film and was reprised numerous times throughout the feature, including the final scene.

The recording used in the movie is that of soprano Dame Kiri Te Kanawa and the London Philharmonic Orchestra conducted by Sir John Pritchard. It immediately sets the perfect tone and setting for this period romantic adventure as we see young Lucy Honeychurch and her chaperone, Charlotte Bartlett, on Lucy's first trip to Florence. Her only request is a room with a view. She experiences a bit of disappointment after discovering that her hotel room windows offers a very limited and quite unexciting view. This minor letdown propels the story and evokes the manners and mores of a different era in an often hilarious way.

In addition to Richard Robbins's wonderful orchestral score, we hear another Puccini aria entitled "Chi il bel sogno di Doretta" from his opera *La Rondine* (also recorded by Dame Kiri Te Kanawa and the London Philharmonic conducted by Sir John Pritchard), as well as excerpts from Victor Herbert's operetta *Mademoiselle Modiste* recorded by The Eastman-Dryden Orchestra conducted by Donald Hunsberger. —DD

Early Baroque (1600–1650)

COMPOSERS TAKE CHARGE

As the Renaissance gave way to Baroque music, the way in which instruments were used was perhaps the biggest change. Notable Baroque composers (such as Monteverdi in his opera scores, namely *L'Orfeo*) began to compose certain types of lines for specific instruments. The flute, for example, with its easy facility, was oftentimes used as a virtuosic instrument, playing trills and fluttering melodies.

In addition, the Baroque era brought an increased use of dynamics. Of course, performers had previously played with differing degrees of louds and softs, but for the first time composers began to write down their intention in that regard. The composer no longer simply trusted the musician to play the piece correctly; they instead gave instructions, perhaps understanding that music would inevitably become a tradition passed down by tangible, written scores instead of solely aural means.

Finally, tonality as we know it at last began to emerge. Instead of individual melodic notes acting as the primary leader in moving the piece forward, the bass line and accompanying chords were the driving force. This idea is what eventually created harmony and linear movement in music.

The primary composers who wrote within this *seconda practica* (as opposed to the older Renaissance style of composition referred to as "prima practica") were Monteverdi, Giovanni Gabrieli, and Heinrich Schütz. —SL

LISTENING HOMEWORK

Monteverdi's L'Orfeo

Gabrieli's In Ecclessis

Schütz's Magnificat

Inner Forms 4: The Period

FOR EVERY QUESTION, THERE IS AN ANSWER

One of the biggest issues for a composer creating a musical structure is to keep the action going forward while maintaining a sense of unity. To keep the flow of ideas from one phrase to the next, composers often mimic the idea of a question and answer or a statement and response. These phrases are related thematically, but the cadence of the first phrase—the antecedent—is weaker, suggesting a question mark or comma. The second phrase—the consequent—ends with a stronger cadence, conclusively ending this particular idea. These two phrases together are called a "period," and music that employs these series of periods is called "periodic music."

Periods are so effective at extending small ideas that they can be extended into asymmetric periods or double periods. The double period organizes four phrases to make two antecedent phrases and two consequent phrases, typically ABAB.

The example here from Haydn's Symphony No. 104 has the pattern ABAC. The A phrases end with a weak cadence, and the first B phrase also ends with a weak cadence, keeping the energy flowing forward. The C phrase has a strong cadence to finish the whole idea. Asymmetric periods have three or five phrases linked together by the weak and strong cadences, but are less common because of their uneven nature. —SS

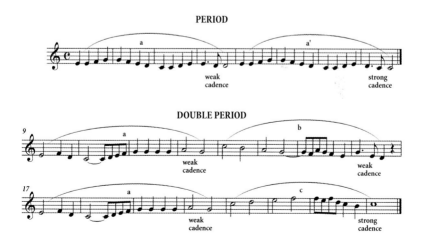

PERIOD

weak cadence   strong cadence

DOUBLE PERIOD

weak cadence   weak cadence

weak cadence   strong cadence

Franz Liszt (1811–1886)

GOD, WOMEN, AND SONG

In some ways, the life of Hungarian composer Franz Liszt began much like Mozart's. He was a child prodigy, managed and promoted by his father. Liszt also struggled deeply in the transition from "child star" to adult. However, where Mozart never seemed to make that transition, Liszt traversed the troubled waters and went on to have a long, productive career.

Liszt was known more as a performer than a composer. An unmatched piano virtuoso and showman, he often left audiences wide-eyed. His earlier works, such as the Hungarian Rhapsodies, basically showcased his abilities. Not until his mid-30s, when he "officially" ended his performance career, did Lizst fully mature as a composer, writing many of the richer works for which he is best remembered, including his 12 symphonic poems.

Like others of the Romantic period, Liszt lived a life of contradictions and extremes. In his darker moments, he turned to religion, several times seriously considering the priesthood. In happier times, it seems he turned to women, particularly women of the nobility—which often gave the public much to talk about.[1] Yet the constant thread between the extremes was his remarkable gift for music—a gift he freely shared with people, not only in performing but in teaching (for most of his adult life he never charged a fee for music lessons).[2] —JJM

Canon in D major

BY JOHANN PACHELBEL, CA. 1700

The layered cycles of Johann Pachelbel's *Canon* are so endlessly pretty that they have single-handedly brought him lasting fame as a composer. Sure, he was respected and productive in the Baroque world, but the soothing tranquillity of this one piece continues to touch us in a way that transcends time, setting, or genre.

In terms of musical form, a canon is made up of repeated melodies that build upon one another to form a harmonious whole. It takes some cleverness to make one work, but a more special kind of musical talent is needed to create a canon as beautiful as Pachelbel's. From a basic eight-note bass progression, the work blossoms through a total of 28 variations as three violins seamlessly imitate and embellish each other in continuously inventive ways.

The short work was intended to precede a livelier gigue movement, but the two movements are rarely performed or recorded together. Instead, *Canon* has taken on a life of its own and has become the official soundtrack for slow-motion bridal party entrances everywhere. Its swirling melodies seem as if they could (and should) go on forever, and it is perhaps the combination of permanence and purity exuded by the piece that makes it not only a fitting reflection of the marriage commitment but also a recurring favorite in each new generation. —CKG

RECOMMENDED RECORDING

Pachelbel: **Canon** *and Other Baroque Hits / RCA / 1991*

L'elisir d'amore (The Elixir of Love)

GAETANO DONIZETTI (1797–1848)

A beautiful landowner, Adina, and a poor peasant, Nemorino, are brought together by the mysterious magic of a special love potion in Gaetano Donizetti's comic opera *L'elisir d'amore (The Elixir of Love)*. Though the elixir contains only wine, it uncovers the true love that has always existed between Adina and Nemorino and, in the process, provides audience members with two acts of laughter and moving bel canto melodies. Written in 1832 in just two weeks, the opera was an immediate hit and has remained a favorite of listeners around the world ever since.

The product of a collaboration with famed Italian librettist Felice Romani, the story of Donizetti's *L'elisir d'amore* is actually based on Eugène Scribe's libretto for Daniel-François-Esprit Auber's 1831 French opera *Le Philter*. Donizetti and Romani took a slightly different approach and transformed a simplistic and predictable romantic comedy into a profoundly touching and heartwarming piece with timeless appeal. The ultimate example of this lies in Nemorino's famed Act II romanza, "Una Furtiva Lagrima" ("A Furtive Tear"), which has become one of the most beloved tenor arias today. The straightforward nature of each vocal phrase, hauntingly echoed by the bassoon, displays a raw vulnerability unusual for this genre. Equally sincere in a completely opposite

manner is Adina's Act II aria, "Prendi, per me sei libero" ("Take it, I have freed you"), in which she finally admits her love for Nemorino. The sentimental melody is tastefully ornamented to perfectly express the excitement and innocence of young love.

—CCD

Leah Partride as Adina, Peter Strummer as Dr. Dulcamara. Photo by Tim Wilkerson (www.timwilkersonphotography.com); courtesy Atlanta Opera (www.atlantaopera.org).

The Clarinet

TRICKY, BUT WORTH IT

A member of the woodwind family, this single reed instrument, closed at one end and employing a cylindrical bore design, generates only odd harmonics when blown through. It is the absence of even harmonics that creates its warm, inviting tone.

The invention of the clarinet is attributed to Johann Christoph Denner, who added two register keys to the Baroque chalumeau in the late 17th century. Clarinets were built in many musical keys until the mid-1800s when Hyacinthe Klosé, impressed with the mechanical key system of Theobald Boehm's flute, devised a new arrangement of keys and finger holes to create a chromatic clarinet.

Because of the complex key system, a player's fingering differs in each octave, making it difficult to play a clarinet in musical keys with many sharps and flats. For this reason clarinets have continued to be built in different keys. In addition to the standard B flat, the concert clarinetist is usually required to play the rounder-sounding A clarinet, sometimes alternating between them in the same piece. Tchaikovsky and Richard Strauss wrote specifically for the brighter C clarinet.

While there are many works of chamber music written for the clarinet, the Classical and Romantic periods yielded a long list of clarinet concertos for this favored solo instrument. Outside of the classical genre, the clarinet is very popular in klezmer and Dixieland music, and the pop group Supertramp embraced this aerophone to help define their unique sound. —LMC

Melody

HUM A FEW BARS

Melody is commonly defined as one pitch or note after another in time. A more purely musical definition: It's the first thing you think of when a song starts running through your mind.

The above C major scale is a melodic ascending scale, left to right, from C to C, encompassing a range of eight letter-named notes, or an "octave." To play it, set a metronome to 60 beats per minute and play one note for each beat.

Of course, that doesn't qualify as a real melody that anyone would remember. A real melody would have more repeated pitches and varied rhythms with interesting patterns, like this:

To count the right beat for this melody, take out your metronome, break the measures down into eighth notes (the smallest note value in the tune), and go "ONE and two and three and, ONE and two and three and" for each bar. The quarter note = 100 is the *tempo,* or metronome mark.

A dot (.) increases the time value of the note preceding it by half. So the first note, quarter-note middle C, lasts one and a half beats, taking up all of beat one and the first half of beat two, leaving the flagged eighth note D to come in on the second half of beat two. The two barred eighth notes, E and F, take up the third beat. —TH

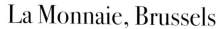

La Monnaie, Brussels

A VENUE THAT HELPED CREATE A NATION

Belgium's most important opera house also tells the intricate story of the journey of Belgian classical music and its significance in the history of Belgium. The venue known as De Munt in Dutch and La Monnaie in French has been through several rounds of construction, demolition, reconstruction, and renovation, a fitting parallel to the turbulence that the Belgian nation itself experienced.

La Monnaie (The Mint) may seem a strange name for a music venue, but the building was constructed on land that had once been a coin mint. Constructed in the late 17th century, it was the first purpose-built public opera theater in Belgium. French repertoire was the dominant offering at La Monnaie until Napoleon ordered it demolished in the early 1800s, to be replaced by a larger, more impressive structure.

The new La Monnaie bore little resemblance to the original, but its significance in Belgian history gave it a life all its own. A single performance there of an opera banned by the reigning Dutch ruler sparked a riot that eventually led to the Belgian Revolution. Unfortunately this second building succumbed to fire in 1855.

Although the third version of La Monnaie has undergone extensive renovations, expansions, and reconstructions, the structure is still there, demonstrating the strength of spirit and openness to change that has been the hallmark both of this great venue and of Belgium. —MM

La Monnaie. Photo courtesy Marco Chiesa.

Newport Music Festival
LOCATION, LOCATION, LOCATION

At the Newport Music Festival in Newport, Rhode Island, music lovers experience 19th-century chamber music the way it was meant to be heard: in the grand rooms of grand mansions. While getting lost in the sounds, audience members also take in *trompe l'oeil* ceilings, sweeping double staircases, stained glass, and flourishes like wraparound balconies, colonnades, and massive chandeliers. From vast terraces they can hear the sea lapping on the shore nearby.

For roughly two weeks in July, giant mansions built by the robber barons of the 19th century—the Vanderbilts and their friends—as "summer cottages" become the venue for some 60 concerts featuring vocal repertoire and Romantic-era piano literature.

The festival was founded in 1969 after an earlier attempt by the Metropolitan Opera to establish a summer season of outdoor opera there failed—the fog rolled in, the sopranos couldn't sing, and one instrument fell apart on stage. Instead, some local creative types realized the mansions would provide the perfect venue of elegant concert halls. Among the palaces used are The Breakers, an Italian Renaissance–style palazzo, and The Elms, modeled after an 18th-century French chateau.

The festival's hallmark is presenting young international and American artists in their North American debuts and highlighting seldom played pieces. The

repertoire covers works from Bach to Berio with a particular focus on the Romantic era, while also featuring contemporary composers and forgotten minor masterpieces such as Rachmaninoff's "Prelude," discovered by long-time artistic director Mark Malkovich at the Library of Congress in Washington, D.C. —KFG

Chamber music concert in The Great Hall of The Breakers in Newport, Rhode Island.

All That Jazz—and Vivaldi Too

"SHOWTIME!"

B ob Fosse's semi-autobiographical film *All That Jazz* is filled with wonderful contemporary songs and music that let show dancers create their
magic on stage, in rehearsal studios, and even at home. The often stress-filled,
drug-fueled lives of those in the worlds of entertainment and the fine arts are
of no surprise to most. Bob Fosse's life was no exception, as he drove himself
to the extreme every day and night. In the film, Fosse's daily morning routine
is perfectly and repeatedly accompanied by music from the Baroque period
of European history.

A brief section of composer Antonio Vivaldi's *Concerto alla rustica for strings
and continuo in G major* is used every time we see Joe Gideon (Fosse's character) preparing for the day in the bathroom each morning after little or no
sleep. The character's self-destruction seems to be fueled by Vivaldi's driving
and bouncing rhythm, as if yet another energizing drug is being taken. Each
brief bathroom scene concludes with Gideon (played by Roy Scheider) looking at himself in the mirror and declaring "Showtime!" The repeated use of
the music in these short scenes almost makes it become the theme of Joe
Gideon. —DD

Fun Fact

*Vivaldi's most popular composition, The Four Seasons,
is a piece of music you hear almost daily, not only in films, TV shows,
and commercials, but also as a ringtone, in your vacation hotel lobby,
and even in the train station during your daily trek to the office.*

Middle Baroque (1650–1700)

HAIL TO THE CHIEF!

Imagine that each government had its own musicians, complete with an orchestra, a full choir, a conductor, and several composers, all vying for attention and approval from the commander in chief.

In the heart of the Baroque era, this is exactly what happened. Court musicians were by far the most respected, and courts with established musicians were thought to be the most successful.

Louis XIV had a musical ensemble that went above and beyond anything ever before; in fact, his "24 Violins of the King" is considered the first established orchestra, consisting of (of course) violins, but also violas, cellos, and basses.

The Sun King's chief composer was Jean-Baptiste Lully. He knew just how to compose in a way that the King adored, and in fact wrote orchestrated ballets that he and the king danced together. Times have changed.

Lully had the honor of complete control of the music of Louis XIV's court; he was so successful largely because he knew how to pull the very best from his musicians. In an era without tuning standards, his orchestra was noted for its remarkable pitch. His music had a wonderful contrast between full orchestration and more soloistic aria passages, and he had a remarkable gift for harmony.[1] Without Lully, our vision of the string-based orchestra would be entirely different. —SL

LISTENING HOMEWORK

Lully's Le Bourgeois Gentilhomme
Lully's Le Triomphe de l'Amour

Rondo

TO EVERYTHING, RETURN, RETURN, RETURN

Think about the pleasure of returning to the kitchen several times to smell the apple pie baking in the oven. Or the relief of returning home after a long trip. Perhaps it is the joy of seeing a familiar face yet again. Each of these sources of satisfaction relies on returning to something, which means that you must first leave it for something different.

The rondo plays upon this desire to return by setting up a refrain from which you depart two or three times but always return to. It is always in the tonic key, so we feel at home when it comes around. The refrains (which may be short phrases or periods or longer binary forms) are separated by episodes that contrast sharply in key and mood.

Using our system of letters to signify sections, the two most common types of rondo are ABACA (the small rondo) or ABACABA (the large rondo), though plenty of composers have used even more sections.

The origins of the rondo can be traced back to an old Medieval song form known as a "forme fixe." In this form the music could repeat, but the text always alternated. By the 18th century the term was used for instrumental music, often found in the title of the work, such as Mozart's *Rondo alla Turca* or Beethoven's *Rondo e Capriccio* "Rage Over a Lost Penny" (both for piano). —SS

Hector Berlioz (1803–1869)

AN OBSESSIVE GENIUS

Hector Berlioz is a key figure in music history, effectively bridging the transition between the Classical and Romantic periods. Like most transitional composers, though, his contributions were not fully appreciated until after his death.

Portrait of Hector Berlioz. Image courtesy Musée Hector-Berlioz.

Prior to Berlioz, music was highly structured and consistent in form. Beethoven had begun pushing the envelope by writing music that adhered to style but evoked more emotion; almost on cue, Berlioz took the next step by *ignoring* structures and writing his music expressly to depict feelings and tell stories, a concept known as "program music." At the time it drew much criticism.

Berlioz himself epitomized the turbulence of Romanticism—a life plagued by drug use, suicide attempts, tumultuous relationships, even a foiled murder plot. His most remembered composition, *Symphonie Fantastique,* was actually a representation of dreams induced by an overdose of opium, and an imagined suicide attempt over unrequited love.[1] The real-life muse behind the piece was actress Harriet Smithson, with whom Berlioz had a lifelong obsession. The five-movement *Symphonie* was his macabre attempt to immortalize his feelings for her. In later years, when Smithson discovered his masterpiece was about her, she eventually entered into an unhappy marriage with him.[2]

Despite Berlioz's emotional torments and addictions, his genius and lasting influence on music's evolution cannot be understated or ignored. The passions that fed into his compositions set the stage for a whole new era of musical expression. The musical landscape was forever changed in his wake. —JJM

Three Gymnopédies

BY ERIK SATIE, 1888

This modest little trio of piano works is profound in its simplicity. Each of the three short pieces is a different manifestation of a single melodic idea, like viewing the same quaint scene from three separate angles. Instead of crafting elaborate melodies, the French composer is content to explore the atmospheric possibilities created by subtle structural manipulation. Unsteady chord changes sway in 3/4 time, occasionally drifting into areas of mild dissonance while toying with resolution. The result is a moody and contemplative grouping that has intrigued and beguiled listeners since Satie wrote it.

In ancient Greece, festivals honoring the dead were called "Gymnopedia," and most scholars assume Satie titled the work after poetry that references the Greek rituals. Regardless of what muse inspired the composer, though, the rich ambience of the interconnected pieces stands on its own.

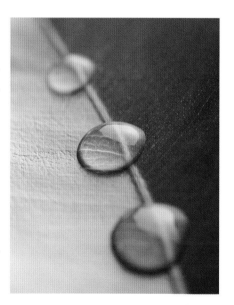

Debussy was so fascinated by this music that he rearranged the first and third *Gymnopedie* for orchestra.[1] Since that time, the works have been exhaustively reimagined in a colorful assortment of styles, including everything from jazz to techno. —CKG

RECOMMENDED RECORDING

Satie: Piano Works; Aldo Ciccolini; EMI Classics; 1992

Lucia di Lammermoor

GAETANO DONIZETTI (1797–1848)

"Ecco il ministro! Porgime la destra! Oh lieto giorno! Al fin son tua, al fin sei mia." ("Here is the minister! Give me your right hand! Oh, joyous day! At last I am yours, at last you are mine.")[1]

Anyone reading these lyrics would imagine the bride singing them while beaming with happiness. Yet the wild eyes of the young woman who emerges clutching a dagger covered with blood tell a different story. That woman is Lucia, and this is Act III, Scene 2, also known as "The Mad Scene" of Gaetano Donizetti's 50th and most popular opera, *Lucia di Lammermoor*.

Written in 1835 in collaboration with Italian librettist Salvadore Cammarano, the three-act tragic opera was loosely based on Sir Walter Scott's Scottish historical novel *The Bride of Lammermoor*. In addition to the coloratura soprano showpiece that is "The Mad Scene," audiences may recognize Lucia's famous Act I aria, "Regnava nel Silenzio" ("Silence Over All Was Reigning"), an exquisite example of bel canto lyricism.

The story revolves around a feud between the Ashton and Ravenswood families. In order to gain political protection for his family, Lucia's brother, Enrico Ashton, forces her to marry Lord Arturo Bucklaw. However, Lucia is in love with Edgardo Ravenswood. In a fit of madness on her wedding night, Lucia kills Enrico and envisions finally marrying Edgardo. When Edgardo learns Lucia is dying of delirium, he stabs himself and hopes to be reunited with his true love in the afterlife. —CCD

Jennifer Welch-Babidge as Lucia. Photo by Carol Rosegg; courtesy New York City Opera.

The Oboe

JUST ABOUT PERFECT PITCH

The oboe is a double reed wood-wind instrument invented in the mid-1600s. Borrowing many of its features from the medieval shawm, this new Baroque instrument produced a softer, more refined sound than its predecessor. It utilized six holes and three keys for modifying pitch and was generally made of boxwood.

The double reed of the oboe is usually made from two blades of cane. Most professional players make their own reeds, as the adjustments are very delicate and need to suit each individual player. The space between the blades allows only a narrow stream of air to pass through, requiring a great deal of pressure and leaving the player with a surplus of air during each breath. Because of this, many oboists practice circular breathing and are able to hold a note longer than other woodwind players.

In the early 1700s, musicians used this expressive instrument in nearly every kind of music, and composers created an abundance of solo music for it. Handel and J. S. Bach featured obbligato solos for oboe with voice, while Vivaldi, Tomaso Albinoni, Mozart, and Haydn wrote inspiring solo concertos.

Like the Boehm flute, today's oboe is a keyed instrument and a member of the orchestral woodwind section. Because of its pure, clear tone, it is used to play the note that the entire orchestra tunes to. A most notable 20th-century performance is found in the children's orchestral piece *Peter and the Wolf* by Sergei Prokofiev, in which the oboe "plays" the duck character. —LMC

Harmony and Chords

ALL TOGETHER NOW

Harmony is two or more pitches or notes played or sung at the same time. *Harmony* is the general topical term, and *chord* means one specific harmony.

TRIADS IN SCALE FORM

You can build a chord on any note of the scale. If you have three notes stacked on top of each other, as above, you have a full three-note chord (triad). You hear all three pitches at once. There are seven scale degrees altogether. Number VIII is a repeat of the pitches of number I, an octave higher. It's another C triad, and its repetition at the end of the scale pointedly identifies it as belonging to the key, or tonality, of C.

The bottom note on which the triad is built is called the "root" of the chord. Roman numeral I is a C triad, II is a D triad, III is an E triad, etc. These triads are in root position, with the root pitch on the bottom. Chordal harmonies are always identified by Roman numerals in music theory to differentiate them from the scale degrees of single melodic notes. Theoretically you can have as many notes in a chord as you want, up and down the staff.

The next note up in the triad stack is the third, and the top note of the root-position triad is the fifth. The major triads have one and a half step intervals (the step-distance between pitches) between the root and the third. The major triads have two whole steps between the root and the third. The VII triad is diminished, as it has only one and a half steps between each pitch. —TH

Suntory Hall, Tokyo
IT'S ALL IN THE SEATING ARRANGEMENT

In the 1970s and '80s, Japan wanted to show that it was making an effort to be a significant player on the international classical music scene. Not a country to do things by halves, Japan's goal was a venue that would be a jewel among concert halls, one that would be renowned for its fine acoustics and architectural originality. Skilled advisors were brought in to advise and oversee the design and construction of the building that would become Suntory Hall.[1]

The most significant of these advisors was Herbert von Karajan, who suggested that Suntory Hall, like the Berlin Philharmonie before it, would benefit greatly from a vineyard-style seating arrangement.[2] Designs were drawn up with the stage in the middle and terraced seating on all sides. This type of presentation, along with the absence of an orchestra pit, generates a double benefit: the performers and the audience are very close to each other, and acoustically, there's not a bad seat in the house. No matter where you are sitting, you will have an experience that feels more like interacting than merely listening.[3]

Suntory Hall owes much to Karajan, and the debt has not been forgotten: In a memorial to the late conductor, a plaza constructed in front of the venue in 1998 proudly bears the name Herbert von Karajan Plaza.[4] —MM

Puccini Festival

ARIAS BY THE LAKE

What better way to experience the music of one of the world's greatest opera composers than in the place that inspired his major works and the place where he lived for 30 years? Each summer some 40,000 opera lovers from around the world converge in Tuscany for the Puccini Festival along the quiet banks of Lake Massaciuccoli in the charming hamlet of Torre del Lago. It is the only festival dedicated to Giacomo Puccini, the Italian composer of ballets and operas that have become staples of opera houses today.

Puccini arrived in Torre del Lago in 1891 in his early 30s while searching for a place "separated from the world"[1] where he could cultivate his two passions, hunting and music. The composer wanted his creations to come to life in the natural setting he so loved. In a 1924 letter to his friend Giovacchino Forzano shortly before his death, Puccini wrote, "I would like to come here and listen to one of my operas in the open air."[2] Forzano made good on Puccini's wish—in 1930 he directed *La Bohème* in a provisional theater with the stage built on piles stuck in the lake in front of Puccini's villa.

Today in July and August, theatergoers watch *Tosca, Madama Butterfly,* and *La Fanciulla del West* performed by some of the biggest names in the opera world and staged in a new open-air theater just a few steps from Puccini's house and museum, where visitors can find such relics as the pianos on which he composed his masterpieces, as well as his human remains. —KFG

The Planets Are Everywhere
GUSTAV HOLST'S STELLAR FAVORITE

Between 1914 and 1916 British composer Gustav Holst wrote his famous symphonic suite *The Planets*. (See page 190.) The work consists of seven beautiful, exciting, and dynamic orchestral tone poems, each representing one of the seven known planets in our solar system at the time. Holst supplemented each planet name with a descriptive title: "Mars, Bringer of War"; "Venus, Bringer of Peace"; "Mercury, the Winged Messenger"; "Jupiter, Bringer of Jollity"; "Saturn, Bringer of Old Age"; "Uranus, the Magician"; and "Neptune, the Mystic."

The Planets has become a favorite of many film/television producers and composers. In 1999 BBC Productions used the pieces in their brilliant miniseries *The Planets.* Holst's music can be heard many times throughout each show in the series in addition to the original score by Jim Meacock.

Two short excerpts of the suite are brilliantly woven into Bill Conti's score for the 1983 film *The Right Stuff.* As astronaut John Glenn makes the first complete orbit of Earth in the *Friendship 7* spacecraft, Conti's score masterfully incorporates an excerpt from both "Mars" and "Jupiter" into his own composition.

Excerpts from the suite can also be heard in many planetarium shows all around the world, the feature films *Annie Hall* and *Shooting Fish,* and numerous television commercials. —DD

Late Baroque (1680-1750)

HERE COME THE GREATS

This era produced composers that everyone knows. Vivaldi. Telemann. Handel. Bach. Rock stars of the genre.

Vivaldi was one of the first composers to support himself as a freelancer without being associated with a court. Prolific beyond words (he wrote 550 concerti!), Vivaldi created massive volumes of trio sonatas and violin works, and established the fast-slow-fast pattern that we still cling to today. (See page 240.)

Johann Sebastian Bach, German composer and organist.

Handel wrote music on a larger scale than Vivaldi, concentrating on oratorios and operas. He studied singers and reflected their ornamentation in his instrumental music. (See page 290.)

Telemann wrote both secular and sacred music, promoting himself by establishing a music periodical that included large amounts of his music. This journal gave him international fame in a time when such a thing was nearly unheard of.

Surprisingly, Bach, that giant of Baroque repertoire, was not all that famous while alive. He was a church musician, writing cantatas for the Lutheran church service each week and acting as music director for the church choir. It wasn't until after his death that the subtleties and genius of his works were truly discovered. (See page 140.)

These composers are all important to the Baroque era for individual reasons; together, they represent the beginning of our common-practice canon. —SL

LISTENING HOMEWORK

Vivaldi's Four Seasons

Handel's Messiah

Telemann's Der Tag des Gerichts (The Day of Judgement)

Bach's Preludes and Fugues

Concerto Grosso

ALL FOR ONE, AND ONE FOR ALL!

Like the three musketeers battling King Louis's army to save their twin brother, a *concerto grosso* pits a small group of musicians against a larger group, but with less bloodshed.

Popular in the Baroque era, this form of music features three to six soloists (the concertino) who play either together or singly while accompanied by the orchestra (the ripieno). Arcangelo Corelli was well known for expanding his trio sonatas to concerti grossi by alternating between the two violins and cello of the concertino and the string orchestra of the ripieno.

In three movements like the solo concerto, the concerto grosso could be designed in suite form or *ritornello* form. Typically the ripieno would play one theme, the ritornello, with the concertino interjecting new material in between.

A good example of this is Bach's *Brandenburg* Concerto No. 2. The concertino in the concerto consists of the trumpet, recorder, oboe, and violin. In the first movement, the opening ritornello is played by all the concertino members and the ripieno strings. Then each of the concertino members gets a brief solo accompanied by the ripieno strings and harpsichord. The ritornello with the whole orchestra comes between each soloist. Then the concertino plays an extended fugue by itself (with harpsichord), before a return of the ritornello. But this time the concertino still plays variations of the ritornello theme as a group. —SS

Antonín Dvořák (1841–1904)

THE CLASSICAL BOHEMIAN

Born in Bohemia (now the Czech Republic) during the rise of Romanticism, Antonín Dvořák pursued a music career despite the objections of his innkeeper father. He developed a keen interest in musical nationalism from fellow composer Smetana, whom he met while studying in Prague. Along with Smetana, Dvořák helped develop a national sound for his homeland, masterfully blending elements of Bohemian and Slavic folk music with the traditional German forms espoused by Brahms and Mendelssohn.[1]

Ironically, Dvořák's most famous work carries folk influences of another kind. An established composer by the early 1890s with numerous orchestral and chamber works already to his credit, he accepted a position in America as director of the National Conservatory in New York. During his three years in the States, Dvořák was deeply moved by the sounds of the Native American and African American traditions. These served as inspiration for his Symphony No. 9 ("From the New World"), containing some of the most hauntingly beautiful melodies he ever wrote.

Dvořák himself challenged American composers to draw from these sounds, claiming that they contained "all that is needed for a great and noble school of music."[2] This challenge was passed to his American students (including Rubin Goldmark, who eventually taught Aaron Copland and George Gershwin). Thus, Dvořák not only developed a unique sound for his homeland, he helped America find hers as well. —JJM

Symphony No. 9 ("From the New World")

BY ANTONÍN DVOŘÁK, 1893

When Dvořák came to the United States in 1892, he was immediately fascinated by the distinctive spirituality of Native American and African American music. During his stay, he created his ninth symphony, which remains his most exciting work. The Czech composer intentionally bathed the symphony in the vivid hues of raw, traditional folk music, though he denied incorporating specific themes into the work (such as "Swing Low, Sweet Chariot"). The effect of his influences is unmistakable—bold melodies, sturdy rhythms, and blunt instrumentation fill the four movements with all the heartiness and diversity of American culture.

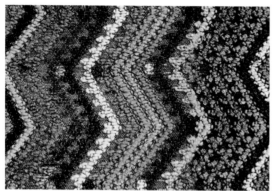

In his earlier symphonies, Dvořák had skillfully woven the texture of traditional Czech folk music into symphonic themes, and in "From the New World" he meant to show how the same could be done with the unique blend of traditional sounds found in the United States. He revives themes throughout the work, even across movements, and in the final allegro, bits and pieces of all three preceding movements share the stage for a rousing finale. —CKG

RECOMMENDED RECORDING

Dvořák: Symphony No. 9; Istvan Kertsz (conductor); London Symphony Orchestra; Penguin Music Classics Series; 1998

Rigoletto

GIUSEPPE VERDI (1813–1901)

It all begins with a cast of caricatures: Gilda, a virtuous young girl whose only errand is to go to church; her father, Rigoletto, a hunchbacked jester in the Duke of Mantua's court; and the Duke himself, a despicable womanizer predictably in love with Gilda. Audiences are amused by the Duke's famous Act I aria, "Questa o quella" ("This woman or that"), and they may at first believe they are in for the typical operatic fare of clichés. Yet as Giuseppe Verdi's *Rigoletto* progresses, a profound human drama emerges, reminding audiences of the indispensability of this beloved piece in today's operatic repertoire.

Ailyn Perez as Gilda and Gordon Hawkins as Rigoletto. Photo courtesy Opera Carolina (Charlotte, North Carolina, www.operacarolina.org).

Composed in 1851 through collaboration with Italian librettist Francesco Maria Piave, the story is based on Victor Hugo's play *Le roi s'amuse (The King's Fool).* The intrigue begins when Monterone, whose daughter was one of the Duke's conquests, places a curse on the Duke and Rigoletto, who ridicules him at a ball. In the delicate Act I aria, "Caro nome" ("Dear name"), Gilda reveals she has fallen in love with Gualtier Malde, a student she met in church, who is actually the Duke.

Noblemen kidnap Gilda and deliver her to the Duke, but Rigoletto soon comes to her rescue. Vowing revenge, he hires an assassin to kill the Duke, but his attempts to protect his daughter backfire when she disguises herself as a man so she will be killed in place of the Duke. Rigoletto realizes that Monterone's curse has been fulfilled as his daughter dies in his arms. —CCD

The Bassoon

DON'T UNDERESTIMATE IT

Related to the oboe, the bassoon is a woodwind instrument and member of the double reed family. Differing from the clarinet, it utilizes a conical bore design for its distinctive sound and is rich with both odd and even harmonics. The double back architecture of the bore allows the tube length to be almost twice that of the instrument's size.

Developed from the Renaissance dulcian in the mid-17th century, the bassoon provides the tenor and bass for the orchestral woodwind section. Pitched in C, today's bassoon generally shares the stage only with its lower-octave sibling, the contrabassoon.

The bassoon did not grow up without its own developmental difficulties, and the early 1800s found it falling behind other woodwinds in its ability to satisfy composer and player demands. It was during this period that virtuoso bas-

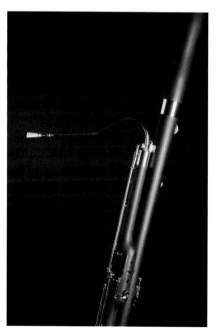

soonist Carl Almenraeder began experimental work at the Schott factory in Germany to improve the instrument's intonation, tone, and playability.

The bassoon's full sonorous bottom and plaintive upper range make it equally popular for comedic effect as well as melancholy passages. With such a wide range of tonal delights, it's considered one of the most versatile members of the orchestra. Vivaldi's 39 concerti, sonatas by Zelenki, and Igor Stravinsky's opening in *The Rite of Spring* are moving classical examples, but the Smokey Robinson and the Miracles' song *Tears of a Clown* may offer the most heard bassoon in history. —LMC

Intervals, Modes, and Emotions

THE MAJOR MODE

The term *interval* as used in music is the distance in pitch from high to low and vice versa between one pitch and any other pitch. This distance is measured in whole steps and half steps. In terms of sound vibrations, half steps are closer together than whole steps. This is unconsciously detectable to most untrained ears, but as with most sensory disciplines, the distance of the pitches from one another becomes more conscious with intensive training.

Have you heard the musical terms "major" and "minor" or "major and minor modes"? In school we were told that music based on major modes sounds "happy," while music based on minor modes sounds "sad." I prefer "light" and "dark."

Beethoven's Fifth Symphony in C minor is a good example. For the first movement, the symphony opens in the serious and dark key of C in the minor mode. But the music "morphs" or modulates into the much brighter, triumphant key of C in the major mode for an optimistic finale and a happy ending. This is a tremendous shift in the emotion of the music.

And exactly what aspect of this highly technical discussion of musical structure can make our mood go from dark and fatalistic in Beethoven's First Movement to optimistic and joyous in his Fourth Movement? It's the placement of the half step and whole step intervals in the C scale that provokes Beethoven's beautiful shifts from light to dark and back again. —TH

Mariinsky Theatre

HOME OF THE KIROV

Few institutions in the classical world are household names, but mention the word "Kirov" on the street and most people will have at least heard of the famous opera and ballet companies. Less well known, however, is the home of these illustrious companies, the Mariinsky Theatre in St. Petersburg, Russia, even though the venue is as historically important as the performances held there.

The theatre opened its doors in 1860, and at the time the dedicated opera and ballet house boasted the largest stage in the world. By the turn of the 20th century the Mariinsky was undoubtedly the leader among Russian theatres. Prokofiev, Tchaikovsky, Mussorgsky, Rimsky-Korsakov, and Khachaturian all premiered there. Great Russian performers and conductors from across the land have performed on the Mariinsky stage for a century and a half, making it one of the most musically significant venues in all Europe.

In recent years the Mariinsky has spread its wings and developed from a single venue into an entire complex of performance spaces, a project that some compare to the creation of the Lincoln Center in New York. In 2007, a dedicated concert hall opened to complement the original Mariinsky Theatre, and work is currently continuing on what will eventually be called "The Second Stage," the first major opera house to open in Russia in nearly a century. —MM

Glimmerglass Opera

LAKESIDE LISTENING

What started in 1975 with four performances of *La Bohème* staged in a high school auditorium for 1,200 local residents has grown into a summerlong festival with national prominence.

Glimmerglass Opera's Alice Busch Opera Theater. Photograph by Peyton Lea/Glimmerglass Opera.

Known for its innovative productions of new and lesser-known works as well as familiar classics, New York's Glimmerglass Opera attracts some of opera's finest performers, designers, and directors, and has produced works from Claudio Monteverdi to Stephen Hartke. Focused on opera's future, the company established its Young American Artists Program in 1988, which brings emerging professional singers to study and perform in appropriate roles in the four main stage productions. The *Financial Times* wrote, "They dare to take chances here—on new talent, on unorthodox concepts, on uncertain repertory."[1]

Each July and August some 30,000 visitors flock to Glimmerglass and its bucolic setting. The Alice Busch Opera Theater, which opened in 1987, is located on about 25 acres of farmland on the shore of Otsego Lake, eight miles north of scenic Cooperstown, New York, home to the Baseball Hall of Fame and the boyhood home of author James Fenimore Cooper—who referred to the lake as the "Glimmerglass" in his *Leatherstocking Tales.*

The intimate theater has a single wraparound balcony and barn-like architecture evoking central New York's rural culture. At intermission, rolling walls mounted on tracks slide open, giving the audience fresh air during hot summer nights. In between performances, visitors can picnic on the surrounding acreage or stroll along trails and boardwalks through a small nature sanctuary. —KFG

Inside the Alice Busch Opera Theater. Photo by Peyton Lea/Glimmerglass Opera.

Bach and *The Silence of the Lambs*

KILLER MELODIES

Serenely, majestically, and with almost mathematic precision we hear a section of Bach's the *Goldberg* Variations projecting from a small cassette player inside of the high-security prison cell of psychopath murderer Dr. Hannibal Lecter as he executes his escape. You can almost see the serial killer's mind work as he calculates each step of deceiving the guards who are bringing his meal to him while taking every precaution to prevent what is about to happen. Bach's music is the perfect accompaniment in spite of the brutal violence that follows.

The scene is from *The Silence of the Lambs,* considered one of the most thrilling horror/drama films ever made. Released in 1991 and directed by Jonathan Demme, the film features an original orchestral score by Howard Shore. The only classical piece that we hear in the entire film is this section of the *Goldberg* Variations recorded by pianist Jerry Zimmerman, presented in the story as a favorite of Dr. Lecter's. The music continues after the violence and ultimate escape, acting as a segue to the next scene.

Bach was one of the most prolific composers. He not only wrote works for harpsichord and piano but also for organ, chamber orchestra, and large choral groups with orchestra. If you enjoy this piece of piano music, you'll surely love the 32 variations that make up the complete work. —DD

Classical Period (1750–1825)

VIENNA IS THE PLACE TO BE

The Classical period in music history is when all the big shots come into play. Yup, we've already had Bach and Vivaldi and plenty of other famous guys.

But now? Now we're up to the common-practice era where the music in and around Vienna was really flourishing, and where it continues to do so today.

Some people use the term "classical music" to refer to anything that is instrumental and sounds like it should be in a concert hall. However, that usage is merely colloquial. When musicians talk about Classical music, or the Classical period, they are really referring to the time period from 1750–1825, or the time of Viennese classicism. Although only 75 or so years long, this was perhaps one of the most important ages in musical history.

In addition to all the musical and compositional developments, it is also when the *First Viennese School* was alive and kicking. The First Viennese School was a group of composers led by Haydn, Mozart, Beethoven, and their pupils.

Although differing in time of influence and strength of career, all three major composers had similar goals: to push the Baroque envelope in terms of compositional form (sonata form became the norm; Baroque dances were considered old-fashioned); length (by the end of the Classical era, symphonies were bordering on the hourlong territory); and instrumentation (say goodbye to the harpsichord, enter the piano).[1]

How did they do all this? Keep reading to find out…. —SL

Canon

THE CHASE IS ON!

W hile children are generally discouraged from playing with cannons (that go boom), one of their first experiences with music is a popular canon (that goes every which way). *Row Row Row Your Boat* takes a single melodic line and creates wonderful counterpoint by staggering the entrances of that line. The generation of complex polyphony from a single melodic idea is the whole point of canon. The number of these imitating voices varies depending on the structure of the melody. *Row Row Row Your Boat* and *Frère Jacques* can have four staggered voices, whereas Pachelbel's *Canon in D* has three voices.

Described as the strictest form of imitation, canon literally means "rule." However, the melody may be altered in some ways during the imitation without breaking these rules. The first and most trivial alteration is to shift the imitating voice up or down by an octave, creating "canon at the octave." The melody can be imitated with all the rhythms doubled in length (canon by augmentation), all the rhythms halved (canon by diminution), with the melody flipped upside down (canon by inversion), or the imitating melody played backwards (crab canon).

Composers such as J. S. Bach and Josquin des Prez regarded canons as ways to show off their skills in counterpoint by creating elaborate polyphony through strict imitation of carefully constructed melodies. —SS

LISTENING HOMEWORK

J. S. Bach—Musical Offering, *BWV 1079*
Josquin des Prez—Missa L'Homme armé *sung by the Tallis Scholars*
Henryck Gorecki—Symphony No. 3

Giuseppe Verdi (1813-1901)

"VIVA VERDI!"

Anyone who loves opera will likely recognize the name Giuseppe Verdi. Born near Bussetto, Italy, he showed interest in the organ as a child, and while furthering his studies in Milan, Verdi discovered opera, the art form that would define his career.

After writing a successful first opera, *Oberto*, Verdi's career was nearly cut short by tragedy. During the composition of his second opera, Verdi's two children and his first wife died, one after the other. Adding to his pain, the opera failed miserably. His spirit broken, Verdi determined to quit composing, but encouraged by the impresario at La Scala, he tried one more opera, *Nabucco*. It was a great success, and Verdi was catapulted into fame.[1]

During this time, Italy was struggling against Austrian dominance; being a staunch nationalist whose operas were sometimes scrutinized by the censors,[2] Verdi became a national hero. Chants of "Viva Verdi!" were often heard at the close of his operas—a chant that was also code for "Long live the king of Italy." (Verdi happened to be an acronym for the king's name.) Verdi wrote a prolific stream of operas during this season and beyond, including his masterworks, *Rigoletto* and *Aida*. Later, he also wrote the Requiem, one of his most beloved works.

Verdi remained immensely popular even beyond his death in 1901; today he is still one of the most celebrated icons in Italy's history. —JJM

Ave Maria

BY FRANZ SCHUBERT, 1825

Here is a case where the work in question is the source of a common misconception. It is a perfectly reasonable mistake to make, though, considering the familiarity of the title. The lovely *Ave Maria* melody written by Schubert is almost always heard today with the Latin text from the Catholic Ave Maria (or Hail Mary) prayer. However, Schubert did not intend it to be so. The song was originally titled *Ellens Gesang III,* which translates from German to mean "Ellen's Song III," and it was meant to feature translated text from Sir Walter Scott's poem *The Lady of the Lake.*[1]

That said, the intended text is itself an appeal to the Virgin Mary made by one of Scott's characters (Ellen), so the deviation in meaning is not too drastic. After the song was first performed, Schubert wrote to his parents that he felt genuine religious devotion while composing the melody, and considering how deeply it resonates with both the devout and secular, he seems to have infused the song with that authentic spiritual feeling. When the voice ascends and soars over a landscape of gentle arpeggios, the work's supernatural quality emerges in all its glory. —CKG

RECOMMENDED RECORDING

Schubert: Lieder; Anne Sofie van Otter; Bengt Forsberg (piano);
Deutsche Grammophon; 1997

La Traviata (The Woman Who Strayed)

GIUSEPPE VERDI (1813–1901)

Violetta Valéry, a well-known Parisian courtesan, is celebrating her recovery from illness at a party with friends when Alfredo Germont, a young nobleman, professes that he has secretly loved her since the day they met. Violetta eventually falls in love with him, gives up her life as a courtesan and moves to the country. Though suffering from financial woes, the couple is happy until Alfredo's father, Giorgio Germont, demands that Violetta end the relationship because her reputation as a former courtesan is negatively impacting his family.

Though reluctant at first, she eventually leaves for the sake of Alfredo's family. When Alfredo accuses Violetta of infidelity and publicly denounces her, she collapses from a relapse of tuberculosis. Shortly thereafter, Dr. Grenvil determines that Violetta does not have long to live. When Giorgio hears of this, he informs his son of Violetta's sacrifice. Alfredo rushes to see her, and she dies in his arms.

Based on the novel *La dame aux Camélias (The Lady of the Camellias)* by Alexandre Dumas, fils, with a libretto by Francesco Maria Piave, the moving story of *La Traviata* alone is enough to gain the lifelong devotion of many opera fans. Combined with Giuseppe Verdi's brilliant score, however, the three-act opera is an immortal contribution to the art form. The work contains many pieces synonymous with Italian opera, including the celebratory Act I duet with chorus, "Libiamo ne' lieti calici" ("Let's drink from this merry chalice"), and Violetta's dramatic coloratura Act I aria, "Sempre Libera" ("Always Free"). —CCD

Elizabeth Futral as Violetta, Sébastian Guèze as Alfredo. Photo by O'Neil Arnold, courtesy Kentucky Opera.

The Brass Section

HORNS APLENTY

The instruments in the brass family all find a common heritage in the horns of antiquity. Often held as a mark of power and status, horns have an elite history of performance for military signaling, battle entrances and exits, and the heralding of kings and queens.

A brass instrument produces sound when a player's vibrating lips, or *embouchure,* cause the air column inside of a tube to vibrate. Tightening or loosening the lips and changing the length of the tube are two ways to change pitch. Valves and slides added a way to instantly change the tube length while performing, advancing their use in the music of the day.

The brass quintet, popular in 16th- and 17th-century Europe with composers like Giovanni Gabrieli and Johann Pezel, is today made up of two trumpets, one French horn, one tenor trombone, and one bass trombone or tuba. The brass quintet is beautifully exemplified in Beethoven's "Für Elise."

Since the beginning of the 19th century, the majesty of the symphony orchestra brass section is largely created by three trumpets, four horns, three trombones, and one tuba. The section is seated toward the back of the orchestra behind the woodwinds, with the principal trumpet usually considered the section leader. The horns are placed to the conductor's left, the trumpets in the center, and the trombones and tuba to the right. —LMC

The Minor Modes

LOWERED SCALE DEGREES

As we come to the placement of half steps and whole steps within the mode, it's time to take a look at the minor mode. Compare it with the major mode and you can see where the placement of the half steps is different. We modify the placement of the half steps by adding three flats. Each flat lowers the pitch of the note immediately following it by one half step. This gives a darker implication to any melodic statement. Play the following minor scales/modes. (Note that today most musicians consider the terms "scale" and "mode" interchangeable.)

This is called the "melodic minor mode." It is only one of several minor modes, and has different ascending and descending forms. It's illustrated here in a scale form to make the placement of the half steps apparent:

MELODIC MINOR SCALE ON "C"

The natural minor has the same lowered third, sixth, and seventh ascending *and* descending:

NATURAL MINOR MODE

In this harmonic (or gypsy) minor example, it is correct to notate the B-natural *without* the natural sign because no B-flat or B-sharp immediately preceded it. If a note has no flat or sharp in front of it, it is considered natural. Sharps and flats that are not in the key signature of a composition are called "accidentals." —TH

HARMONIC MINOR ON C

Fun Fact

Why were these modes called "harmonic" and "natural"? One guess is that they stem from a relatively old and unscientific form of nomenclature that predates the rise of science (as does the art of music itself). Natural is used in the sense of "normal" or "basic" when applied to scales.

Musikverein, Vienna

TOO BEAUTIFUL FOR MUSIC?

"Musikverein" refers to two things: one, the Society of Music Lovers in Vienna; and two, the magnificent concert hall that hosts the society's season of performances. That both institutions use the same name shows just how much the society relies on the concert hall, and vice versa. In the minds of the Viennese, the two are inextricably linked, and both elements are stronger because of the bond.[1]

The Musikverein hall is home to the Vienna Philharmonic, and acoustically it is known as one of the three finest concert halls in the world. The superior quality of the sound appears to have been a fortunate accident; architect Theophil von Hansen aimed only to create a building that was structurally and visually impressive, surrounding its visitors with beauty and opulence from every angle. Not only did he succeed, but some thought he had done his job too well. During the opening festivities in January 1870, Vienna's leading music critic commented that perhaps the Musikverein was a bit too beautiful for a concert hall.[2] Nonetheless, most visitors seem to agree that the physical magnificence only enhances the appreciation of the music.

As well as an impressive roster of soloists and ensembles that grace its stage, the Musikverein has another prized possession: its collection of music archives, which is one of the largest in the world. The society regularly hosts exhibitions of original handwritten scores, photographs, recordings, and musical instruments, generously displaying these historic items for public viewing.[3] —MM

Festival d'Aix en Provence

A COURTYARD THEATER TRADITION IS BORN

Born in the whirl of postwar enthusiasm, the Festival d'Aix en Provence began in July 1948 in the archbishop's courtyard when a group of artists transformed the outdoor space into a colorful backdrop for music, theater, and song. About three or four concerts were held in the courtyard, another in St. Sauveur Cathedral, and six concerts and recitals in other locations around town. The mostly French audience was introduced to an unfamiliar opera, *Cosi fan tutte*, by Mozart. To this day the composer and his operas are a festival mainstay.

With its long tradition of courtyard open-air theater, the festival attracts some 60,000 visitors each summer for several weeks. When festivalgoers aren't enjoying the splendid town, wonderful food, or beautiful surrounding countryside, they can choose from opera, orchestral, choral, and chamber concerts.

Today three of the five venues are located outdoors. Among them are Théâtre de l'Archevêché, located in the former garden and courtyard of the archbishop's palace. Festivalgoers also can head to the shady courtyard of the Hôtel Maynier d'Oppède, opposite the archbishop's palace, or outside of town to a theater located within a courtyard on the expansive Grand Saint-Jean property. Indoor venues include a restored 18th-century Italian-style theater, or the newly built Grand Théâtre de Provence. —KFG

Aix en Provence festival attendees enjoy events all over the city.

Pachelbel and *Ordinary People*

A SHOWCASE FOR THE CANON

The Robert Redford–directed motion picture *Ordinary People* became a unique showcase for German Baroque composer Johann Pachelbel's *Canon in D major*. The film was responsible for opening up a completely new audience for the composition.

The 1980 film presents it three times, each time taking advantage of the following different versions.

We first hear the music at the very beginning of the film, performed as a choral piece with solo piano accompaniment. It's here that the story's main character is introduced as a member of his school's choir. Conrad, played by Timothy Hutton, is living with the pain of his self-imposed guilt about the accidental death of his older brother, which eventually leads him to seek professional therapy.

It's during a breakthrough session that we hear Pachelbel's *Canon* again, this time performed on solo piano. The reprise of the melody accompanies Conrad's relief as he discovers the truth and begins to understand the dynamics of his complicated family relationships, especially those of his seemingly loveless mother.

Finally we hear the piece again when Conrad and his father accept their future and reveal their love for each other at the end of the film. This time it's performed by a chamber orchestra, giving the theme a rich and full sound.
—DD

Rococo/Galant

MORE IS MORE

You know those people who decorate their houses to the umpteenth degree every single holiday? The ones whose front yards boast gargoyles and flashing skeletons for Halloween and full manger scenes for Christmas? Well, those people are the modern-day embodiment of the rococo—or galant—music written in the first half of the 18th century.

The term "rococo" originated in 1796 in the realm of art and architecture. It referred to a relaxing of the severe Baroque lines and rules. Literally, rococo means "shellwork"; only the outside frame was affected. So, as the Rococo ideals took over, ornamentation on churches and official structures became the norm. To understand the aura of these new buildings, think of a seventh-grade girl's handwriting, complete with curlicue script and heart-dotted i's.

Now imagine that architectural prototype applied to music. Trills and ornaments were utilized with abandon, and players freely improvised on the main melody, oftentimes to the point of making the main musical line almost unrecognizable.

The musical line itself, however, was still within the framework of the Baroque time period, and this rococo music is not considered part of the Classical era. Early 18th-century composers, particularly "The Famous Bach's" sons (J. C. Bach and C. P. E Bach), Franz Couperin, and Jean-Philippe Rameau, pushed the expected limits and helped redefine musical language through rococo.

We should definitely be thankful, no matter how tacky the giant inflatable Easter bunny! —SL

LISTENING HOMEWORK

C. P. E. Bach's Sonata in A minor for flute alone

Couperin's 4 Concerts royaux

Rameau's Les Indes galantes

Scherzo

SURELY, YOU MUST BE JOKING

As composers began experimenting with the traditional dance form of the minuet and trio in the third movements of symphonies and sonatas, they began to choose faster tempos. Haydn's minuets were fast and humorous, and eventually he used the term "scherzo" (Italian for "joke") to label the dance movement of his Opus 33 string quartets. But it is Beethoven who is particularly associated with the scherzo, starting with his Second Symphony. This was followed quickly by Franz Schubert, who used the form quite often in his string quartets and piano sonatas.

One common alteration in the scherzo was to add a second trio, either a repeat of the original trio or a completely new one. This shifted the form from a compound ternary form—ABA—to a rondo, ABAB (or C) A. These second trios are found in Beethoven's Symphonies Nos. 4, 6, and 7; and Schumann's four symphonies. Beethoven and Schumann sometimes shifted the scherzo to the second movement or composed the initial scherzo in a complete sonata form, as in Beethoven's Ninth Symphony. Beethoven also didn't write "scherzo" in the scores to his symphonies 4, 6, and 7, though the form was still used.

The term began being used in musical circles in the 1600s to describe madrigals and arias, though the form was usually strophic in those cases. In the Romantic era some individual scherzos were composed, but these tended to be character pieces rather than modified minuet and trio forms. —SS

Johann Sebastian Bach (1685–1750)

MORE THAN JUST A GOOD ORGANIST

Perhaps no other composer in history has had a greater reach than Johann Sebastian Bach—a thought made even more profound considering that Bach was one of history's least-traveled composers (living and dying in Germany); that he was known in his day more for his organ playing than his compositions;[1] and that his works were largely forgotten for more than 50 years after his death.

Born into a musical family at the height of the Baroque period, Bach earned his keep with music throughout his life, mostly through church positions. A prolific composer, he was at one point responsible for the music of four different churches at once;[2] yet he also wrote numerous instrumental solo and orchestral works, including a number of keyboard pieces designed to instruct his many children. A devout Lutheran, he dedicated every composition "to the glory of God alone."[3] Surprisingly, though, with all his other projects, less than half his total output was actually written for the church.[4]

Bach's compositional genius was not fully realized during his lifetime. A master of counterpoint, Bach wrote with an intricacy and complexity that often set him at odds with church leaders. Yet deeper analysis of his pieces reveals layers of numerology and mathematic consistency that continue to astound theorists today. More than just a good organist, Bach is recognized today as one of the masters of composition. —JJM

Symphony No. 94 ("Surprise")

BY FRANZ JOSEF HAYDN, 1791

Haydn is sometimes called the "father of the symphony" for his vital role in developing the genre. Incredibly, the Austrian composer produced more than 100 symphonies during his illustrious career, and most of them are expertly crafted.

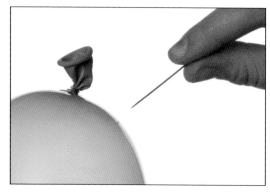

So what's so special about his 94th attempt? The source of the nickname "Surprise" certainly has something to do with its exceptional fame. During the symphony's supposedly calm and relaxing second movement, a seemingly innocent melody has grown steadily quieter, lulling the listener into a defenseless state, when an aggressive tympani stroke and forceful chord from the orchestra delivers a startling wake-up call.

Haydn was known to inject his compositions with a healthy dose of humor, so it is commonly suspected that he had mischief in mind when writing the surprise, perhaps in order to rouse any audience members who might have become too comfortable and nodded off in their seats.

It is not only the andante's musical joke that makes Symphony No. 94 memorable, though. As one of his *London* Symphonies, it displays the invaluable structural contribution Haydn made to the genre. The melodies are not without their charm, either, especially in the blossoming theme of the opening allegro and the spirited finale. —CKG

RECOMMENDED RECORDING

Haydn: Early London Symphonies; *George Szell (conductor);*
Cleveland Orchestra; Sony Classics; 2009

Aida

GIUSEPPE VERDI (1813–1901)

The quintessential example of *grand opera,* a genre characterized by historically significant subject matter and elaborate stage productions, can be found in Giuseppe Verdi's tragic opera *Aida.* With a cast of eight principal roles, usually more than 100 chorus members, actors, and dancers, and even sometimes live elephants and horses onstage, the sheer manpower involved in a production of this magnitude is impressive. Add to that the elaborate sets, costumes, and stage effects, and this opera is a spectacle in every sense of the word.

While *Aida* may be visually stunning, it is Verdi's music that makes this four-act opera timeless. Simply listening to a recording of the epic Act II Triumphal March can inspire courage, while Aida's Act III aria, "O patria mia" ("Oh, my country") may bring tears, even to those who do not understand the meaning of the lyrics.

Verdi masterfully sets the Italian libretto of Antonio Ghislanzoni to present a moving scenario first conceived by French Egyptologist Auguste Mariette. The story involves the Egyptian general Radames, who is in love with the captured Ethiopian Princess Aida. Her father, the Ethiopian king Amonasro, convinces his daughter to obtain the Egyptian battle plans from Radames. The Egyptian Princess Amneris is in love with Radames and jealous of Aida, so she demands that Radames be put to death for giving away the battle plans. He is sealed in a tomb to die when he discovers Aida, who hid herself there to be by his side for eternity. —CCD

Photo courtesy Opera Carolina (Charlotte, North Carolina, www.operacarolina.org).

The Trumpet
FROM THEIR LIPS TO YOUR EARS

A member of the brass family, the trumpet produces sound via air blown through vibrating lips into a mouthpiece at one end of a long, flared tube. Among the oldest of instruments, their loud, brash sound was historically used for military signals and fanfares. Two trumpets found in the tomb of King Tutankhamun give this wind instrument a birthday of more than 3,300 years ago.

The long, straight trumpet of medieval Europe was altered in the 1400s with the addition of two U-bends, forming a loop in the tube and the basis for the trumpet of the Renaissance and Baroque periods. One of the earliest musical uses is found in the beginning of the 17th century in Monteverdi's opera *L'Orfeo*.

This "natural" trumpet was not an easy instrument to play. Lacking finger holes or any way to alter pitch beyond the proficiency of the player's lips, its notes were normally limited to a harmonic series until the 1790s, when a trumpet with mechanical keys was invented by Anton Weidinger. It was for this instrument that Joseph Haydn and Johann Hummel wrote the two great trumpet concertos of the Classical period.

By the early 1800s valves were introduced, heralding the modern trumpet. They continued to be made in many sizes and pitches, including the higher piccolo trumpet. Bach made the soprano in D famous, and the piccolo has been immortalized on the Beatles' song "Penny Lane." In addition to its place in the orchestral brass section, the trumpet has recognized popularity in the jazz field with virtuosos like Miles Davis, Dizzy Gillespie, and Louis Armstrong. —LMC

Flats, Sharps, and Naturals

You've already seen the flat sign. Here are its partners, the sharp and the natural.

A-FLAT, A-SHARP, AND A-NATURAL

Just as the flat lowers any pitch by a half step (or semitone), a sharp raises any pitch a half step. The natural "A," not A-sharp or A-flat, is just the pitch of the corresponding line or space.

In the gypsy or "harmonic" minor (see page 134), you'll remember that all the intervals are the same as in the natural or basic minor, but that in the seventh scale degree, the pitch "B" is not lowered with a flat sign. When the sixth degree is lowered but the seventh is left "natural" or "as is," one and a half steps are created between steps six and seven, the A-flat and the B. This is called an "augmented second."

Musicians often omit the word "mode" when discussing major or minor modes. It's just a shorthand way of speech. So Beethoven's Fifth is just called Symphony in C minor. The presence of the word "mode" is understood. —TH

Place des Arts, Montreal

THE ARTISTIC PULSE OF THE CITY

Without a doubt, the 1960s was Montreal's most active decade in terms of cultural architecture. Expo 67, a metro system, and countless buildings and plazas injected new life into a city that was already teeming with excitement.

When the Place des Arts, a multivenue complex in the heart of the city, opened in 1963, it immediately became the focal point of performing arts and culture in Montreal.[1] Today it would be difficult to imagine the city without this all-important artistic hub.

It is difficult to talk about Place des Arts in terms of its relatively short history, as the momentum of the complex has always encouraged looking to the future rather than the past. What started out as a simple desire to have a grand performance venue quickly developed into no fewer than five concert halls specializing in everything from classical music to modern dance.

Place des Arts keeps an intense performance schedule of symphonic music, opera, and ballet, and in addition hosts a number of international arts festivals. Each passing season brings a torrent of new projects, fresh faces, and the greatest talents in the international arts community. Whether you prefer traditional classical music, eclectic modern compositions, or an outdoor music festival, there is plenty at Place des Arts to suit every taste. —MM

Dresden Music Festival

FOUNDED BY DECREE DURING THE COLD WAR

When the Dresden Music Festival was founded in 1978 by government decree, the city's residents were officially East Germans, the government communist, and foreign journalists were likely to be followed by secret policemen.

Much has changed since then. But a constant has been the quality of the music staged by the world's finest orchestras, ensembles, and performers for three weeks in May and June.

One of the most distinctive features of the festival is its yearly theme. The 2009 "New World" motto reflected the abundance of American works in the program. In 2010, some 20 years after the fall of the Iron Curtain, the (East) Berlin-born cellist and festival director Jan Vogler turned to Russia for a "fresh look at works by Russian composers" under the motto "Russlandia."[1]

The many festivalgoers come not only for the music, but also for the stunning architecture in this city on the river Elbe. Among the many venues are several treasures that were destroyed during the 1945 bombing of Dresden and later rebuilt: Frauenkirche, the 18th-century high Baroque church, and the Italian high Renaissance–style Semper Opera House. —KFG

Cellist and intendant Jan Vogler and the Symphony Orchestra of Hessian Radio conducted by Kristjan Järvi perform the Dresden premiere of Lieder von einer Insel (Songs from an Island) *during the Dresden Music Festival 2009. Photo by Mirko Joerg Kellner/DMF.*

Mozart in *Out of Africa*

SOUNDS LIKE ROMANCE

In December 1985, Sydney Pollack's wonderful romantic film *Out Of Africa* was released to theatres around the world. Based on the books by the main character in the film, Karen Blixen (Isak Dinesen), the story reveals a passionate and doomed love affair in 1913 Kenya. John Barry's film score is big, slow, and full of breath as it accompanies gorgeous shots of the wide-open African countryside. In addition to the original orchestral score, the audience is treated to recordings of four of Mozart's compositions.

The Adagio from Clarinet Concerto in A major, K. 622, and excerpts from Sinfonia Concertante for Violin, Viola, and Orchestra in E Flat Major, K. 364, *Three Divertimenti,* and Sonata for Piano in A major, K. 331 "Ronda Alla Turca" are heard when Karen's lover Denys Finch Hatton enters and re-enters the story. Denys brings many gifts to Karen during their friendship and affair, but perhaps the most rewarding are the Gramophone and the discs of recorded music. Along with Karen's crystal vases, china plates, fine pieces of art, and her designer clothing shipped from home in Denmark, hearing Mozart's music brings Europe a bit closer to her strange new home of Kenya.

The film won seven Oscars, including Best Director for Sydney Pollack. The recordings of Mozart's works used in the film were by maestro Sir Neville Marriner conducting the Academy of St. Martin-in-the-Fields, clarinetist Jack Brymer, and solo pianist András Schiff. —DD

Classicism: First Viennese School (1760–1775)

HAYDN GAVE US MORE THAN ONE FEELING

Until 1760 or so, each movement of a certain piece was written with one affect, or feeling. If the movement was sad, for example, it was sad all the way through, and the same process followed for more upbeat movements.

And here comes a surprise. If you had to name a famous classical composer, who would first come to your mind? Mozart, perhaps? Early Beethoven, maybe? Those are both great answers, but one of the most influential classical composers is quite commonly overlooked: Joseph Haydn.

Haydn introduced and developed the idea of having more than one important motivic attitude. Music was suddenly allowed to have mood changes. This was a huge liberation from the forced control of the Baroque period.

The first example of this new philosophy is Haydn's 1761 triptych *Morning, Noon, and Evening.* From that early work, he wrote over a hundred symphonies, all following the new writing style. One of his more famous and mature pieces, the "Farewell" Symphony, perfectly exemplifies the changing attitudes as well as some of Haydn's other breakthroughs.[1]

What are those breakthroughs, you ask? Just sit down, relax, and listen to the piece to make that judgment for yourself. Make sure you listen all the way to the end.* —SL

(*Hint: Up until the 1760s, symphonies were always expected to end bombastically.)

LISTENING HOMEWORK

Haydn's Morning, Noon, and Evening
"Farewell" Symphony, No. 45 in F sharp minor
String Quartets, Op. 20

Sarabande

MUSIC TO DANCE BY

Many dances from the Renaissance ended up as musical forms divorced from the original physical moves. The sarabande, also called the sarabanda or zarabanda, is one of those dances, found quite often in Baroque suites.

The dance originated in South America around the 16th century, and was eventually transported to Europe. It was deemed obscene in Spain, yet it was adored by Queen Anne of France. The sarabande (with or without the e) is based on the same three-beat measure as the minuet and the waltz, but it is distinguished by the slower tempo and the tendency to use the rhythms in the example below.

[quarter dotted quarter, eighth; or quarter half]

The dancers, usually a group of women accompanying themselves on the castanets, would drag their feet on the longer notes and undulate their bodies in a sexually suggestive manner.

This eroticism is not usually associated with the Baroque and Romantic examples. Instead, they evoke a melancholic nostalgia, more looking back at past romantic adventures rather than enacting current ones. Baroque examples of sarabandes can be found in Bach's unaccompanied 'cello suites, violin partitas, and keyboard suites; Handel's Concerto in G minor (listen to the performance by trumpeter Maurice André) and keyboard suites; and Telemann's *Trumpet Suites*.

Falling out of favor during the 19th century, the sarabande was reimagined in the beginning of the 20th century. The rhythms aren't exactly the same, but the slow, melancholic feel in three-beat measures is kept in the sarabande movements of Benjamin Britten's *Simple* Symphony and Claude Debussy's *Pour le Piano*. —SS

Aaron Copland (1900–1990)

AMERICA'S COMPOSER

Probably no American composer has gained more prominence than Aaron Copland. Born in humble surroundings to Russian Jewish immigrants at the turn of the last century, Copland's life and music have come to represent the American "everyman."

In his early 20s, Copland studied under Nadia Boulanger in Paris; it was she who first identified his compositional style and unique rhythmic patterns as distinctly "American," something she had not previously heard.[1] In the years that followed, Copland focused on developing that unique sound, writing several innovative works without any apparent external influences.[2]

Copland soon softened his style in the hope that the average person would connect with his music. Among his noted pieces at this time were the ballets *Appalachian Spring* and *Billy the Kid,* and several film scores. His "Fanfare for the Common Man" celebrates the human spirit with its unmistakable dual-trumpet melody line, and is possibly his most played work. In his later years, seeking fresh inspiration, he wrote several works using the 12-tone serialism of Arnold Schoenberg.

A gifted pianist, conductor, and teacher, Copland was also an advocate for the furthering of American music and composers' rights. He formed the American Composers Alliance in 1936 and participated in other groups. He was not a prolific composer, but as one conductor observed, everything he wrote was quality.[3] His style changed over time, but with his unique sound, America gained a distinct voice of its own in the world of music. —JJM

Peter and the Wolf

BY SERGEY PROKOFIEV, 1936

Classical music is often considered intrinsically highbrow, cerebral, and adult-oriented, but one listen to Prokofiev's whimsical *Peter and the Wolf* is enough to topple that stuffy stereotype. The Russian composer wrote the narrated orchestral work for a children's theatre and authored the story along with the music. Interspersed with the music, a narrator tells the tale of the brave boy Peter who heroically captures a menacing wolf. The delightful piece has not lost any popularity among kids or grown-ups.

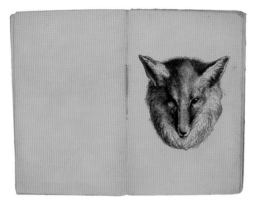

Prokofiev intended *Peter and the Wolf* to teach children about the various sections in the orchestra, so each character in the story is represented by a different instrument. The effect is wonderful, as the quality of each instrument reveals the personality of the character, and vice versa. Every scene is magically brought to life by the music, such as the unfortunate moment when the oboe-voiced duck is swallowed by ominous horns playing the part of the wolf. Peter himself is illustrated through the string section's famous theme, which captures all the innocent zeal of childhood.

Despite the cleverness required to create such a work, *Peter and the Wolf* cuts through any snobbery and proves that classical music can be fun after all.
—CKG

RECOMMENDED RECORDING

David Bowie Narrates Prokofiev's Peter and the Wolf; *Philadelphia Orchestra; Eugene Ormandy; RCA Victor; 1992*

Otello (Othello)

GIUSEPPE VERDI (1813–1901)

Following the successful premiere of *Aida*, Giuseppe Verdi decided to retire in 1871. Eight years later, he found himself unable to resist a proposal to partner with Italian librettist Arrigo Boito for an adaptation of William Shakespeare's play *Othello*. His return to the Italian opera scene resulted in what many critics consider to be his finest piece, *Otello*.

Boito's adaptation follows Shakespeare's play closely, telling the story of Otello, a Moor and mercenary serving in the Venetian Army. Iago, Otello's ensign, vows revenge when Cassio is promoted instead of him. Iago plots to make Otello believe that his wife, Desdemona, is cheating on him with Cassio. Otello kills Cassio and Desdemona, discovering too late that she was faithful. He then stabs himself and dies by Desdemona's side.

Kelly Kaduce as Desdemona, John Mac Master as Otello. Photo by J. David Levy; courtesy Kentucky Opera.

Filled with characterizations more detailed than those typically allowed by the melodrama of opera, Verdi brings depth to the three main roles. The title character's frustration is most evident in his Act II aria, "Ora e per sempre addio" ("Now and forever farewell"). The score also provides shades of gray to the black and white sketch of the evil Iago. His famous Act II aria, "Credo in un Dio crudel" ("I believe in a cruel God") is mesmerizing, as the orchestra relies on accented notes in the depths of the lower register. In contrast, the weeping innocence of Desdemona is portrayed with simultaneous sophistication and folklike simplicity in her Act IV aria, "Salce," also known as the "Willow Song."
—CCD

The French Horn

PLAYING WITH HAND AND MOUTH

Developed from the ancient hunting horn in France during the mid-17th century, the orchestral horn, commonly referred to as a French horn, is a conical bore brass instrument made from over 11 feet of tubing coiled in a circle.

This primitive "natural" horn used changes in the player's lips and breath and the insertion of the player's hand into the instrument's bell to sound different notes. It was therefore limited to about 12 tones in the harmonic series of the instrument's natural key. Short add-on tubes, called crooks, enabled the musician to change the key of the instrument and provide the musical horn used by most Baroque and Classical era composers.

In the early 19th century, valves replaced crooks as a way to adjust the tube length and change pitch, and the horn became a more versatile, chromatic instrument. This escalated the creation of horn works and solos throughout the 19th century by, among others, Beethoven, Chopin, Dvorak, and Tchaikovsky.

The requirement of an orchestral player to use both a deeper, more mellow F horn and a brighter, more agile B-flat horn led to the late-19th-century invention of the double horn. Combining the two instruments into one frame and adding a valve to switch between them created what was to become today's standard orchestral horn.

Although the typical symphony orchestra uses four horns, Gustav Holst's orchestral suite *The Planets* calls for six, and composer Richard Strauss scored for 20 in his tone poem *Eine Alpensinfonie.* —LMC

Gravity and Tonality in Music

THAT SOUNDS HEAVY

Repetition of harmonies is key to musical tonality (gravity).
Musical gravity, in turn, defines musical form.

Yes, music not only has form, but like the visual arts, it has *gravity*.

Take a moment now and listen to any good recording of just the first movement of Beethoven's Symphony No. 5 in C minor. Listen all the way to the

end. The last chords say to our ears, un-equivocally, "END! The END, the END, the END, the END, the END!" Now that's what we call musical gravity in action! There are 11 chords like that at the end of the 1st Movement.

These chords sound final not just because they're repeated again and again. It's which degree of the scale they're built on that gives them such finality.

Refer to the below chart of chords, numbered I through VII. In terms of sound, they operate in their own little "solar system" subject to their own tonal gravitational field.

The Roman numerals represent the same Roman numeral chords on the staff, except that their arrangement here shows how musical tonal gravity functions
in all tonal music, classical or otherwise.

Inside the three concentric circles, at the target's bull's-
eye, is the I chord, built on the first scale degree, called
the "tonic." In the key of C, major or minor, it's the C
chord (major or minor). —TH

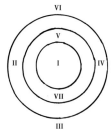

Chart of tonal gravity

Royal Opera House, London

THE QUEEN'S PRIDE

A theme of destruction by fire runs through the story of many of the world's great historic classical music venues. Candles made concerts possible, but they also presented a constant risk of burning the place to the ground. Add to that the lack of modern firefighting equipment, and you have a recipe for repeated disaster.

Royal Opera House, Covent Garden. Photo courtesy of Flavio Ferrari.

There have been three venues at the Covent Garden site that holds the current Royal Opera House in London. The previous two were destroyed by—you guessed it—fire.

The current incarnation began its story in 1858, hosting both ballet and opera performances for the public. Two world wars saw the building converted into a furniture repository and then into a dance hall, and had it not been for music publishers Boosey and Hawkes intervening, the venue might never have hosted a music event again.

When the Royal Opera reopened in 1946, there was no opera company waiting to reside there. So the directors began to assemble a company from available singers, and what started as a patchwork quilt of musicians eventually earned a charter as the official Royal Opera Company in 1968.[1]

These days the Opera House has been renovated to equip it with both the facilities and the technology to make it an integral part of the Covent Garden experience. Shops, restaurants, improved performance spaces, and beautiful design have transformed the Opera House into the crown jewel of the London musical community. —MM

Glyndebourne

SOMETHING OLD, SOMETHING NEW

An evening at Glyndebourne, a family-run summer festival in the English countryside, has been likened to a fairy tale. There are rituals—men in bow ties, women in evening dresses, picnics on the lawn (occasionally with cows grazing nearby), and extraordinary opera productions that aim to provoke, challenge, and entertain. The experience is similar to "the feeling of stepping back into *Brideshead Revisited*," wrote the *Times*.[1]

The curtain first rose on the Glyndebourne Opera Festival on May 28, 1934, at the estate of John Christie, who "felt that [opera] was almost nonexistent…in England, so we ought to begin to bring it here."[2] "We" referred to Christie and his wife, Audrey Mildmay, a professional singer. The festival's birth coincided with the rise of Hitler, when many artists were forced from Germany into exile. Christie drew three of them—conductor Fritz Busch, director Carl Ebert, and the impresario Rudolf Bing—to run his new festival. They produced *The Marriage of Figaro*.[3]

Sixty years to the day after the festival's inauguration, John Christie's son, George, who took over from his father, oversaw the opening of a rebuilt opera house, seating 1,200.

Internationally renowned, Glyndebourne aims to balance the expected with the unexpected, challenging audiencegoers with new productions of established works and premieres of commissioned new operas. More than 90,000 people attend its annual May to August season, and another 55,000 attend performances by Glyndebourne on Tour, which takes productions mounted at the festival to a wider audience at venues around the country. —KFG

Barber and *Platoon*

ANTIDOTE AND ACCOMPANIMENT TO WAR

American composer Samuel Barber finished his most famous work, *Adagio for Strings,* in 1936. The adagio is actually the second movement to his first *String Quartet.* This second movement is so passionate, heart wrenching, and beautiful that it has taken on a life of its own. Since its radio broadcast premiere by Arthur Toscanini and the NBC Symphony Orchestra, a number of arrangements and transcriptions of the work have been created.

The music is so powerful and profound that it became a major part of the score for Oliver Stone's Academy Award–winning 1986 film *Platoon.* Not only do we hear Barber's *Adagio for Strings* at the opening and close of the film, we hear it constantly throughout. This repeated use is very unique and makes for a poignant and important addition to composer/conductor Georges Delerue's original score for this Vietnam War epic.

Barber's *Adagio* came to director Oliver Stone's attention through his editor, Claire Simpson (who won an Oscar for her work here). Simpson, who found it very difficult to watch much of the footage depicting the horrors of war day after day, would hum Barber's famous *Adagio for Strings* to help her get through it. Ultimately, Stone found it to be the perfect accompaniment to much of the film. —DD

Classicism: First Viennese School (1775–1790)

MOZART STEPS UP

While Haydn was the most important figure in the early Classical period, Mozart was certainly the most significant composer of the middle Classical years.

Haydn had worked to expand the emotional ability of the repertoire while also elongating the pieces in general. While Baroque and pre-Baroque symphonies had commonly reached 10–12 minutes in length, music written in the Classical period had less limitation.

With Mozart's 1781 arrival in Vienna, though, Classicism was able to reach entirely new heights. Mozart brought Haydn's innovations to the world by touring throughout Europe. Mozart also had great interest in creating popular operas—ones that would create lasting fame in cities everywhere.

So while Haydn perhaps worked more seriously at the symphony genre, Mozart nearly perfected the classical opera. He added extended virtuosic woodwind melodies and expanded the breadth of the orchestral timbre by greatly increasing the size of the orchestra.

The only other composer who could even partially live up to these two musical giants was a famous pianist (and piano composer) named Clementi. During a piano improv competition, Clementi once tied with Mozart—imagine how much that infuriated Mozart! Clementi wrote innumerable piano sonatas, pieces that are now the basis for beginning conservatory students everywhere. Clementi is important in his own right because his performance in and around London greatly contributed to the expansion of Classical music. —SL

LISTENING HOMEWORK

Mozart's The Magic Flute
& The Marriage of Figaro
Clementi's Piano Sonatas (listen to any of them… you'll get the idea quickly!)

Fugue

IS THAT YOUR FINAL ANSWER?

The fugue was considered the pinnacle of compositional forms in the Renaissance because it required the perfect balance of rules and freedom. The term comes from the Latin *fuga* (flight) and has been used to signify three or more "voices" that imitate each other. These voices were real singers in the Renaissance, but in the Baroque era and forward, fugues were also performed by a keyboard instrument or an instrumental ensemble.

In the beginning of the fugue, called the "exposition," each voice enters singly with the theme. The first voice's theme is called the "subject," and the subsequent voices' imitations of the subject are called the "answer." The answer is always transposed in some way, usually a perfect fifth higher. If the transposition is exact, so all the intervals of the melody remain the same, the answer is "real" and the key has been switched. If some of the intervals of the melody have been altered to keep the melody in the original key, the answer is "tonal." When the new voices

BACH FUGUE IN C# MINOR FROM WELL-TEMPERED CLAVIER BOOK 1

enter, the previous voice continues with free counterpoint accompanying the answers. After this the fugue alternates freely between further statements of the subject and "episodes" that might use completely new ideas. The fugue usually finishes with a final statement of the subject.

It is fun to count how often the subject is performed in the fugue, made challenging by inversion, augmentation, diminution, or *stretto* (overlapping statements of the subject). —SS

Charles Ives (1874–1954)

LIVING IN THE TENSION

American composer Charles Ives lived a life that reflected the dual nature of his writing. A successful businessman by day and an eccentric composer by night,[1] Ives wrote a body of work that swung wildly between conventional and experimental.

Ives's music reflects several profound influences. His father, George, the town bandmaster, loved to experiment with sound. The folk music and hymnody of his native New England also affected him deeply. Finally there was transcendental philosophy, espoused by Romantic writers like Emerson, a belief in self-determination that Ives embraced.[2]

Ives's compositions draw from folk, sacred, and classic influences, yet become wildly creative and experimental, incorporating polytonality, polyrhythms and polymetrics (multiple key signatures at once), tone clusters, chance elements, and sometimes what seems like utter chaos. All of it was music to him.[3]

Ives lived in the tension between the music he longed to make and the music people would accept. Realizing his radical approach could not make him a living, he worked in insurance so he could be free to write as he wished. Yet he lived long enough to see even his more experimental pieces recognized for their artistic value. —JJM

FUN FACT

George Ives was by far the most profound influence on Charles' musical direction. The respected yet eccentric bandmaster of Danbury, Connecticut, once defended the off-key singing of a local workman, saying, "Look into his face and hear the music of the ages. Don't pay too much attention to the sounds—for if you do, you may miss the music."

"Moonlight" Sonata

BY LUDWIG VAN BEETHOVEN, 1801

Beethoven wrote over 30 piano sonatas during his lifetime, many of which are brilliant and beautiful, yet none is as famous as the beloved Piano Sonata No. 14 in C sharp minor, or "Moonlight Sonata." Its wild popularity is due in large part to its mournful first movement, but there is more to the sonata than the brooding melody and arpeggios of the adagio.

The fact that the sonata begins with an adagio, with such a lamenting tone, is rather unusual, especially since it is not in true sonata form. In "Moonlight Sonata," the traditional sonata-allegro is saved for the end, when the adagio's formerly pensive theme returns with a fiery vengeance. Between the related bookends is a brief, docile allegretto that temporarily lightens the mood, allowing a deep breath before the urgent final sprint.

The work's celestial nickname was not Beethoven's idea but rather was coined by a German music critic who likened the tranquility of the first movement to the luminous twinkling of the moon's reflection on Lake Lucerne.[1] —CKG

RECOMMENDED RECORDING

Beethoven: Moonlight, Waldstein, Appassionata; Vladimir Ashkenazy (piano); Penguin Classics; 1998

Der fliegende Holländer (THE FLYING DUTCHMAN)

RICHARD WAGNER (1813–1883)

German composer Richard Wagner revolutionized the art form with his fourth opera, *Der fliegende Holländer (The Flying Dutchman)*. Discarding standard composition techniques, he paved the way for his larger-scale music dramas, including *Der Ring Des Nibelungen (The Ring of the Nibelung)*, through this pioneering effort. Most significantly, Wagner introduced the use of *leitmotifs* (leading motifs), recurring musical themes that represent particular characters, places, events, or ideas within the story. These leitmotifs are introduced in the overture and recur throughout the opera, adding symbolism and further unifying the piece. Wagner also wrote *Der fliegende Holländer* to be performed without intermission in order to maintain the unity of the piece. However, many modern productions divide the opera into three acts.

Mark Delavon as the Dutchman. Photo by Tim Wilkerson (www.timwilkersonphotography.com); courtesy of Atlanta Opera (www.atlantaopera.org).

Wagner wrote his own libretto for the opera, basing it on Heinrich Heine's novel, *Aus den Memoiren des Herrn von Schnabelewopski (The Memoirs of Mister von Schnabelewopski)*. The story recounts the legend of a ship captain who has been condemned by Satan to sail the seas forever. During the brief time he is allowed to venture ashore every seven years, the Dutchman's only hope to be released from his torture is to find the unconditional love of a woman. When he docks in Norway, Senta is intrigued by the legend and vows to save him. Flirtations with a local huntsman make the Dutchman believe Senta has betrayed him. Without hope for redemption, he departs. Still faithful to the Dutchman, Senta throws herself into the sea. The two ascend into heaven together. —CCD

The Trombone
A MOST FORTUNATE NAME CHANGE

Originally known as a sackbut, the trombone emerged during the mid-15th century and is thought to have evolved from the Renaissance slide trumpet. Although it has been made in many sizes over the years, from piccolo to bass, it is one of the few instruments whose original shape has not changed.

A member of the brass family, the trombone is characterized by the telescoping, U-shaped sliding section of the tube. The slide is moved through seven different positions. As the slide is pushed out, lengthening the tube, each position lowers the pitch by a semitone.

With its tendency to be loud and boisterous, the trombone is popular in fanfares, outdoor events, and military bands, and it can be heard in the marches of John Philip Sousa. When played quietly, its clear, focused sound and subtle articulation have found favor in church music, doubling the lower voices, and it is often paired with the cornett as natural accompanists for choral music.

J. S. Bach and Frederic Handel used this aerophone in the early 1700s, while mid-century Austrian virtuoso trombonist Thomas Gschladt inspired works by Mozart and Haydn. It wasn't until 1808 that Ludwig van Beethoven is credited with first using the trombone in a symphony in his Symphony No. 5 in C minor.

In addition to being the tenor voice in the orchestral brass section, the trombone is popular in jazz, swing, R&B, and rock. It has been played on many hit songs by James Pankow in the pop group Chicago. —LMC

Tonic Rules

EVEN WITHOUT THE GIN

The tonic note and chord (I = major; i = minor) are the tonal center, and are heard more often in a musical piece than any other. In the next ring out, we have the V, or dominant chord, and the VII, or leading tone chord. It's called "leading tone" because it leads up to the tonic (on eight this time) again.

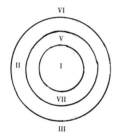

II (supertonic) and IV (subdominant) are the next furthest from the tonic gravitational center. They often lead away from the tonic at the start of a musical phrase or other composition, then back "home" to the tonic at the end.

The "farthest-out" chords are on III (mediant) and VI (submediant).

Chart of tonal gravity

As further proof that the tonic rules, it can be judiciously inserted between any other two chords according to the rules of tonal music. Of course, all this use of the tonic chord keeps the ear focused on it. The music-processing part of the brain often hears all of the other chords first with reference to the "mighty" tonic, and second with reference to each other.

So repetition in musical sound is important in harmony too because it establishes where our musical ear wants to go by repeating the tonic chord in a musical composition. As you might expect, the dominant (V) and leading tone (VII) are heard slightly less, the supertonic (II) and subdominant (IV) less than that, and the median (VI) and submediant (III) the least.

Remember, this chart illustrates how you hear and feel the music, not how it's notated. —TH

Vigado, Budapest

IT'S NOT ALWAYS ABOUT ACOUSTICS

While most noted concert halls possess an almost mysterious ability to carry and enhance sound, in some venues the mystery is more about why such an average-sounding place has become so popular.

The Vigado has had as rough a time as most famous European venues; war and bombings have certainly taken their toll on more than one occasion. The original hall was destroyed in 1848 during the Hungarian War of Independence, and a completely new

building was constructed in its place.[1] Although acoustically the Vigado was nothing special, architecturally it was one of the most celebrated structures in Budapest, and its popularity drew the presence of such renowned composers as Bartok and Kodaly.

The attraction of the Vigado may lie in its versatility. In addition to classical music, the hall was also a popular venue for balls and galas. Its heyday in the late 19th century saw performances from Brahms, Debussy, and, of course, Liszt, the beloved Hungarian pianist and composer.[2]

World War II also took its toll on the Vigado, and the resulting damage kept the venue closed until 1980. Another major renovation took place in 2004, restoring decaying parts of the auditorium and giving the façade a general cosmetic freshening.[3] Today the Vigado is run by the Foundation for Art and Community Culture, and it hosts both music works as well as other art exhibitions.[4] —MM

Oregon Bach Festival

A CLASSICAL WORLD EVENT IN THE PACIFIC NORTHWEST

A "Bach mobile"—colorful 40-foot banners reading "Oregon Bach Festival"—twirls in the sunlit lobby of the Hult Center for the Performing Arts, reflecting the inspiration for this yearly celebration that specializes in large choral works and presents the best of Bach's masterpieces and the works of composers he influenced. The festival has been called "astonishing" by the *Washington Post* and "a musical enterprise virtually without equal in America" by the *Los Angeles Times.*[1]

Located in the college town of Eugene, nestled in the Willamette Valley about 100 miles south of Portland, the festival started quietly in 1970 when German organist and conductor Helmuth Rilling came to the University of Oregon for a series of small choral workshops and an informal concert—and stayed to co-found the festival. The annual event attracts hundreds of musicians from around the world and some 35,000 visitors every year.

Festivalgoers can choose from major choral-orchestra works, instrumental and chamber concerts, solo recitals, workshops, lectures, and master classes over a nearly three-week period in June and July. While the repertoire focuses on great works of the past, Rilling, the festival's artistic director and conductor, is also committed to commissioning new work, including Krzysztof Penderecki's *Credo,* for which the Oregon Bach Festival won a Grammy Award in 2001 for the best choral performance of the year. —KFG

Performance at the Oregon Bach Festival of composer Sven-David Sandström's Messiah. *Pictured are conductor Helmuth Rilling and vocalists Robin Johannsen and Roxana Constantinescu. Photo by Jon Christopher Meyers; courtesy the Oregon Bach Festival.*

Bellini and *The Bridges of Madison County*

MUSIC THAT MAKES THE HEART SING

In 1995, director/actor Clint Eastwood decided to make a very different film from what he was known for, delivering his interpretation of the Robert James Waller novel *The Bridges of Madison County*. The story and film are pure rhapsodic romance. Starring next to Mr. Eastwood, who portrays *Life* photographer Robert Kincaid, is the amazing Meryl Streep, playing housewife Francesca Johnson living on a farm in the American heartland.

Francesca finds herself alone at home when she decides not to attend a state fair in Illinois with her family. Even though she's happy and loves her family, this time alone finds her recalling her days as a young single girl in Europe during and after World War II. The audience senses her longing for those days of freedom and excitement. These feelings are stirred even more when Robert Kincaid appears at her door asking for directions. This meeting evolves into a wonderful and aching romance that would last to the end of their lives.

The radio in her kitchen often connected Francesca to her past. In an especially profound moment in the film we see her listening to a broadcast of an aria from Vincenzo Bellini's opera *Norma* entitled "Casta Diva." It seems as if her heart is singing with the soprano; the realization of her newfound feelings for someone other than her husband and her longing for the past seem almost like regret. The music dramatically underscores this revelation. —DD

Classicism: First Viennese School (1790–1825)

BYE BYE BAROQUE

We've talked about Haydn reigning over the early Classical period and Mozart as king of the middle Classical period. Who do you think might be the musical giant of the late Classical period?

If you said "Beethoven," you are 100 percent right. Beethoven might be more known as a Romantic composer, but he grew from Classical roots. You could even say he was responsible for the entire transition period from Classical to Romantic music. So while Beethoven scholars concentrate on late Beethoven and talk about his string quartets until they're blue in the face, I think it is equally important to look at his early influence.

If, by the early 1800s, there was any Baroque feel left in the musical palettes of composers, Beethoven obliterated it. Because of him, figured bass was no longer a means of driving the piece forward; instead, importance lay in using differing modes, varying the melodic drive through the available instruments (and thus bringing texture to the forefront), and of course continuing to elongate the length of symphonic repertoire.[1]

All in all, young Beethoven and his contemporaries were interested in a more complex type of music; they wanted to challenge both each other and their listeners, and they were oh so eager for the next musical era to open up before them. —SL

LISTENING HOMEWORK

Beethoven's Symphony No. 1
Beethoven's Fidelio
Schubert's Symphony No. 8 ("The Unfinished Symphony")

Sonata

NOT TO BE CONFUSED WITH SINATRA

Sonatas are first and foremost instrumental works in three or four move-ments for either solo piano or piano and one or two other instruments. Works for more than just piano always have the piano as an equal partner rather than a subservient accompaniment. However, in the 19th century, theorist A. B. Marx noticed that all of Beethoven's piano sonatas began with the same compositional structure, which was also found in the first movements of concertos, symphonies, and multimovement chamber works by a variety of composers.

This structure, called the "sonata form," is basically the rounded binary form on steroids. The three parts, rather than ABA, are called the "exposition," "development," and "recapitulation." The exposition can have several themes, but always has two different keys, usually tonic and dominant. The exposition is supposed to repeat, but often the repeat is skipped in performances. The development places the previous themes in new contexts, from different keys to fragmented versions to new orchestrations. The recapitulation returns all the original themes in their original order (usually), but now all the themes are in the tonic key. The development and recapitulation are theoretically supposed to repeat together, like the B A in the rounded binary form, but this hardly ever happens.

Sometimes there is a *coda,* new or developmental music that closes the whole movement, or an introduction that is slower in tempo than the rest of the movement. —SS

FUN FACT

Beethoven was known to compose codas that were longer than the rest of the movement, like the first movement of his Third Symphony.

Igor Stravinsky (1882–1971)
A LIFE OF EVOLUTION, AN AGENT OF CHANGE

Comparing an Igor Stravinsky piece from his early years with one from his latter years, you would not know they were written by the same man. Indeed, it seemed Stravinsky's entire life reflected a personal progression: Russian-born, later becoming a French citizen, and eventually dying an American citizen. In a similar odyssey, his compositional style evolved from the late Russian Romanticism of his famous composer-teacher Rimsky-Korsakov into neoclassicism (writing modern tonalities into older classical forms), and later into Arnold Schoenberg's 12-tone method of composition.

The defining moment of Stravinsky's career was the 1913 Paris debut of his ballet *The Rite of Spring*. A depiction of ancient Russian paganism, it broke with convention in nearly every way imaginable. The music departed from traditional tonality, and the provocative content crossed moral boundaries.[1] The audience rioted, their sensibilities completely offended. Stravinsky remembered later, "I have never again been that angry…I could not understand why people who had not yet heard it wanted to protest in advance."[2] Yet that moment in time permanently altered the musical landscape, influencing the direction of music for years to come.

Stravinsky's body of work, much of which he eventually recorded, includes compositions for piano, vocal, choir, orchestra, opera, and ballet. The common thread weaving through Stravinsky's evolution of style is his remarkable creativity and innovation, driven by an insatiable curiosity and desire to grow.
—JJM

Blue Danube

BY JOHANN STRAUSS II, 1867

Probably the most famous waltz in the history of music, the *Blue Danube* needs little introduction. Strauss II is the reigning "waltz king," and this particular piece is easily his most celebrated. It's almost impossible to listen to the spritely main theme without envisioning the extravagant ballroom dances of 19th-century Vienna.

However, the work was not an immediate success upon its Viennese premiere, where it was performed with words sung by a four-person choir. It wasn't until Strauss removed voices from the score that the world began to catch on. The original title, *An der Schonen, Blauen Donau,* translates to *On the Beautiful, Blue Danube,* and might have been borrowed from the poetry of Karl Beck.[1]

Because of its frequent, sometimes frivolous use in popular culture, the waltz may not always receive the appreciation it deserves. Shortened versions exist to provide modern listeners with a quick fix of the well-known melody, but the complete work is really quite intricate. Five "mini-waltzes"—each with two sections—compose the piece, and they flow together effortlessly despite frequent changes in tempo and key. Truly, the *Blue Danube* is as suited to the concert hall as the ballroom. —CKG

Lohengrin

RICHARD WAGNER (1813-1883)

Each year, millions of brides march down the aisle to the tune of "Here Comes the Bride." Many do not realize that this music is actually the "Bridal Chorus" ("Treulich geführt") from Act III of Richard Wagner's German opera *Lohengrin*. Composed in 1850, this three-act opera is more similar to traditional Italian opera than any other written by Wagner, as evidenced by the abundance of choruses and arias, as well as the lyrical writing style.[1]

Ryan McKinny as Royal Herald, Richard Paul Fink as Friedrich of Telramund, Simon O'Neill as Lohengrin. Photo by Felix Sanchez; courtesy Houston Grand Opera.

With a libretto written by Wagner himself, the story is based on the German mythological tale of the knight of the Holy Grail, also known as the son of Parzival. Lohengrin is led to Antwerp by a swan to rescue Princess Elsa of Brabant from an unwanted suitor. Lohengrin saves her, and they marry. Even though Elsa is forbidden to ask Lohengrin's identity, she cannot temper her curiosity and inquires. Lohengrin is, therefore, sent back to the castle of the Grail. The swan returns and Lohengrin's prayers transform him into Elsa's lost brother, Gottfried. Lohengrin departs, and Elsa collapses, having died from the grief of losing her beloved.

In addition to the "Bridal Chorus," Wagner's *Lohengrin* is well known for several other pieces, including the opening music to Act II, Scene 4, "Elsa's Procession to the Cathedral," which is frequently used as a concert band arrangement. Equally famous is Lohengrin's Act III aria, "In fernem Land" ("In a Distant Land"), in which he reveals his true identity. —CCD

The Tuba

PLAYING WITH THE BIG BOYS

The tuba is the largest and lowest-pitched member of the brass family. Over the years, its size and design have varied greatly. It is a valved, metal tube instrument using a wide conical bore, with the tubing usually coiled into an elliptical shape and terminating into a very wide bell. In contrast to its cousins, the trumpet and trombone, the tuba is usually played in the vertical position with the bell facing upward or forward.

The original patent for the tuba was granted to Wilhelm Friedrich Wieprecht and Carl Moritz in Prussia in 1835. Following the shape of the ophicleide, the tuba used valves, similar to the trumpet, instead of padded keys and sound holes, to soon replace its Renaissance predecessor.

Other 19th-century versions designed to wear over the shoulder include the helicon and the sousaphone. The larger sousaphone was developed in the 1890s for composer and bandmaster John Philip Sousa in an attempt to create a tuba that was easier to hold and that could project its sound up and over the band.

The Wagner tuba is specially designed by composer Richard Wagner for his epic opera work *The Ring* in an attempt to bridge the gap between horns and trombones. While many composers, including Bruckner, Schoenberg, and Richard Strauss, have written for this unique brass instrument, Stravinsky's *The Rite of Spring* is a superb example.

In addition to being a member of the symphonic orchestra, the tuba plays a prominent role in jazz, ragtime, and big-band music. —LMC

Cadences

MUSIC'S TRAFFIC LIGHT

When chords change from one to another, it's called a "harmonic progression," a "chord progression," or simply "changes." (This last term is from the jazz and pop world.)

The chord change from IV to I or V to I at the end of a section or a piece is called a "cadence." Cadences, like modes, chords, and other aspects of music, have several forms, but share one thing: They bring the music back to a point of rest, almost always on the tonic chord. Cadences claim more of the listener's attention when they occur at a climactic point.

To hear what a dominant-tonic chord progression sounds like, listen again to the closing measures of Beethoven's Fifth, and you'll hear that Beethoven used one of the strongest sets of changes and one of the purest cadences available in classical music: He goes from the chord nearest the center of gravity to the center…and back.

And in a move that threatens the propriety of the austere classical symphony, he does it again and again, driving home the cadence in true Romantic fashion. (You want the end? I'll give you the end!) It's called an "authentic" cadence. Others include:

- plagal cadence (IV—I): another ending cadence. Sounds like the "amen" at the end of a hymn
- deceptive cadence: substitutes the VI chord for the I; can feel like a temporary harmonic pause
- half cadence: another chord moving to the V chord; also feels like a temporary pause —TH

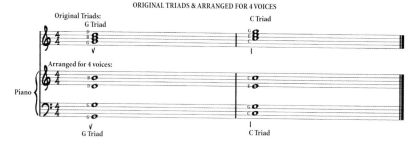

PERFECT AUTHENTIC CADENCE

ORIGINAL TRIADS & ARRANGED FOR 4 VOICES

Royal Festival Hall, London
PROBLEMATIC, YET STILL BELOVED

If you visit the Royal Festival Hall in London, you may note that it is not the most striking venue you've ever seen, and indeed it seems to be completely overshadowed in this city full of beautiful and historic concert halls. But the Royal Festival Hall is important enough in British culture that the government officially designated it a protected building, and in addition, it is the home of the London Philharmonic Orchestra, once led by the great Sir Georg Solti.

In 1948, commissioning architect Hugh Casson decided to give young architects in Britain a chance to show their talent. The result was a bold statement of modernism that got a very mixed reception from the public. In addition, the acoustics of the hall were not up to the high standards of the era. After several revisions to both the internal and external structure, the building still resembles what some have called "a giant chicken coop," and the sound quality remains sketchy at best.

So why is the Royal Festival Hall considered a great venue? Simply put, it is a triumph of function over form. Despite its troubles, management has been extremely well handled, and it has become an important center for classical concerts and music festivals. The foyer areas of the hall remain open during the day and are one of the most popular meeting places in all London. —MM

Royal Festival Hall. Photo courtesy Ewan Munro.

Rossini Opera Festival
REVIVING LOST MASTERPIECES

The seaside resort town of Pesaro on the eastern Italian coast boasts sandy beaches, a medieval town center, surrounding hills, and artistic landmarks. Pesaro is also the birthplace of one of Italy's most famous opera composers: Gioachino Rossini.

Born in 1792, Rossini wrote 36 operas during his lifetime. Many have been lost or ignored. The Rossini Opera Festival held annually in August aims to study, revive, and stage his musical legacy. Founded in 1980, the festival has played a pivotal role in bringing back Rossini's rarely performed operas and ones thought to be lost. The most significant revival was the recovery of *Il viaggio a Reims*, the mythical score that disappeared after its first performance in 1825. Its rediscovery and revival in Pesaro in 1984 under Italian conductor Claudio Abbado marked one of the most important musical events of the century.[1]

"No great composer's fame rests upon so few works as Rossini's, and no one wrote more masterpieces still awaiting full appreciation," wrote the *Telegraph*. "That's good news for the Rossini Opera Festival…for it has plenty of ground to cover before it begins recycling itself."[2]

When Rossini opera lovers aren't attending a performance, they can visit the modest house where the composer was born, located on Via Rossini. Today it is a small museum with a portrait gallery, the spinet on which the maestro studied as a boy, some autographs, and other memorabilia. —KFG

Photo courtesy Studio Amati Bacciardi.

Moon Music

A BIT OF DEBUSSY IS JUST THE RIGHT STUFF

One of composer Claude Debussy's most famous works, "Clair de Lune" is heard during a very unique scene in director Philip Kaufman's 1983 film adaptation of the Tom Wolfe book *The Right Stuff*.

The film and book tell the story of the United States Air Force test pilots who broke speed and altitude barriers and were eventually chosen to be part of the Mercury and Apollo missions by NASA. The trials and triumphs of those first missions to space are well documented and brilliantly played.

The scene in which an orchestral version of Debussy's famous piece is played stands out in a film made up of mostly exciting action and wonderful adventure. We see the chosen Mercury astronauts being honored by President Johnson in Texas. Part of the entertainment during this event is a young female dancer who performs an almost erotic dance choreographed to "Clair de Lune." The music plays above the sound of the audience and no dialogue is heard. However, we see the astronauts acknowledge their special place and elite status as they make eye contact with each other during this very peaceful performance.

"Clair de Lune" is not only a great choice for this surreal moment, but it also points forward toward John F. Kennedy's seemingly impossible goal of reaching the moon before the end of the 1960s. —DD

Romanticism

AN EMOTIONAL APPEAL

When you think of the 1960s, you automatically imagine hippies, peace marches, and a general sense of hope, right? Well, it must be true that history repeats itself, because a similar feeling was in the air through much of the 19th century. During the Romantic period, the spirit of freedom and rebellion was all consuming, and the term "Romanticism" could safely be applied to all areas of life then, especially the arts, but also philosophy, politics, and even science.

All these genres replaced strict form and function with an emphasis on feeling and emotion. Nature stories, fairy tales, and anything regarding omnipotent "hero worship" were all the rage.

The Romantic era is generally divided into three subcategories. During the first, Sturm und Drang (Storm and Stress), there were still Classical roots, but feeling in music was intensified. The other two categories—Early and Late Romantic—show the evolution of Romantic music and the beginnings of a transition into modern music.

Within Romantic music as a whole, though, you can hear composers stepping out of line for the first time, as if they're experimenting with their own protests and petitions. From Beethoven and Weber in Germany to Ravel and Debussy in France, Romantic music broke down some incredibly strong barriers. —SL

LISTENING HOMEWORK

Beethoven's Symphony No. 6 ("Pastorale" Symphony)
Ravel's **Daphnis et Chloe**
Weber's **Der Freischutz**

Waltz

I COULD'VE DANCED ALL NIGHT...

With the minuet, sarabande, and suite, we have already seen that classical composers loved to use dances as compositional forms. Well, dust off your ballroom slippers, because we are now tackling the waltz.

This is yet another dance in triple meter, with a quick tempo and a strong emphasis on the first beat. The term comes through German from the Latin *volvere,* for the revolving and turning that is an essential part of the dance.

Waltzes were composed for orchestra and for piano, starting as accompaniment to dancers but eventually switching to concert waltzes. Franz Schubert wrote many waltzes for the piano that reveal the evolution of the form from short binary forms to short ternary forms to longer composite ternary forms with the addition of a trio.[1] Certainly the most popular waltz composers were father and son Johann Strauss I and II, the latter known as the "waltz king." Junior's famous *Blue Danube* and *Emperor Waltz* are good examples of concert waltzes, with many tempo shifts that would make dancing difficult.

The waltz was found everywhere in the 19th century: ballrooms, plays, operas, operettas, ballets, symphonies, piano music, and chamber music. Later composers like Ravel and Stravinsky used waltzes to evoke 19th-century Vienna either fondly or critically, because it was so strongly associated with that time and place. —SS

Béla Bartók (1881–1945)

NO ONE ELSE COMPARES

Due to numerous illnesses as a child, Hungarian composer Béla Bartók spent much of his youth in isolation, and he almost didn't live to age 20—which likely contributed to his quiet, terse nature as an adult. One associate of his remarked that his outward demeanor was "exactly the opposite of the revolutionary vigour of his art."[1]

Many of Bartók's compositions inspired intrigue but were largely misunderstood. His style was actually derived from a wide range of influences gleaned from his insatiable curiosity—from the Romanticism of Strauss, to Debussy's impressionism, to the atonality of Stravinsky and Schoenberg.

His greatest inspiration by far, however, was the folk music of his own people, largely unaffected by Western tonality. When he first heard it, he was forever captivated; collaborating with Zoltán Kodály, he collected thousands of folk songs from the Magyar, Transylvanian, and Slavic regions. Of Magyar descent himself, Bartók considered Magyar peasant songs to be true Hungarian folk music. His work in this area helped found a new field of music study, ethnomusicology.[2]

The cumulative result of these influences on Bartók was a body of some of the most innovative music ever written—an exploration of polytonality (multiple key signatures at once), irregular rhythms, modal scales, and percussive playing styles. His music is at times hauntingly melodic, at times harshly dissonant, at times wildly tribal—but always distinctly Hungarian and uniquely *Bartók.* —JJM

Missa Papae Marcelli

BY GIOVANNI PIERLUIGI DA PALESTRINA, 1567

Prior to the Baroque era, which began around 1600, Western music was predominantly religious in nature, written to glorify or invoke the supernatural. In the Middle Ages and into the Renaissance, choral music was an integral part of worship, and as time went by, compositional structures became more complex. By the late Renaissance, polyphonic layers of melody and harmony were interwoven to create gorgeous layers of textured sound. Palestrina was the preeminent composer of that time, creating hundreds of masses, motets, and madrigals that combined technical innovation with transcendent beauty.

His most famous mass, *Missa Papae Marcelli,* was written to honor Pope Marcellus II. Each of its sections—Kyrie, Gloria, Credo, and Sanctus—is a vehicle for church liturgy, and as such is meditative in tone and restrained in composition. By no means is this music boring, however. The cascading voices that begin the Kyrie are enough to bring chills as layers of harmony build and reverberate in heavenly echoes. It is a testament to Palestrina's talent that, with only six voices, he can create so much depth and evoke so much emotion. —CKG

RECOMMENDED RECORDING

Palestrina: Missa Papae Marcelli, Missa Aeterna; *Oxford Camerata; Jeremy Summerly (conductor); Naxos; 1994*

Tristan und Isolde

RICHARD WAGNER (1813–1883)

The single most famous chord in the history of opera opens Richard Wagner's 11th opera, *Tristan und Isolde*, an intensely psychological tragedy in three acts. Known as the "Tristan chord," the opera's initial harmony contains two dissonances that leave the listener in expectation of resolution. This never completely arrives until the conclusion of the drama, mirroring the constant state of tension the title characters feel.

Isolde, daughter of the Irish king, is being carried by Tristan's ship to Cornwall, as she is being forced to marry its king, Marke, instead of the Irish champion Marold, whom Tristan killed in battle. Isolde, miserable and riddled with guilt because she healed the wound Tristan received in battle from Marold when he came to her in disguise, determines death would be a better alternative for both herself and Tristan. She sends her maid, Brangäne, to make a death potion, but Brangäne instead serves them a love potion, and Tristan and Isolde begin a passionate affair. Their love is eventually exposed, and Tristan, wounded in battle, returns to his childhood home to die. Isolde quickly follows, and Tristan dies in her arms. King Marke, having learned the truth of the love potion from Brangäne, arrives to forgive them, but is too late. The lovers are finally joined in death. —CCD

The Percussion Section

ACCESSORIZING WITH A SNAP, CRACKLE, AND POP

The largest variety of instruments can be found in the percussion section of the symphonic orchestra. Yet the orchestral percussion section typically contains just two to five percussionists.

Percussion instruments are generally divided into two categories—those that produce sound of a definite pitch, like the xylophone and tympani; and those that don't, like cymbals, triangles, and snare drums.

Typically there is a section leader, and he or she will determine how the parts are distributed among the players so they have time to switch from one instrument to another between parts. Although some players do specialize, as with the tympani and marimba, most professional percussionists are able to play many instruments.

Percussion instruments are, by definition, things that are struck, but the orchestral percussion section bends that rule. Wind players do not blow whistles, a

violinist does not bow the saw, and the conductor does not crack the whip. The orchestral percussionist handles all this as well as banging anvils and popping paper bags.

Because many of its instruments require a lot of space and can easily be heard over the others, the percussion section lives at the back of the orchestra. Rarely designated to provide continuous rhythm like rock and jazz drummers, orchestral percussionists are relied on for accents, textures, and melody. From Lully to Beethoven to Tchaikovsky to Cage, composers have always used percussion to enhance the classical music experience. —LMC

Diatonic and Chromatic Scales

STEPPING IT UP BY HALVES

Up until now, we've been working with a seven-tone scale from C up to B on the keyboard, with C repeated at the top, and with half steps only between the third and fourth, and the seventh and eighth scale degrees: the scale of C major. All these major and minor scales are *diatonic scales.*

Ever notice the five black keys on the piano? If we include them in our octave from C to C, it's goodbye diatonic! We will then have a scale composed entirely of half steps, called a "chromatic scale." Chromatic pitch inflections are often used throughout classical music of all styles to add color, nuance, and expression to "plain vanilla" major and minor music.

Those keys also allow us to make any note in both the diatonic and chromatic scales the center of a key. This means we can replicate the major and minor scales, or *modes,* on any key, including any line or space on the staff. Thus we have the key of E-flat major or minor, D major or minor, and so on. Notationally, this is indicated by the use of *sharps* and *flats,* moving notes up or down a half step.

In the ascending scale, sharps are used to create the half steps between every pitch except where they happen naturally, between B and C, and between E and F. In the descending scale, the same succession of half step intervals is accomplished by putting a flat in front of the note. These sharps and flats are called "accidentals." —TH

Festspielhaus, Bayreuth

WAGNER, WAGNER EVERYWHERE

Many of the world's most important classical composers were happy to let orchestras and artists interpret their music, at least up to a certain point. Others, however, exhibited a desire to have more control over their music and how it was played. Richard Wagner was known for being obsessed with the presentation of his works, and it was this obsession that led to the construction of one of the world's most unusual opera houses, the Bayreuth Festspielhaus.

What makes the Festspielhaus so special is not the theater's construction itself—though it does have some interesting features, such as the recessed orchestra pit that prevents the audience from seeing the musicians. Rather, the main curiosity behind the theater is how it is used. That is to say, it only has one function: to serve as a performance venue for the operas of Wagner. Wagner himself had the hall constructed specifically for this purpose, as he felt an audience could only appreciate his operas fully if they were performed under circumstances that he could control, with every last detail organized to his specifications.

Of course, after Wagner's death in 1883, the Festspielhaus would necessarily come under new direction. Over the years it has had quite a number of artistic and financial leaders, some who have made more controversial decisions than others. It is impossible to say whether Wagner would have approved of the changes, but one thing is for certain: The annual Bayreuth Festival in the Festspielhaus is wildly popular with Wagner fans the world over. —MM

Edinburgh International Festival
TRANSFORMATION, THE SCOTTISH WAY

Out of the rubble of World War II grew the Edinburgh International Festival. Founded in 1947 in the capital city of Scotland, the festival is based on the belief that the arts have the power to transform. Its founders aimed to provide "a platform for the flowering of the human spirit" and enliven the cultural life of Europe, Britain, and Scotland.[1]

The festival has done just that. Each year hundreds of thousands of visitors converge on Edinburgh, where they can choose from classical music, opera, ballet, and theater at some 180 events during the three-week summer festival. The repertoire ranges from Handel and Haydn to premieres of new commissioned works.

The *Daily Telegraph* called the city's atmosphere "not just the most thrilling, beguiling, preposterously enjoyable place on Earth; it is also wonderfully addictive." The *Spectator* wrote, "You can sleep in September."[2]

The events are scattered at venues throughout the city. Catch a concert of Baroque music in Usher Hall, a landmark in the heart of Edinburgh; or the premiere of a new opera at The Edinburgh Playhouse; or head to The Hub. With its prominent spire that can be seen for miles, The Hub forms an integral part of the architectural fabric of the city, and each summer it becomes the buzzing center of the festival.
—KFG

The gothic building The Hub serves as the center of the festival. Photo courtesy Edinburgh International Festival.

Mozart's "Romance: Andante" and *Alien*

KEEPING MONSTERS AT BAY

A lien, one of the most shocking science fiction/horror films ever made, was so successful that it spawned three sequels. Directed by Ridley Scott and released to theatres in 1979, the film kept audiences on the edge of their seats by telling the story of a space mining crew returning home to Earth but diverted to another planet in order to investigate an SOS. While tracking the source of the signal on this alien planet, one of the crew is stricken by a parasite springing from an egg and attaching itself to his face. Thus begins the horrifying series of events that brings a killer alien on board the ship *Nostromo,* killing almost the entire crew.

At one point in the movie, after many horrific events, Captain Dallas (played by actor Tom Skerritt) decides to take a break, finding sanctuary and a bit of peace in the rarely used shuttle located in a bay at the bottom of the ship. It's there that the audience discovers him listening to Mozart. The particular piece, "Romance: Andante" from Serenade in G, K. 525, is a beautiful melodic composition written for chamber orchestra. Not only does Dallas seem to find relief from the madness and terror in the ship, but it also allows the audience a chance to catch its collective breath and prepare for what is to come.

The original score for the film was composed by the incomparable Jerry Goldsmith. —DD

Sturm und Drang (Storm and Stress)

MUSIC TO SHOCK AND AWE

One way to explain the Sturm und Drang movement is to compare it to a TV special that asks you for money to support starving children in a Third World country. When you see those commercials, tears inevitably well up, you feel jolted out of your luxurious American couch, and you almost want to look away. So too was the effect of music written in the latter part of the 18th century in Germany.

Between 1750 and 1800, there was a new stirring in Germany. As the Classical era ended and the Romantic era began, composers found themselves at a crossroads. No longer attempting to portray the literal and straightforward, artists aimed to stun, surprise, and overwhelm. Composers joined the thrall and began to write music that sounded increasingly sad and purposely inappropriate.

Now, this music might not sound weird to us as modern listeners. But back then, writing an entire symphony in a minor key (Mozart's Symphony No. 25) or including programmatic elements that required players to walk off the stage while the piece was still being performed (Haydn's "Farewell" Symphony) was totally bizarre—and also kind of scary.

Serving as a meeting place for music and drama, musical theater is actually the medium that best describes Sturm und Drang. Gluck's operatic depiction of *Don Juan,* for example, even had explicit instructions within the program notes that the D minor finale was intended to scare the listener!

So next time you're watching TV and feeling jaded about life in general, listen to a recording of late Haydn or Mozart. Pretend you're sitting in a late-18th-century audience, and imagine the amazed and distressed reactions around you when the final chord of the symphony is a huge blast of minor dissonance. —SL

LISTENING HOMEWORK

Gluck's Don Juan
Haydn's "Farewell" Symphony
Mozart's Symphony No. 25 in D minor

Concerto

ONE AGAINST MANY

There is nothing like the thrill of performing as a soloist in front of a huge orchestra. But it is also scary, as the awesome might of the large ensemble threatens to overwhelm the soloist. It is no accident that *concerto* comes from the Latin word that means both "to fight or contend" and "to join together." Composers often set the large forces of the orchestra against the smaller soloist in a musical argument.

Concertos are usually in three movements, following a fast-slow-fast pattern. The first movement is often a variant of sonata form, where the orchestra gets its own exposition followed by the soloist or small chamber playing a separate exposition, accompanied by the orchestra. The second movement can be a slow ternary, binary, or hybrid form, but it is usually very lyrical in nature. The last movement is often a rondo. In most cases a cadenza is placed at the end of the first movement, though sometimes it is placed in the last movement or even in both. The *cadenza* is a moment when the orchestra pauses on the dominant chord and allows the soloist to either improvise on the themes of the concerto or to perform a precomposed fantasia.

The most common concertos are written for piano or violin soloists, though there are concertos written for almost all orchestral instruments, and some concertos for two, three, or four soloists, such as Beethoven's *Triple Concerto* for piano, violin, and 'cello. —SS

RECOMMENDED RECORDING

Beethoven: **Triple Concerto/Choral Fantasy;** *Yo-Yo Ma, Itzhak Perlman, and Daniel Berenboim*

Gustav Holst (1874–1934)

HE'S OUT OF THIS WORLD

Despite his Swedish name, Gustav Holst was from England, the son of a Swedish father and English mother. His works, consisting largely of orchestral suites, opera, ballet, and choral pieces, were part of an English rebirth—a return of the British to the world musical stage after two centuries of dominance by Austria, Germany, and Italy.[1]

Influenced by late Romantic composers like Wagner, and later by contemporaries like lifelong friend Ralph Vaughan Williams, Holst soon began to venture beyond the conventions of Romanticism. Ever intrigued by the mystical, Holst was drawn to Eastern religions, especially Hinduism. Several of his works were derived from ancient Hindi texts, including his opera *Sita,* for which he learned Sanskrit in order to translate the text correctly. *The Planets,* Holst's most famous work, was deeply rooted in astrology, another of his interests. These influences affected not only the themes but the structures of his pieces—a reality that often backfired because audiences failed to connect with Holst's esoteric sounds and themes.[2] Most of his later works garnered tepid responses.

Beset with lifelong frail health, Holst struggled with poor eyesight, asthma, and a nerve condition affecting his right hand. He died in 1934 due to complications from stomach surgery. As music has evolved, however, his legacy continues to be felt, even in popular culture. Today, excerpts and adaptations of *The Planets* regularly find their way into movie scores and modern rock recordings. —JJM

Peer Gynt

BY EDVARD GRIEG, 1874–1875

In 1874, the great Norwegian composer Edvard Grieg received a letter from his compatriot Henrik Ibsen, a prominent writer who had recently adapted his dramatic story *Peer Gynt* for the stage. In the letter, Ibsen invited Grieg to write incidental music for the new play, and the resulting score was an immediate hit. Years later, Grieg picked highlights from the original 26 sections and compiled them into two suites, for a total of eight selections.[1]

The first suite begins with the bright radiance of "Morning," but storm clouds abruptly darken the mood with the dissonant echoes of "Aase's Death." The remainder of the two suites is marked by similarly bipolar mood swings, from the manic chorus of "In the Hall of the Mountain King"

Photo by Colin Gilbert.

to the melancholic elegance of "Solveig's Song." Ultimately, the work is unified by a hearty melodic core. Even when utterly detached from their earliest role as program music, these pieces make sense together because of their extraordinary compositional quality and dynamism. —CKG

RECOMMENDED RECORDING

Grieg: Peer Gynt; Symphonic Dance No. 2; In Autumn; Old Norwegian Folksong with Variations; *Thomas Beecham (conductor); Royal Philharmonic Orchestra; EMI Classics; 1999*

Faust

CHARLES GOUNOD (1818–1893)

When the curtain rose on the stage of the Metropolitan Opera House in New York City for the first time on October 22, 1883, audiences witnessed the old scholar Faust seated at a table with an open book before him and heard the music of French composer Charles Gounod. The grand opening at the Metropolitan Opera was a success, and Gounod's five-act Romantic opera *Faust* became one of their most performed pieces for the following century.

Loosely based on Goethe's play of the same name, the story was adapted for the opera stage by librettists Jules Barbier and Michel Carré. The aging philosopher Faust sells his soul to the devil Mephistopheles in exchange for youth and the love of the virtuous maiden Marguerite. Valentin, Marguerite's brother, prepares to go to war and asks his friend, Siébel, to protect his sister. When Valentin returns, however, he finds that Marguerite has been condemned to death for killing her illegitimate child by Faust, who has now abandoned her. Marguerite resists Mephistopheles's attempts to claim her soul as angels proclaim her salvation and Faust is dragged down to hell.[1]

Maureen O'Flynn as Marguerite and Chester Patton as Mephistopheles. Photo courtesy Opera Carolina (Charlotte, North Carolina, www.operacarolina.org).

Several arias from *Faust* remain favorites of opera lovers, including Faust's Act III cavatina, "Salut, demeure chaste et pure" ("I greet you, home chaste and pure"), and Marguerite's famous Act III aria, The Jewel Song, "Ah! je ris de me voir si belle en ce miroir" ("I laugh to see myself so beautiful in this mirror"). —CCD

The Timpani
WORLD'S OLDEST BEAT

The use of large, loud drums dates back to ancient cultures. Tree trunks, clay bowls, and even large tortoise shells covered with hide were used to send military signals, motivate marches, celebrate victories, and provide the rhythm for tribal dance. This is where the timpani, or kettledrum, comes from.

Considered the most important percussion instrument in the orchestra because of its ability to produce notes of a definite pitch, the timpani is a drum consisting of a kettle-shaped shell, usually of brass or copper, and a goatskin or calfskin head stretched over a hoop. The drum is played with a pair of sticks called "mallets" or "beaters."

The drum's pitch is altered using T-shaped hand screws or foot pedals to tighten or loosen the skin. Retuning a drum during a performance while the orchestra is playing in a different key is one of the most challenging aspects of being a timpanist.

Prior to 1800, the use of two drums was popular. The higher drum was tuned to the tonic of the piece being played and the lower to the dominant pitch. Today's timpani range from 51 cm to 84 cm in diameter, and no orchestra is complete without three or more.

Traditionally played in consort with trumpets and choir sections, the timpani has been handsomely featured by composers Bach, Haydn, Berlioz, Beethoven, and Mozart, as well as rock bands Led Zeppelin and the Beach Boys.

—LMC

Key Relationships

THE CIRCLE OF FIFTHS

Songs, sonatas, and symphonies are pitched in different major and minor keys, or tonal centers. These are indicated by sharps and flats in key signatures at the beginning of each staff. Each time you add a sharp, the tonal center moves up a fifth or down a fourth. Each time you add a flat, the tonal center moves up a fourth or down a fifth.

The following notational illustrations show how sharps and flats are used to make a tonal center on any pitch in the chromatic scale.

As you can see, the key of C major has no sharps or flats. Each major key has a relative minor key, and vice versa. So the key signature for C major or its relative minor, A minor (A is a minor third down from C or a major sixth up from C, the submediant), is the same.

Summing up, sharps and flats can be used two ways: as *accidentals* to give more tonal color and nuance to a diatonic major or minor key; and in *key signatures* as an indicator of the tonic location (line or space). —TH

KEY SIGNATURES

RELATIVE MAJORS AND MINORS

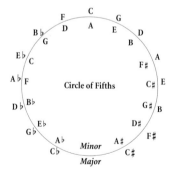

Konzerthaus, Vienna

A VENUE FOR THE PEOPLE

Built in the early 20th century, the Vienna Konzerthaus is certainly not the oldest or most prestigious venue in Austria; nonetheless, it has carved a niche for itself in both the local and international classical music scenes. Its relative youth works well as a metaphor for the novel idea behind the construction of the building: to provide a place where anyone, not just aristocrats, could come and enjoy quality music. This idea, which was quite innovative in Vienna at the time, set off an entire strategy of taking unconventional approaches to music.

Photo courtesy Andrea Puggioni.

The original drawings for the Konzerthaus included a bicycle club and an ice skating rink in an effort to commit to the theme of catering to the common people. In the end, however, the venue ended up being a little more traditional, and at first the music was too. After the end of World War I, the Konzerthaus began to expand its repertoire into more avant-garde areas like modern dance, and although its reputation suffered somewhat during World War II, in the years following the war the artistic directors of the venue concentrated on rebuilding its damaged status, with great success.[1]

To this day, the Konzerthaus remains a venue of the people, giving new and lesser-known musicians a chance to make their names on the international stage. It also hosts concerts for the Wien Modern, the most prominent festival of contemporary music in Austria. —MM

Banff Summer Arts Festival

SOMETHING FOR EVERYONE

Cultural fiends take note: There's something for everyone at this cultural smorgasbord in the Canadian Rockies. Artists of all stripes—classical musicians, dancers, jazz and opera performers, visual artists, filmmakers, writers, and multimedia artists—converge at the Banff Summer Arts Festival from May to August.

A typical day at the festival—which features more than 150 events—might include a string quartet performance in a downtown park, followed by a mid-afternoon chamber music concert and an evening opera or dance in the Eric Harvie Theatre. In between those performances, festivalgoers can view contemporary art exhibits and adventure film screenings, listen to literary readings, attend late-night jazz performances, and participate in GPS-enabled multimedia art explorations.

An arts, cultural, and educational institution and conference facility, the Banff Centre, which runs the festival, has provided professional development in the performing and fine arts since 1933. The festival started in 1971 as a weeklong event and developed into the summerlong festival at which Canadian home-grown and international artists, both emerging and established, perform. The festival has seen premieres of Canadian new works, including Michael Daughtery's opera *Jackie O,* and new dances by Canada's up-and-coming choreographers Peter Quanz and Sabrina Matthews.

Expect the unexpected here: In recent years mathematicians have mingled with artists when a group of international mathematicians attending a symposium didn't just discuss theorems and algorithms, but also met with artists to explore how other forms of creativity can contribute to their field.[1] —KFG

Grace Adams, Betty Allison, Andrea Casola, Leslie Davis, Michael Sheridan, Amanda Casola, and Rowan Lalonde in the opera The Cunning Little Vixen *at The Banff Centre. Photo by Donald Lee.*

Walt Disney's *Fantasia*

ANIMATION BASED ON CLASSICAL MUSIC

The 1940 animated classic by Walt Disney's team of brilliant animators, directors, and producers is a treat even in our age of computer-generated film images and dynamic digital audio. Each scene and story is based on a particular piece of classical music, and the characters' movements are perfectly choreographed. Conductor Leopold Stokowski was brought on board with the wonderful Philadelphia Orchestra to record all the pieces used in the film (with the exception of "The Sorcerer's Apprentice," which was recorded a year earlier by members of the Los Angeles Philharmonic and Stokowski).

The classical pieces on which each segment is based are: Stokowski's orchestral transcription of Bach's *Tocatta and Fugue in D minor;* six dance scenes from Tchaikovsky's *The Nutcracker;* Paul Dukas's wonderful tone poem, "The Sorcerer's Apprentice"; Stravinksy's intense *The Rite of Spring;* the first three movements of Beethoven's "Pastorale" Symphony; "The Dance of the Hours" from Ponchielli's opera *La Gioconda;* Mussorgsky's "A Night On Bald Mountain"; and Franz Schubert's *Ave Maria.*

Fantasia is now available on DVD with a newly remastered and enhanced audio soundtrack so that the original recordings made for the film can be fully appreciated. —DD

Early Romanticism

ESCAPE TO ANOTHER TIME AND PLACE

As the Romantic era developed, music began to take on a new form. Between the years 1800 and 1850, music actually began to resemble a fantasy novel. Bearing emphasis on love, nature, and even Greek mythology, early Romantic compositions oftentimes took the listener on a journey to a faraway land.

There was also a much greater importance placed on extreme emotion. Keep in mind, however, that although early Romantic music certainly "sounded" freer, it was still written within the strict Classical framework.

Beethoven's Symphony No. 3 ("Eroica") is a perfect example. While the piece exemplifies all the traits of Romantic music—with its death of the hero and references to Prometheus, the god who gave humans their independence— the symphony is still written in the standard four-movement form. It was not until Beethoven's Symphony No. 6 ("Pastorale") that these hard and fast rules began to break down. The 6th Symphony's 5-movement format replaced the formerly accepted 4, and its last three movements are played *attaca* (continuously).

Another trademark of the early Romantic era was the many types of pieces. No longer trapped in traditional multimovement sonata format, composers such as Robert Schumann and Frederick Chopin wrote well-received shorter song cycles and piano compositions that previously would have been considered insufficient. —SL

LISTENING HOMEWORK

Beethoven's "Pastorale" Symphony
Chopin's 24 Preludes, Op. 28
Schumann's 5 Lieder, Op. 40

Madrigal
COUNTERPOINT WITHOUT ALL THAT RELIGION

In the 16th century, Italian musicians began to reuse *madrigal,* songs that had fallen out of fashion 100 years earlier. These new pieces had little in common with the 14th-century madrigal other than being texts in Italian. The famous poet Petrarch wrote a series of lyrics that were very in rhythmic effect because he alternated between 7-syllable and 11-syllable lines. In the 1500s his poems became very much in fashion, encouraging musicians to set his verse and those of his followers in a related free style.

Madrigals became known as secular verse set for three to six voices, occasionally for solo voice with instrumental accompaniment. In all cases madrigals shifted between polyphony (each voice has its own independent line) and homophony (all voices have the same basic rhythm with the top voice as clear leader).

Styles changed over the century as composers like Palestrina and Lassus created more ornate counterpoint and Monteverdi and Gesualdo intensified the emotions through much more chromaticism and dissonance. But in all cases the madrigal was considered a difficult song to perform, whether it was the choral madrigal, which required independent voices, or the solo madrigal with very heavy ornamentation over the bass instrument and chords (keyboard or lute).

At the end of the 1500s, the madrigal also became popular in England, inspired by all the Italian musicians imported there by Queen Elizabeth I. The most popular of these English madrigalists were William Byrd and Thomas Morley. —SS

Franz Schubert (1797–1828)

FOLLOW THE "LIEDER"

Franz Schubert was one of the last composers in the Classical tradition, living during the transition between the Classical and Romantic eras.[1] A master of melody, Schubert is most noted for his German *lieder* (art songs)— he wrote over 600 of them. In addition, he wrote operas, choral music, and symphonies, hundreds in all. Despite his short life span, Schubert was one of history's most prolific composers, remembered for pieces like *The Erlking,* the "Great" Symphony No. 9, and others too numerous to mention.

Ironically, Schubert was also possibly the most nonpublished among the Classical masters. Although he had many admirers in his native Vienna, Schubert had great difficulty getting publishers to accept his pieces.[2] Most performances of his works occurred in the drawing rooms of Vienna's growing middle class; in his lifetime, Schubert saw only one public concert completely devoted to his work, just months before his death. Impoverished, he often lived in other people's homes, composing on borrowed pianos.

Schubert's writing style matured with age, and his last works are widely considered his best. He was finally beginning to see public recognition when he fell ill, possibly with typhoid fever. In the decades following his death, hundreds of his unpublished works were discovered, and the scope of his musical genius was more widely recognized. Today he is an icon among the great composers, having written some of the most recognizable melodies in music history. —JJM

The Rite of Spring

BY IGOR STRAVINSKY, 1911–1913

The 1913 Paris premiere of *The Rite of Spring* was a riot. No, really. Shortly after it began, audience members began shouting, and before long fists were flying. By the intermission, the police had arrived to restore order. What exactly sparked the outrage is a matter of debate—the ballet's pagan themes and bizarre choreography may have been the major culprit—but the music's jarring dissonance and erratic, primitive rhythms undoubtedly contributed to the chaos. Years later, a Bostonian newspaper reviewer poetically expressed a popular opinion of the music:

> *Who wrote this fiendish* Rite of Spring
> *What right had he to write the thing,*
> *Against our helpless ears to fling*
> *Its crash, crash, cling, clang, bing, bang, bing?*[1]

There are those who might today feel the same hostility toward *The Rite of Spring,* which is now performed as a concert piece rather than a ballet, but by and large its notoriety has been transformed into renown. There is something fundamentally human in its primeval passion, and Stravinsky's blinding ingenuity shines through the densely layered compositional lines. By boldly going where no work had gone before, *The Rite of Spring* proved once and for all that nothing is off limits in the universe of music, and that liberating message has inspired the world ever since. —CKG

RECOMMENDED RECORDING

Stravinsky conducts Stravinsky: Petrushka / Le Sacre du Printemps; Columbia Symphony Orchestra; Sony; 1990

Roméo et Juliette (Romeo and Juliet)

CHARLES GOUNOD (1818–1893)

For more than 400 years, audiences have enjoyed *Romeo and Juliet*, William Shakespeare's immortal tragedy of star-crossed lovers. French composer Charles Gounod fell in love with the story at age 19 when he attended a rehearsal of Hector Berlioz's symphony *Roméo et Juliette*. Decades later, in 1864, he decided to compose his own operatic version of the story.

Gounod enlisted the help of librettists Jules Barbier and Michel Carré, who followed the original play closely. Their adaptation simplified the plot, eliminated several minor characters, and added scenes to give it more operatic flair. They also created the role of the comic character Stephano, Roméo's page, and included the wedding of Roméo and Juliette. In addition, Juliette wakes from her drug-induced sleep before Roméo dies, which allows the lovers to see each other one last time.[1]

The result was instant success, both in France and abroad. In fact, *Roméo et Juliette* was Gounod's most popular opera during his lifetime, even surpassing *Faust*, which later came to be his most enduring work.

Though the popularity of *Roméo et Juliette* has faded somewhat in recent years, audiences will recognize Juliette's famous Act I aria (Juliette's Waltz),

"Je veux vivre" ("I want to live"), which is often excerpted as a performance piece for lyric coloratura sopranos. Equally captivating is the Act I duet, "Madrigal: Ange Adorable" ("Madrigal: Adorable Angel"), in which Roméo and Juliette acknowledge their newfound love for one another. —CCD

Gaston Rivero as Romeo, Sari Gruber as Juliette, and Philip Cokorinos as Frère Laurent. Photo courtesy Opera Carolina (Charlotte, North Carolina, www.operacarolina.org).

Tuned Percussion

XYLOPHONE AND MARIMBA CHIME IN

With its origin in Africa and Asia, the first xylophone appeared in Europe in the early 1500s. This simple instrument of 15 to 25 wooden bars loosely strung together with ropes of straw and struck with wooden beaters was often called a straw fiddle. Following a rise to prominence in the 19th century, when virtuoso xylophonist Michał Guzikow attracted the attention of composers Mendelssohn, Chopin, and Liszt, today's modern orchestral xylophone emerged.

The bars are made of rosewood and are graduated in size, with smaller bars producing higher notes. Their layout follows that of the piano keyboard with the accidentals behind and vertically raised above the natural notes. Each bar has a tuned resonator tube hanging beneath it to amplify the sound. Saint-Saëns's use of the xylophone to represent the rattling of bones in his *Danse Macabre* is a chilling example of this instrument's unique sound.

Classical marimbist Vida Chenoweth "elevated the instrument to concert status" and has been inducted in two music halls of fame. Photo courtesy the Percussive Arts Society.

Latin American cousin to the xylophone, the lower-pitched marimba is the most popular solo instrument of the tuned percussion family. It is a bigger instrument than the xylophone, since deeper tones require larger bars, and its warmer sound is attributed to the use of softer mallets. Today's orchestral marimba replaces the traditional gourd resonators with long metal tubes. —LMC

FUN FACT

Vida Chenoweth is considered to be the first professional solo classical marimbist, and her remarkable talents have been captured in many recordings.

Seventh Chords

BULKING UP THE SOUND

Earlier we showed that it's possible to not only build triads, but also to stack the chord up as high as it will go. The next note added on top of a triad (root, third, and fifth) in root position is the 7th—after that, the 9th, 13th, and so on. The sound is thicker (see examples below) in these taller chords because of the added notes. To the classical ear, a total of four voices is ideal for most instrumental textures. Here it is in a typical V^7 (dominant seventh)—I cadence (see "Cadences," page 174).

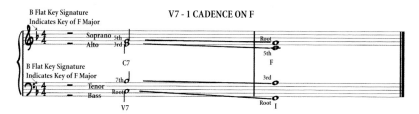

So now we have two ways of identifying any note according to its harmonic or melodic musical function: according to its melodic scale degree—one, two, three, etc.—or according to its harmonic function as the root, third, or fifth of the chord.

Chords themselves have a function, as noted above, and since the C7 is constructed on the fifth scale degree of the key of F, it is the V^7 chord of the key of F, and naturally moves to its center of tonal gravity, the F-major triad, or tonic. From the bass voice up, the root of the dominant C7 (V^7) moves to the root of the F major or tonic. The Seventh of the V^7 moves to the third; the third of the V^7 moves to the fifth; and the fifth of the V^7 also goes to the root of the tonic. —TH

(Confused? Refer to "Key Relationships," page 194.)

Hungarian State Opera House
THE JEWEL IN THE HUNGARIAN CROWN

Hungary has its share of revered classical music venues, but none quite as prestigious as its famed State Opera House in Budapest. The chief performance center of opera and classical music in Hungary, the State Opera House has been honored with the likes of Gustav Mahler and Otto Klemperer as musical directors. Ferenc Erkel, the composer who wrote the Hungarian national anthem, was not only the first musical director of the Opera House, but he also founded the Budapest Philharmonic Orchestra. In addition, the Hungarian National Ballet also calls the venue its home. Between music and dance programs, the Opera House hosts over 50 new productions per season, many of which play to a full house.

Performances are a stately affair at the State Opera House, and the lavish appearance of the venue is rivaled only by that of the patrons. Although there is no formal dress code, people generally dress to the nines, with gentlemen in suits and ladies in evening gowns.

The Opera House itself is a sight to behold, noteworthy even in a land of countless noteworthy buildings, and is said to be the finest work of designer Miklós Ybl, one of the top 19th-century Hungarian architects. The building is so beautiful and historically important, in fact, that guided tours help visitors gain a more in-depth understanding of how the venue was constructed. The tours have become so popular that they are now conducted daily in six different languages.[1] —MM

Beethovenfest Bonn

ROLL OVER, BEETHOVEN

Beethovenfest Bonn is no staid event. Like the composer himself, the annual festival is innovative and unconventional.

Music is not treated as a museum piece at this celebration located in Beethoven's birthplace. Instead, each year festival organizers seek new ways to confront the composer and his oeuvre. And new works are commissioned. A recent festival, for example, explored the potential for new formats of the string quartet—which experienced its heyday with Beethoven. Since 2006 the festival has served as a rendezvous for young filmmakers, who visualize their own approach to Beethoven through short films and installations.

Some 40,000 German and international tourists attend each year and listen to well-known soloists, major ensembles, promising young performers, and top international orchestras—including the New York Philharmonic and the Philadelphia Orchestra. Some 60 concerts are held in 25 venues, including churches, concert halls, museums, former parliament buildings, modern office buildings, and castles in the city of Bonn and the surrounding rural region. Since 2004 the festival director has organized the lively celebration around a theme, such as a cultural region, politics and music, or the artist as celebrity.

Beethovenfest Bonn has existed in its modern form—a four-and-a-half-week annual festival—since 1999, but its tradition stretches back to 1845, when a three-day music event was held to help dedicate the Beethoven Monument on the city's Münsterplatz.

For music lovers who can't make it in person, excerpts of concert recordings are available as podcasts, accessible through the festival Web site. —KFG

Public viewing in Bonn market. Photo by Barbara Frommann ©2008.

Ravel and *10*

THE "BOLERO" AND THE BEAUTIFUL

In 1928 composer, pianist, and orchestrator Maurice Ravel presented what would become his most famous work: *Boléro*. Originally intended for the ballet, the work took on a life of its own as a performance piece for large orchestra. A large theme is repeated many times as it's played on different instruments in a gradual and very grand crescendo. The piece is only one movement based on a musical form of Spanish dance called "bolero."

Who would have thought it would one day become the love theme of a major Hollywood motion picture?

Blake Edwards's hilarious story and film *10* was released in 1979. It's the story of a successful middle-aged composer/songwriter name George (played by Dudley Moore) who is going through a midlife crisis. Feeling like his sex life is passing him by, he chases after a young woman named Jenny (played by Bo Derek), whom he sees as a "10" on a scale of 1 to 10. After many comical events, George finds himself being seduced by Jenny in spite of her marriage. Jenny asks George; "Did you ever do it to Ravel's *Boléro?*" and then attempts to seduce George using the music's gradual and big crescendo. —DD

FUN FACT

The music became so associated with the film that it became known as "The Love Theme From 10." A disco version of Boléro was even produced for the dance clubs by Nardello and the Philadelphia Luv Ensemble.

Late Romanticism

NOW IT'S GETTING PERSONAL

The late Romantic era had two distinct musical characteristics. The first was the emergence of a nationalistic pride and the use of folk melodies. The second was the development of "programmatic music," where the piece itself told a specific story, and certain musical motives represented recurring characters in the story.

Nationalism ran strong throughout post-Napoleon Europe. Countries strived to rediscover their national identity in the face of occupation or oppression, and composers joined forces in that quest. Corresponding with the overarching natural trend within all Romantic music, composers wrote about the landscapes and other natural wonders within their respective countries. Bedrich Smetana, for example, wrote about the Czech Moldau River in a piece entitled *Ma Vlast* (My Fatherland).

To understand the programmatic concept, think of the music from a recent Harry Potter movie. John Williams (perhaps the most famous and successful film composer of all time) composed Harry's triumphant theme, and every time Harry appears in a scene, his music accompanies him. Each character from the movie has their own theme (even Harry's mode of transportation—the Nimbus 2000 broomstick); the themes intertwine and develop along with the characters throughout the movie.

In his *Symphonie Fantastique,* Henry Berlioz uses several *idées fixes* (or musical motives) to portray characters, and the piece as a whole tells a fantasy story that could very well be a Harry Potter prequel. —SL

LISTENING HOMEWORK

Berlioz's **Symphonie Fantastique**

Sibelius's **Finlandia**

Smetana's **Moldeau**

Ballad

ONCE UPON A TIME

Many art songs are about emotions or images, but ballads tell a complete story of a historical or supernatural nature. There are two types of ballads in classical music: English folk songs that originated in the Middle Ages, and German art songs from the Romantic era. In both cases, the songs' texts consist of repeated strophes in simple rhyme schemes. The music of the Romantic songs can be through-composed or modified strophes, whereas the music of folk songs are always as strophic as the poems.

The largest collection of folk ballads are the Child Ballads collected by Francis James Child in the 1880s. These 300 ballads include "Barbara Allen," which was recorded by Simon and Garfunkel, and "The Riddle Song," recorded by Joan Baez. They have been a major influence on the modern folk movement, and on popular music in general.

Probably the most famous Romantic ballad is Franz Schubert's "Erlkönig," about a man and his sick boy being pursued through a stormy night by the elf king. The galloping horse is portrayed by the repeated chords in the piano, and each of the characters is given their own motive. The elf king does take the boy's life at the end of the song after promising golden robes and beautiful daughters to dance with him. The text, by the famous poet Johann von Goethe, tempted many composers to set it to music. However, Schubert's setting is the most famous, and it solidified his reputation as an eminent art song composer. —SS

Edvard Grieg (1843–1907)

NORWAY'S MUSICAL TRAILBLAZER

One might surmise that Edvard Grieg was placed in the wrong part of the world for his particular talents. Born into a musical family—but not in a land known for its musical development—Grieg often had to travel far from his homeland to further his career, both in his education and in the performance of his works.

At age 15, Grieg went to Leipzig, Germany, to study and develop his compositional skills in the German Romantic tradition. Acutely aware that Norway lacked an artistic sound of its own, Grieg made it his aim to create music that was distinctly Norwegian. He spent much of his time composing in a small shack by a fjord in the Norwegian wilderness, drawing inspiration both from nature and from the folk music of his land.[1]

But the Norwegian public was indifferent to his craft, so Grieg often took his Norwegian-sounding compositions out of Norway to perform them around Europe. Two of his works in particular—Piano Concerto in A minor and the incidental music for Ibsen's *Peer Gynt*—gained him international acclaim. Eventually Norway honored Grieg's achievements by awarding him a government pension.

Grieg was indeed a trailblazer; he not only brought the arts to Norway—he brought Norway to the arts. —JJM

Adagio for Strings and Organ in G minor

BY REMO GIAZOTTO, 1945

Although it's a term usually reserved for popular musicians, one-hit wonders abound in classical music too. Pachelbel and Barber, for example, would probably not be familiar names (outside the world of music critics and aficionados) if it were not for their most famous works. Despite the fact that he was a gifted and prolific Baroque composer, Italian Tomaso Albinoni is another artist typically associated with a single work—the enigmatic *Adagio*.

The evocative movement has long overshadowed Albinoni's many concertos and other works. As it turns out, though, he did not even write it! The *Adagio* was actually composed by the musicologist Remo Giazotto, who spent much of his career chronicling the life of Albinoni. One version of the story is that Giazotto, while collecting research, came across an authentic Albinoni score fragment that contained the Adagio's bassline, and he expanded and arranged the work from there. However, there is still debate over whether Albinoni had anything to do with it at all.

Regardless of its origin, the *Adagio* is an unforgettable piece of music. Anchored by the steadiness of the organ and a delicately plucked bass line, the string section delivers a panorama of widescreen drama as its mood fluctuates between seductive, mournful, and hot-blooded. If Giazotto truly penned the piece from scratch, perhaps he too should be proclaimed a bona fide one-hit wonder! —CKG

RECOMMENDED RECORDING

Albinoni: The Complete Concertos Op. 9, Adagio for Organ And Strings; Philips; 1997

Les pêcheurs de perles (The Pearl Fishers)

GEORGES BIZET (1838–1875)

One of the most famous tenor and baritone duets in opera, "Au fond du temple saint" ("At the back of the holy temple"), can be heard in Georges Bizet's *Les pêcheurs de perles* (*The Pearl Fishers*). First performed in 1863 at the Théâtre-Lyrique du Châtelet in Paris, the three-act opera was written in collaboration with librettists Eugène Cormon and Michel Carré. Known for its exotic setting and music, *Les pêcheurs de perles* takes place on the island of Sri Lanka.

Zurga has just been elected king of the pearl fishers in the village. He reminisces with his former friend Nadir, who has just returned after a year spent away in the forest, about how their friendship ended when they both fell in love with an unknown priestess. They vow to never again allow their friendship to be threatened. However, when Nadir recognizes Priestess Leila as the woman he and Zurga both loved, the vow of friendship is once again broken. The high priest Nourabad catches Nadir and Leila together, and they are condemned to death as punishment for Leila's broken vow of chastity. Though Zurga feels jealous and betrayed, he learns that Leila saved his life in the past. He then sets fire to the village to allow Nadir and Leila to escape. Zurga is killed when the high priest of Brahman discovers his plot to save the two lovers. —CCD

Stephen Powell as Zurga, William Joyner as Nadir. Photo by John Fitzgerald, courtesy Kentucky Opera.

Carillon

WORTH THEIR WEIGHT IN GOLD

Coming into existence during the late Medieval period is one of the largest and heaviest instruments ever developed: the carillon. While swinging bells were already popular across Europe, the carillon is a set of stationary bronze bells played with a keyboard. It initially found favor during the 15th century in the Netherlands and Flanders.

More than just a signaling bell, carillons became symbols of civic pride that were central to a community's identity. Towns and cities would compete to have the largest and best-sounding bells. Typically located in a town hall or church, the carillon would fill the surrounding streets and cottages with its magnificent melodies.

Commonly housed in a tower, a carillon by definition must have a minimum of 23 bells and, with the exception of the lower three, form a chromatic scale. Modern carillons encompass over four octaves and include bells weighing 25 pounds to more than a ton per bell.

A piano-style keyboard and foot pedals are used to operate a set of clappers to strike each bell. Although the carillon is generally a solo instrument, it is by nature a public instrument, and a carillonneur should have a repertoire of well-known music. —LMC

Fun Fact

The University of California, Berkeley campus houses a five-octave carillon in the Sather Tower and features extensive carillon study.

Monophonic Music

ONE VOICE, ONE MELODY

"Monophonic Music" means one melody line (any voice or instrument) heard alone.

While it's good to have a lot of different sonorities jumping from one consonant or dissonant sound to a contrasting one in the soprano, alto, tenor, and bass (SATB) voices of chords, we mustn't forget that, historically, these chords assumed their forms through those SATB voices singing their own melody lines in harmony together. Musicians speak of the soprano line or the bass line. In the notation on page 204, you'll see that the diagonal lines between the notes show the voice leading: how the notes move in the cadential chord change.

Due to the diatonic and chromatic stepwise nature of melodic movement, if you have three or four voices simultaneously, at any given moment a harmony is occurring as a chord.

But in monophonic music there is no chord, no harmony. The ear of the listener may subjectively try to supply one, more or less successfully. But the composer and/or performer do not. Such music is said to be performed *a cappella*, literally "according to the chapel," as no accompaniment was allowed for the human voice in the early Roman Catholic Church. Catholic and Jewish sources constitute the oldest sources of written music in Western culture. Gregorian chant is monophonic vocal music. Monophonic music exists as a single line (see "Melody," page 104). —TH

FUN FACT

From the Impressionist era, Syrinx, *a piece for solo flute by Claude Debussy, is an example of monophonic instrumental music.*

Theatre des Champs-Elysees

AN OVERNIGHT SENSATION

In terms of venues whose international reputation is built primarily on the strength of the artists who have performed there, the Theatre des Champs-Elysees in Paris is a hard act to follow. Though the theater itself is a gorgeous and rare example of Parisian Art Deco, its appearance is often mentioned only as an afterthought, overshadowed by the rich tales of legendary artists, memorable performances, and even a scandal or two.

The Theatre des Champs-Elysees opened in 1913, just as Stravinsky was ready to premiere his new and groundbreaking piece, *The Rite of Spring*. A rumble of political and social unrest laid the foundation for radical change across Europe, as prewar tensions had people thinking about the implications of the impending upheaval. When Stravinsky added his impassioned musical fire to the mix, the result was explosive. The composer knew his music was risky, but not even he could have predicted a near riot from the audience. People shouted so loudly and caused so much commotion that the music could barely be heard. As the story hit the streets, the theater soared to fame overnight, and to this day it is still referred to as the venue of "the Stravinsky scandal."[1]

Theatre des Champs Elysees. Photo courtesy Elliott Brown.

Perhaps this stormy beginning gave the theater the kick start it needed, as it has certainly held its own over the years. Artists as varied as Maria Callas and Josephine Baker have graced the stage, and the theater boasts performances by such legendary names as Toscanini and Debussy.[2] —MM

Santa Fe Chamber Music Festival

FEAST FOR EYES AND EARS

This summer celebration glances back to chamber music's beginnings and ahead to its future. At its six-week summer season, each July and August the Santa Fe Chamber Music Festival features guest composers and the premieres of new works. Since 1980 the festival has commissioned 47 compositions, contributing significantly to the 20th- and 21st-century chamber music repertoire.

No doubt the artists and listeners who attend the event, founded in 1972, come not only for the beautiful works performed by some of the world's finest musicians and ensembles, but also for the unusual setting, nestled in the Sangre de Cristo Mountains. It's the same environ that attracted the renowned visual artist Georgia O'Keeffe, who first visited Santa Fe in 1929 and eventually moved to the state. So tied to the area was the artist that for the first 20 years of the annual event, the festival's posters and program book covers were designed with O'Keeffe's paintings.

Chamber music lovers can choose from more than 40 concerts at two venues. One is the renovated, state-of-the-art, 82-seat Lensic Theater. The other, more primary venue is the intimate, historic Saint Francis Auditorium in the New Mexico Museum of Fine Art. Designed to look as though it had always been in Santa Fe, the auditorium features *vigas* (large ceiling beams) and *latillas* (peeled sticks used as ceiling material laid between vigas) made from limbs in a herringbone pattern. —KFG

Santa Fe Chamber Music Festival. Photo courtesy Gene Peach Photography.

Elgar and *Elizabeth I*

MUSIC THAT KNOWS NO TIME

Exploring the global influence of England, a small island country, is both overwhelming and fascinating. A brilliant 1998 film directed by Shekhar Kapur entitled *Elizabeth I* passionately captures a small chapter of England's story. The film stars Cate Blanchett as the Virgin Queen and Joseph Fiennes as her romantic interest, potential husband, and lover Lord Robert Dudley. The original score was composed by David Hirschfelder and is accompanied by the use of Sir Edward Elgar's "Nimrod" (from his *Enigma* Variations) during the film's dramatic ending.

Queen Elizabeth I had been under pressure to marry since claiming the throne in 1558. Her choice of a husband had always been lifelong friend and romantic interest Lord Dudley, who had married before Elizabeth's ascension to the throne. After complications and much opposition from Elizabeth's counselors due to the scandal surrounding the accidental death of Dudley's wife, Dudley remarries. Elizabeth does not forgive him, and since he perhaps was her only true love, she decides to never marry.

During a final confrontational scene with Lord Dudley and then during the declaration scene we hear Elgar's "Nimrod." It's a profoundly dynamic use of the music. "Nimrod" was composed almost 300 years later in 1899, but perfectly captures the passion and complicated emotions of Queen Elizabeth I.
—DD

Sir Edward Elgar's "Nimrod" brings Queen Elizabeth I alive to movie audiences.

20th-Century Music

A COMPOSER'S FREE-FOR-ALL

20th-century music is really a big eclectic grab bag—you honestly never know what you're going to get. So when someone says, "Hey, let's go listen to some 20th-century music tonight!" it really could mean absolutely anything. To give you an (overwhelming but true) idea, here's a partial list of what 20th-century music could include:

The transitional Romantic style of Mahler and Sibelius, impressionism by Debussy, expressionism by Bartok and Hindemith, futurism by Stravinsky and Paganini, the Second Viennese School led by Schoenberg, neoclassicism by Prokofiev, electronic music by Varese and Davidovsky, and jazz-influenced music by Gershwin, Copland, and Bernstein.

Sheesh. It makes you tired just thinking about it.

Basically, the 20th century was a time of exploration; composers had free rein for the first time, and anything was possible. Consequently, the sounds of 20th-century music can be hard for some people to accept. Atonality (music with no clear key center) is not easily understood upon first hearing, and has led many people to assume they simply don't like any music written in modern times.

But since there are so many options within 20th-century music, it really isn't fair to judge so hastily. So next time you see an advertisement for a concert with modern music, give it a try. You just might like it. —SL

LISTENING HOMEWORK

Debussy's Prelude de la après mide d'un faune
Stravinsky's The Rite of Spring
Copland's Appalachian Spring

Toccata

WHAT A SHOW-OFF!

While we like to think that all classical music should elevate our understanding of human nature or touch our heart with sublime beauty, sometimes a piece is composed solely to demonstrate that the performer is really, really good. These are called virtuoso pieces, characterized by extremes in speed, range, and dynamics. Compositional artistry is often sacrificed to allow these pyrotechnic displays, but the pieces are still a lot of fun, both for the listener and the performer.

One type of virtuosic piece is the *toccata,* a genre for the keyboard (piano, organ, or harpsichord) that has been around since the Renaissance. The word comes from the Italian verb *toccare* ("to touch"), indicating that the hands of the keyboardist will be very busy touching many keys. There isn't a specific form for the toccata. It can be a fugue, sonata, canon, or prelude. What all toccatas have in common is lots of scales, and usually driving rhythms—continuous sixteenth notes—that continue for a whole section or the whole piece.

The most popular toccatas were composed in the Baroque era, such as Bach's *Toccata and Fugue in D minor* or Alessandro Scarlatti's *Primo e secondo libro di Toccate.* But the style has continued up to today, particularly as works for organ. Many an organist has woken up their congregation on a Sunday morning with the *Toccata* by Charles Widor (1844–1937). —SS

Nadia Boulanger (1887–1979)

INFLUENCING THE INFLUENCERS

Few among the general public would recognize the name Nadia Boulanger as they would Beethoven or Brahms. Among the most prominent talents in 20th-century classical music, however, there are few who do not know who she was. This woman composer, organist, conductor, and teacher became one of the most profound influences on music of our day.

Nadia Boulanger's life was centered around music. By age nine, she was taking classes at the Paris Conservatory, and she began winning awards soon after. Showing promise as a composer, she won second prize at the famed Prix de Rome competition, though politics may have prevented her from going farther. Her younger sister, Lili, eventually went on to take first prize.

When Lili died in 1918, the heartbroken Nadia gave up composition for good, turning primarily to teaching composition. This is where her influence is most felt. Among her pupils were Aaron Copland, Philip Glass, Virgil Thomas, Quincy Jones, and countless others who went on to prominence. At one point, Thomas quipped that every small town in America had a post office and a Boulanger student.[1] Nadia reportedly rejected composer George Gershwin as a student, saying, "What could I give you that you haven't already got?"[2]

By the time of her death in 1979, Nadia Boulanger had quietly reshaped the musical landscape—not directly, but by influencing the influencers. Through her more than 1,200 students,[3] her legacy has affected more people than any other single composer could have done. —JJM

Boléro

BY MAURICE RAVEL, 1928

Many of the greatest works contain at least one dramatic build up to a moving climax. We can't help but feel engaged and excited when music takes us on a journey, and Ravel's great ballet score *Boléro* clearly demonstrates the power of trajectory.

While other works use frequent rhythmic or melodic twists to keep things interesting, this 15-minute piece is little more than a single, slow-burning ascent. Considering the exotic sound of the work, it may surprise some to learn that the composer was French, but he was commissioned to produce a work with such Spanish flair.

Even among works that rise to thrilling peaks of power or emotion, *Boléro* is unique. The primary figures of melody and rhythm scarcely change, yet we remain transfixed, enjoying the added texture created by each new layer of orchestration.

Ravel treated the composition as a sort of experiment, joking that it was "a piece for orchestra without music."[1] The original score is famous for its lack of instructional markings. The musicians are simply required to play the notes in front of them, repeatedly, at steady volume and consistent tempo. Ravel's brilliant exploitation of the orchestra does the rest. —CKG

RECOMMENDED RECORDING

Ravel: Bolero; Pierre Boulez (conductor); Berlin Philharmonic Orchestra;
Deutsche Grammophon; 1994

Carmen

GEORGES BIZET (1838-1875)

Filled with some of the best-known melodies in the history of music, Georges Bizet's *Carmen* is one of the most frequently performed operas today. Yet when the four-act opera premiered in 1875 at the Opéra-Comique of Paris, the reviews were not favorable. In fact, the piece was criticized for its reliance on realism. Many audience members found Carmen's behavior too wild and immoral and also objected to the onstage smoking of the chorus of cigarette factory girls. The greatest critique, however, came in reaction to the onstage murder of Carmen.

Based on the novella *Carmen* by Prosper Mérimée, the libretto was written by Henri Meilhac and Ludovic Halévy. The opera is set in Seville around the year 1830. Don José, the Corporal of Dragoons, is seduced by the gypsy factory-girl Carmen and allows her to escape from custody. He later gives up his life as a soldier and love for the village maiden Micaëla in order to join the smugglers with whom Carmen is associated. However, Don José is consumed with jealousy, especially when Carmen shows a preference for the bullfighter Escamillo. The opera ends tragically when Don Jose kills Carmen outside the bullring when she declares she no longer loves him.

Audiences will recognize Carmen's seductive arias, "Habanera" and "Séguidilla," both Spanish dances, and Escamillo's famous "Toreador Song," as well as Don José's Act II aria "La fleur que tu m'avais jetée" ("The flower that you threw me"). —CCD

Kathryn Allyn as Carmen Photo by Chris Arend, courtesy Anchorage Opera (www. anchorageopera. org).

The Glockenspiel
ARE THOSE BELLS YOU'RE HEARING?

In its infancy, the glockenspiel was an actual set of bells resembling a miniature carillon and often played by multiple people or struck using a complicated clocklike mechanism. Over the 17th and 18th centuries, the "glock's" bells were replaced by metal bars and oriented similar to the keys of a piano, much like its cousin the xylophone.

During the time of Handel and Mozart, a closed version was popular. It was played using a keyboard to operate hammers that struck the bars from underneath. Handel's oratorio *Saul* is considered the first use of this instrument, and Mozart used it about 50 years later in *The Magic Flute* to represent Papageno's magic bells. It is also thought that Puccini's operas *Turandot* and *Madama Butterfly*, Debussy's *La Mer*, Respighi's *Pini di Rom*, and Honegger's Fourth Symphony all intended to use this version.

Today's glockenspiel, often referred to as orchestral bells, is open and played with mallets, offering better sound and a greater variety of tonal colors. A small instrument, typically with a two-and-a-half-octave range, it voices two octaves above the written score. Many composers use it to double the melody of another instrument in an effort to lighten the sound. Examples can be found in the *Dance of the Hours* by Ponchielli, Strauss's *Don Juan*, Tchaikovsky's suite *Nutcracker*, Elgar's *The Dream of Gerontius*, Ravel's *Daphnis et Chloé*, Holst's *The Planets*, and Britten's *The Prince of the Pagodas*. —LMC

Polyphonic Music

VOICES IN PERFECT HARMONY

The first known notated examples of two voices harmonizing with each other come from the 9th and 10th centuries. As if on railroad tracks at the interval of a perfect fifth apart, two voices move up and down a modal scale in a narrow range.

Later, more voices were added, and thus a polyphonic choral musical form called the "motet" was created.

Although the human ear-brain unit has trouble following more than three voices at a time, four to eight voices were not uncommon in the great contrapuntal works of the 17th and 18th centuries.

Polyphonic means "many voiced," and as for counterpoint, the complete term is point-counter-point, meaning "note against note."[1]

The voices enter in melodic imitation of each other at regular time intervals in a way that suggests a canon or a round (such as *Frère Jacques*), or a fugue—all contrapuntal, polyphonic musical forms. —TH

Frère Jacques is completely built on inversions of the F major chord.

Gewandhaus, Leipzig

GROWING PAINS

The Gewandhaus in Leipzig is one of those venues that is so closely tied to its orchestra that it is often difficult to separate their respective histories. The venue itself has been the more obedient of the pair, changing both figuratively and literally to meet the needs of the performers and their ever growing audience. In fact, today's Gewandhaus bears very little relation to either of its two predecessors, except in name and reputation.

In 1781 the Gewandhaus Orchestra moved from its previous home at a local inn into a grand hall that could seat 500 people, the original Gewandhaus concert hall. Within a mere century, attendance figures were so high that a new, larger hall had to be found. In 1884 the orchestra moved to this second Gewandhaus, which held three times as many patrons.

The devastation of World War II left much of Leipzig in ruins, and sadly the Gewandhaus was not spared. Efforts were made to bring the structure back to life, but those failed, resulting in the building being demolished. It wasn't until 1981 that a new Gewandhaus was constructed on the same site as the previous two, but the youth of this venue has not prevented it from becoming one of the premier concert halls of the world, hosting more than 600 events annually.[1] —MM

Neues Gewandhaus, Leipzig. Photo courtesy William Rand.

Handel House Museum

THE ULTIMATE LIVE-WORK SPACE

The former home of the great Baroque composer George Frideric Handel does not lie silent. Restored as faithfully as possible to reflect the early Georgian interiors Handel would have known, the Handel House in London, which opened as a museum in 2001, brings back to life the space where the composer lived, worked, and died—through displays, special exhibitions, and recitals of his works.

Handel's bedroom at the Handel House Museum. Photo by Matthew Hollow.

Handel created many of his masterpieces, including *Messiah,* at 25 Brook Street, the modest townhouse he moved to in 1723. It is located within walking distance of St. James's Palace, where he had official duties, and the King's Theatre, where many of his operas premiered. Handel composed, rehearsed, and held informal performances on the first floor; on the second were his dressing room and bedroom, where he died the morning of April 14, 1759, having said the previous evening that he was "done with the world." From the ground floor, he conducted business: selling copies of his music and tickets to his concerts.

Today, visitors can wander through the upper floors of 25 Brook Street, where they can view portraits and paintings of Handel's contemporaries and 18th-century London, the original staircase, a canopied bed of the type the composer used, and a reproduction of a double manual harpsichord, like the instrument Handel might have owned. —KFG

FUN FACT

In the adjoining 23 Brook Street—which was the home of rock legend Jimi Hendrix in the late 1960s—manuscripts and printed scores from the collection are displayed.

Black & Decker® and Rimsky-Korsakov

THE HANDYMAN'S MUSE

A high-speed and breathtaking orchestral interlude from Russian composer Nicolai Rimsky-Korsakov's 1900 opera *Tale of Tsar Sultan* often accompanies quick-cut television commercials and choreography in dance and figure-skating performances.

Perhaps the best-known use of the piece was in the 1998 Black & Decker cordless power screwdriver ad campaign featuring trumpeter/music professor George Vosburgh playing with superhuman speed and total accuracy. As we see the wonders of the cordless power drill getting all the pending jobs finished in 30 seconds or fewer, "The Flight of the Bumblebee" propels the ad with dizzying speed.

"The Flight of the Bumblebee" is often used as a showcase piece for soloists to display their virtuosity on the trumpet, violin, piano, or flute. Many classical superstar artists include the piece on their recorded collections of short works.

The work was also used in the films *Kill Bill* in 2003 and *Shine* in 1996. Those who are familiar with radio shows from the 1940s and '50s may recall this piece used as the theme for *The Green Hornet* adventure series. More recent television commercials include Pampers Diapers in 2003, Puma in 2005, and Red Bull, also in 2005. —DD

Romantic Style

A BRIDGE OVER CHANGING MUSIC

Instead of being a movement in and of itself, the Romantic style of modern music really represents the transition between bona fide Romantic music and the true eclecticism of modern music.

Arnold Schoenberg is considered the largest contributor to this evolution (see "Arnold Schoenberg," page 60). His *Verklärte Nacht* (*Transfigured Night*) of 1899 was the first piece of programmatic music written for a chamber music ensemble—specifically a string sextet with two violins, two violas, and two cellos.

Schoenberg modeled the composition after the poem of the same name by Richard Dehmel about forgiveness between a man and a woman; he composed the piece in five sections, just like the poem. He also included musical references to the poem's subject matter, thus making it programmatic.

Although traits of Romantic music are readily recognizable, evidence of Schoenberg's atonal future is also obvious. This duality within Schoenberg's early music makes it especially interesting to dissect. Amazingly, this famous work was initially rejected by the Vienna Music Society because of a chord that Schoenberg invented—and this was Schoenberg's reaction:

"And thus (the work) cannot be performed since one cannot perform that which does not exist."[1] —SL

LISTENING HOMEWORK
Schoenberg's Verklärte Nacht

Passacaglia

DIG THAT BASS!

The flip side of the chaconne, the *passacaglia* is a repeated bass line as the basis for a varied melodic line. The bass line creates a groove over which the melody can soar, either aligned or unaligned with the phrase markers of the bass. There are several stock bass lines used, particularly the *lament bass,* so called because of the minor key and the stepwise bass line descending from scale degree one to scale degree five.

Like the chaconne, the passacaglia was produced in Spain in the 17th century. It was distinguished from the chaconne by Giacomo Frescobaldi, who composed many examples of both continuous-variation forms. He usually put passacaglias in minor mode and chaconnes in major mode, but there are plenty of exceptions. Two excellent examples of the passacaglia are "When I am Laid in Earth" from *Dido and Aeneas* by Henry Purcell, and J. S. Bach's *Passacaglia and Fugue in C minor,* BWV 582. Purcell's aria uses a highly chromatic lament bass, over which Dido sings her dismay over her lover leaving, with a soaring lyrical line. Bach's organ piece is also in a minor key, but not so histrionic. Instead, Bach uses the repeating bass line to create increasingly virtuoso variations. The passacaglia has seen modern versions, from "Nacht" in Schoenberg's *Pierrot Lunaire* to "Dirge" in Britten's *Serenade for Tenor, Horn, and Strings.* —SS

Sergei Prokofiev (1891–1953)

ENFANT TERRIBLE

Born at the height of Russian Romanticism, Sergei Prokofiev grew up in a doting household in what is now Ukraine. Immersed in music as a child, he would lie awake nights listening to his mother play the piano[1] and soon showed great proficiency himself. His mother took him to the St. Petersburg Conservatory, where at age 13 he became the youngest student ever to be accepted to the school.

With a precocious confidence bordering on arrogance, the young Prokofiev earned the nickname "enfant terrible" among his instructors,[2] regularly ignoring the rules of compositional style and pushing the envelopes of tonality and harmony in his pieces. Even after graduating, as he emerged onto the world stage, his compositions regularly garnered a mixture of acclaim and scorn. Not only did Prokofiev take this in stride, he remained firmly confident of his own musicality, and even seemed to thrive on the controversy. Not until his latter years, when Stalin's regime began censuring his works, did Prokofiev's self-confidence begin to waver. He didn't survive to see this reproach reversed, dying on the same day as Stalin himself.

Despite the mixed reviews he often received, Prokofiev's contributions to music cannot be overstated. Writing for a full range of genres, he revived many of the classical forms, such as the symphony and concerto, by infusing them with his own progressive style.[3] The enfant terrible grew up to be one of this century's most influential composers. —JJM

Toccata and Fugue in D minor

BY JOHANN SEBASTIAN BACH, CA. 1708

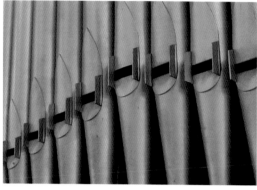

Power, grace, beauty, drama—this one mesmerizing work for solo organ has it all. In about eight minutes the listener is taken on a wild ride through what may seem like the musical equivalent of a Hallow-een fun house. In fact, the opening bars of the *Toccata* have practically become pop culture's theme for all things spooky. In a case like this, it may not be easy to strip the work of its silly modern associations, but only when we look beyond the visions of Dracula's castle can we fully appreciate the genius of Bach that is manifest in the *Toccata and Fugue.*

After about two and a half minutes, when the ominous figures of the *Toccata* have sufficiently terrified the listener and stretched out the organist's hands, everyone can take a quick breath before the dizzying contrapuntal passages of the fugue begin. From there, nimble sequences of imitation and pseudo-improvisation put on a dazzling display that builds to a chilling conclusion. There is some mystery and debate about the original circumstances sur-rounding the work, but those kinds of riddles suit this enigmatic work just fine. —CKG

RECOMMENDED RECORDING

Bach: Toccata and Fugue in D minor; *Prelude and Fugue in B minor; Concerto No. 2 in A minor; Prélude and Fugue in D major; Michael Murray (organ); Telarc; 1990*

Samson et Dalila

CAMILLE SAINT-SAËNS (1835–1921)

"**M**on cœur s'ouvre à ta voix" ("My heart opens itself to your voice"), one of the most famous mezzo-soprano opera arias in history, can be heard in Camille Saint-Saëns's three-act opera *Samson et Dalila* (*Samson and Delilah*). Based on the biblical story from the Old Testament's Book of Judges, chapter 16, *Samson et Dalila* was Saint-Saëns's second opera and the only one from the French composer still performed today. He had originally intended in 1859 to use the legendary tale as inspiration to write an oratorio, but librettist Ferdinand Lemaire convinced him the drama would be better suited to the opera stage.

Samson et Dalila enjoyed a successful premiere in Weimar in 1877 in German translation, but did not receive international attention until the 1890s. Since then the piece has become a staple of the classic opera repertoire.

Set in Gaza circa 1150 B.C.E., the story opens with mighty warrior Samson leading the Hebrews in a rebellion against the Philistines. Samson is seduced by the beautiful Dalila, who has been sent to discover the secret of his strength. When she discovers that Samson's strength is in his long hair, she shaves his head. Samson is then taken prisoner and held in the Temple of Dagon. He prays that God will restore his strength. The opera ends as Samson pulls down the pillars and temple, crushing his enemies and himself in the process. —CCD

Frank Porretta is Samson. Photo by David Bachman; courtesy of Pittsburgh Opera (www.pittsburghopera.org).

Indefinite Pitched Percussion

NOISEMAKERS EXTRAORDINAIRE

Although anything able to be banged, shaken, rubbed, or scraped could be considered an indefinite pitched percussion instrument, three primary noisemakers were found in the early Romantic-era orchestra.

Possibly the most popular, the crash cymbal is able to create a wide range of effects. In addition to being crashed together to accent sections of high dynamics, these metal discs can also be tinkled with sticks, swelled with soft mallets, and scraped with a coin.

The triangle is a bar of metal bent into a triangular shape with one of the angles left open. It is held using a piece of cloth or wire and played with a metal striker, often to enhance movements of excitement. Although Mozart, Haydn, and Beethoven used it, Franz Liszt's Piano Concerto *No. 1* is the first piece to feature a triangle solo.

A shallow frame drum with metal discs called "jingles" hanging loosely in its sides, the tambourine is one of the orchestra's older percussion instruments. It traditionally has a head on one side, and it is most often shaken, hit against the hand or leg, and rubbed to produce its array of energetic sounds.

As composers like Debussy and Richard Strauss experimented with tonal colors and textures, many items began to overflow the orchestral percussionist's tool bag—from wood blocks, anvils, whips, and rattles to castanets, gongs, finger cymbals, and motor horns. But no one has topped Tchaikovsky's thunderous use of volleying cannons in his *1812 Overture.* —LMC

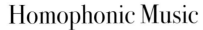

Homophonic Music
ONE LEADER, MANY SUPPORTERS

Homophonic music is one melody above any accompaniment, which may be a guitar, an orchestra, a band, or a choir of supporting voices.

Polyphonic music generated homophony. First, melodies were sung together, each singer listening to his own tune in relation to the others. That's how tonality evolved; if you stopped the music at any point, you could hear harmony—a chord—sung by the voices together. Melody is older than harmony and always has authority over how the chords change.

Before, you saw sample chords all in root position. But historically, when chords resulted from melody lines, they often came up in *inversions,* because it's easier—the path of least resistance—for voices to move stepwise rather than jump around in disjunctive intervals. Musicians call it "voice leading."

Triads have root position and two inversions. Seventh chords have root position and three inversions since they have an added seventh factor.

The horizontal line of top notes historically wound up being the melodic notes; the other notes decreased in importance, and that's how homophonic music was born.

HOMOPHONIC MELODY WITH CHORD INVERSIONS IN ACCOMPANIMENT

The piano left hand has evolved from a contrapuntal melody line to a non-melodic guitar finger-picking style, and is intended only as a graceful rhythmic accompaniment to the melody. —TH

INVERTED TRIADS & 7TH CHORDS

To invert a chord, put the bottom note on the top.

Bolshoi Theatre

THE "GRAND" DAME OF RUSSIA

The word "bolshoi" in Russian means "grand," and the Bolshoi Theatre in Moscow deserves this name without a doubt. Aside from hosting two of the world's leading fine arts institutions (the respective opera and ballet companies that bear the Bolshoi name), the theatre serves as an outward representation of the story of the Russian people, a strong story that has weathered many revisions.

The Bolshoi Theatre was built in 1824 after the opera and ballet companies had spent nearly two decades without any real home. The idea was to create a venue where Russian works could be presented for a Russian audience, but as repertoires and public appetite expanded, eventually the Bolshoi companies began to perform some works from international composers. (Even so, about 70 percent of Bolshoi performances are still based on Russian works.)

Those performances are being held in a completely separate venue at the time of this printing, however, as the Bolshoi undergoes major renovations.[1] Although a substitute theatre was constructed from start to finish in less than six months, the work on the original Bolshoi building, which began in 2005, will be complete in 2013. Originally the project was to be much less involved, but as engineers explored the cosmetic work was to be done, they discovered major structural flaws in the building that must be corrected in order for the venue to be stable. —MM

The Ottawa International Chamber Music Festival

FILLING CANADA'S CAPITAL WITH MUSIC

In 1994, the idea of a chamber music festival in Ottawa came to life to remedy the meager availability of live classical music during the summer months and fill the city's churches with splendid sounds. The festival started with 22 concerts in two churches; the next year the number increased to 48 concerts, and the festival has been growing ever since.[1]

Today the Ottawa International Chamber Music Festival, or Chamberfest, as it is affectionately called, is considered the largest chamber music festival in the world. For two weeks in late July and early August, some 80,000 listeners converge for about 100 concerts—among the performers are the St. Lawrence and Emerson string quartets, pianists Anton Kuerti and Louis Lortie, violinist James Ehnes, and the Gryphon Trio. The repertoire ranges from early music to contemporary.

Located on the banks of the Ottawa River, the city boasts architecturally interesting churches within walking distance of each other. For an informal, relaxed evening of music, some folks head to one of Ottawa's newest hot spots, Saint Brigid's Emerald Club—located in a deconsecrated Roman Catholic church undergoing restoration to become a downtown arts and culture center for late-night concerts.[2] —KFG

The Gryphon Trio perform at the Ottawa International Chamber Music Festival. Cellist Roman Borys is now artistic director for the Ottawa Chamber Music Society, which runs the festival. Photo by John Beebe.

British Airways and "Flower Duet"

"SAFETY AND PEACE IN THE SKIES"

Many people often feel a bit nervous before boarding a plane, especially after having seen a recent newscast of a crash or hijacking. To soothe their jittery customers, British Airways's mad men allowed opera to do the talking for them. In a series of long-running international television and radio commercials through the 1990s, the music of Leo Delibes was heard. The choice of an excerpt of the "Flower Duet" from his opera *Lakmé* made many feel as if two mermaids were singing to them in a dream. It's a most relaxing sound and a beautiful melody. The piece of music sold British Airways's message perfectly…calm, comfort, safety, and peace in the skies.

The duet, composed to be sung by two sopranos, is a lovely, heavenly sounding song that soars over a light string and wind section. The scene in the opera is that of the main character, Lakmé, and her servant gathering flowers growing by a river. The libretto is in French and written by Edmond Gondinet and Philippe Gille. Though not often performed in the opera halls, there are a number of brilliant recordings available of the complete opera.

Various recordings of the "Flower Duet" have been used often in television shows as well as in motion pictures like *The Hunger* and *Someone to Watch Over Me*. The duet is well known, however, as "The British Airways Song."
—DD

Impressionism
THE FRENCH TAKE THE LEAD

It seems like new styles in music are oftentimes revolts from the music of the previous era. Just as "history repeats itself," composers take on the roles of rebellious teenagers, refusing to go along with their predecessors.

The following Debussy quote is a case in point, emphasizing the emergence of impressionism: "I am trying to do 'something different'—what the imbeciles call 'impressionism' is a term which is as poorly used as possible, particularly by art critics."[1]

What were they doing differently, you ask? Well, a lot of things. First there was a dramatic change in tonality—major and minor keys were used together to create a new tonality in and of itself. Whole tone scales (a scale consisting of only the interval of a whole tone, instead of the usual combination of whole and half tones that creates major and minor scales) were used with  abandon. Overall, these different tonalities created more dissonance than in previous Romantic music.

The impressionistic piece was, in general, much shorter; instead of symphonies and concertos, composers concentrated on writing shorter forms such as the nocturne, prelude, and arabesque. Most importantly, impressionistic writers were largely Frenchmen; there were some English contributors (namely Ralph Vaughn Williams), but the main impressionistic school was created and developed in France. This French foothold took the world's musical center away from Italy and Germany. —SL

LISTENING HOMEWORK

Debussy's Prelude de la après mide d'un faune
Ravel's Daphnis and Chloe
Ralph Vaughn William's Fantasia on a Theme of Thomas Tallis

Mazurka

FOLK DANCING GETS FANCY

Like the sarabande, minuet, and gavotte, the mazurka started life as a dance. In fact, it is one of two popular folk dances to come out of Poland, along with its more famous cousin, the polka. But whereas the polka is still danced regularly at Wisconsin weddings, the mazurka has found life on the concert stage thanks to over 50 piano pieces by Polish composer/pianist Frédéric Chopin between 1825 and 1849.

Chopin spent most of his career in Paris, reshaping his native dances for the salon. The characteristic rhythms of the mazurka remained, although Chopin indicated so many tempo shifts that it would be very difficult to actually dance to them. He also added chromaticisms and elaborate counterpoint that were not found in the original dances.

The mazurka is in a triple meter, but with the accent displaced from the first beat to the second or third beat. Usually the first beat is divided, impelling motion forward to the second or third beat. The overall form of the piece is either a rondo or a composite ternary form, and a droning pedal is often used to mimic the *dudy*, the traditional Polish bagpipe.

After Chopin established the mazurka as a concert form, it was used by other composers such as Karol Szymanowski (Poland); Piotr Tchaikovsky, Alexander Borodin, and Mikhail Glinka (Russia); Claude Debussy and Maurice Ravel (France); and Heitor Villa-Lobos (Brazil). —SS

Two basic mazurka rhythms.

Antonio Vivaldi (1678–1741)

HALF-HEARTED PRIEST, WHOLE-HEARTED COMPOSER

Italian composer and violinist Antonio Vivaldi came into prominence during the height of the Baroque period. He was ordained as a Catholic priest but stopped performing masses shortly after his ordination. The official reason was physical ailments, but it was apparent that his heart was in music.

At the time Vivaldi's home town of Venice was a musical center much like Vienna would soon become, and no doubt this fact helped promote his compositions even beyond Venice. A prolific composer, it is believed that he wrote over 700 pieces,[1] many of them concertos, for which Vivaldi was best known. His musical contributions, in fact, helped solidify the forms that would carry into the Classical period. Most famous among his concertos was his series *The Four Seasons.* He also wrote numerous successful operas, although most of these have been lost.

An interesting part of Vivaldi's history is his relationship with the Ospedale della Pietà. These "orphanages" for young girls were more specifically homes for the illegitimate offspring of noblemen; the girls were cared for through many "anonymous" donations, and music was a large part of their training.[2] Vivaldi was appointed a violin instructor at the Ospedale, and eventually became their concert master—a position he held for much of his career. This partially accounts for the large number of his concertos, which were specifically written for the talented young ladies there.[3] —JJM

Requiem

BY GABRIEL FAURÉ, 1887–1900

A requiem is different from a regular mass in that it is focused on commemorating the dead. Musical settings for the traditional Latin requiem have been introduced by a number of composers (most famously Mozart, who was tragically unable to complete his), and in the 19th century it was an especially popular form. Many requiems are known for their overwhelming intensity, but it is the solemn restraint of Fauré's setting that makes it so touching. As he said, "The piece is as gentle as I am myself."[1]

Although the work is immaculately constructed and sounds as if it emerged from Fauré's imagination with divinely inspired ease, it actually underwent many revisions. For 13 years Fauré tinkered with arrangements. He had worked for decades as a church musician but composed the *Requiem* "purely for the pleasure of it," and the joy that he invested in this tenderly elegiac work is transmitted to the listener.[2] In the introspective "Sanctus" and haunting "Pie Jesu," where disembodied voices seem to echo from the infinite beyond, we can palpably feel the mysterious consolation that arises out of mourning. —CKG

RECOMMENDED RECORDING

Fauré: Requiem *and other choral music; John Rutter (conductor);*
London Sinfonia (members of); Collegium; 2000

Les Contes d'Hoffmann

JACQUES OFFENBACH (1819–1880)

The story of Jacques Offenbach's *Les Contes d'Hoffmann* (*The Tales of Hoffmann*) begins during the intermission of another famous opera, Mozart's *Don Giovanni*. As the poet Hoffmann waits in the lobby bar for Stella, a diva in the show, he begins to sing about the ideal woman. This leads him to recount stories of three past loves: Olympia, a mechanical doll; Antonia, a young girl who loves to sing but for whom the activity further endangers her fragile health; and Giuletta, a conniving courtesan. As Hoffmann finishes his stories, Stella appears at the lobby bar to find him drunk. She then decides to leave with his rival, Councilor Lindorf. Hoffmann's friend, Nicklausse, assuming the form of his muse, urges him to return to his writing and reminds him that his heartbreak will make his poetry even more insightful.

Based on the play *Les contes fantastiques d'Hoffmann* (*The Fantastic Tales of Hoffmann*) about the German Romantic author E. T. A. Hoffmann and written by Jules Barbier and Michel Carré, the opera's French libretto was written solely by Barbier. Though Offenbach began composing the opera in 1877, he did not live to see its premiere at Opéra-Comique in 1881. As the composer was not completely finished with the score before he died, there are now several different versions of the opera. Ernest Guiraud's version was used at the opera's premiere, as he had completed Offenbach's scoring and composed the recitatives. —CCD

Hoffmann (tenor Gerard Powers) captivates tavern patrons with his storytelling. Photo by Jeffrey Dunn © 2008; courtesy Boston Lyric Opera.

Indefinite Pitch Orchestral Drums

NO TUNE, LOTS OF BEAT

A s orchestras continued to become louder and more powerful, drums of indefinite pitch added support as accent and rhythm components. The power trio consists of the bass, the snare, and the tenor drums.

The biggest of the orchestral drums is the bass drum. Typically a large round wooden shell with two playable heads, it is mounted on a wheeled stand that can be tilted for ease of playing with soft mallets. It is most commonly used for accent and coloration. Hits in the bass drum's literature are Stravinsky's *The Rite of Spring* and Tchaikovsky's Symphony No. 4 and *1812 Overture.*

The snare drum, often called the side drum, is possibly the most recognizable drum in the orchestra because of its sharp, military-style sound. The snare is accented with a set of wires, or snares, resting on the bottom head, adding a buzzing sound to the drum to increase its brilliance. A famous passage featuring the snare drum is found in Carl Nielsen's Fifth Symphony.

Pitched lower than a snare drum and higher than a bass drum, the tenor drum is similar in diameter to the snare drum but makes use of a deeper body. This tom-tom–style drum experienced a 20th-century boom in popularity in compositions by Benjamin Britten and Aaron Copland, as a member of marching bands, and as part of the rock 'n' roll drum kit. —LMC

Implied Harmony

YOU JUST *THOUGHT* YOU HEARD THAT

A document circulates on the Internet in which all the words have missing letters. Readers are challenged to understand the message despite the letter gaps. A surprisingly high percentage are able to understand the message.

The same principle pertains to the "hearing" of implied harmony. It means you hear only a few of the notes of the chords in the music as it goes by you, but that's enough to let you follow it—all of it—melody, harmony and rhythm. Your mind supplies the rest. Inversions are also implied by which chord voices are left in the bass line after the chord has been "flipped" or inverted through the melody.

Our example is the opening of Johann Sebastian Bach's Two-Part Invention No. 4 in D minor for keyboard.

IMPLIED HARMONY 2-PART INV. IN D MINOR

Johann Sebastian Bach

The bottom staff of each system is not played. It only shows the chords suggested by the two melodies. Even though only two notes are sounding, the ear implies the whole chord. —TH

LISTENING HOMEWORK

Look up a recording of Bach's Two-Part Invention No. 4 in D minor;
play it back several times.

National Theatre, Munich

A HOME FOR GERMAN MUSICAL GENIUS

"Third time's the charm" is often the story for venues being destroyed and rebuilt, and with fire and war both being common in the history of Europe, it's not surprising how many European venues have had to be reconstructed more than once. The National Theatre in Munich has remained stronger than most throughout the three acts of its life, and today remains a symbol of many important historical moments in German music.

The first version of the National Theatre opened in 1818, and within five years had already burned down. This did not discourage the German people, and a second building was constructed on the site two years later. World War II took its share of victims, and in 1943 the National Theatre fell once again. Rebuilding took two decades the second time, but the new National Theatre that opened in 1963 retained all the glory of the original neoclassical design.

The venue is no stranger to famous performances, and many noteworthy artists, conductors, and composers have shared their talents with Munich audiences over the years. Before Wagner went off and built his own concert hall, the National Theatre was the default stage for his opera premieres. Richard Strauss served there as conductor for several years and maintained strong ties with the venue throughout his professional life. —MM

Ravinia Festival

CULTURE WITH A COLORFUL PAST

Founded on land originally purchased in 1902 to be used as an amusement park to lure riders to the fledgling Chicago and Milwaukee Electric Railroad, Ravinia boasts a long, colorful history. After the amusement park failed, a group of North Shore residents made Ravinia a summer venue for classical music in 1911. The era from 1919 to 1931 marked Ravinia's golden age of opera, when some of the world's greatest singers performed on a small wooden outdoor stage. They had to be flexible, though: one noted American tenor, Mario Chamlee, sang as a train rolled past the park.[1]

The golden age came to a close with the onset of the Great Depression, and for five years the park was silent. Music returned in 1936, when Ravinia became the summer residence of the Chicago Symphony Orchestra, which remains the centerpiece of the festival today. Ravinia's program evolved, adding jazz, pop, blues, dance, and opera concert performances. Over the years festivalgoers have enjoyed such luminaries as Louis Armstrong, the Ballet Russe, Leonard Bernstein, Ella Fitzgerald, Janis Joplin, and George Gershwin.

Today many of the 600,000 visitors who enter the festive main gate during the three-month summer season pack a picnic (some complete with candelabra and fine china) and catch a concert by candlelight as they gaze at the stars.
—KFG

During the Ravinia Festival's golden age of opera, the iconic arch over the festival's main entrance bore the name Ravinia Opera. Photo courtesy Ravinia Festival.

Grieg and Nescafé®

A LITTLE *PEER GYNT* WITH YOUR COFFEE

The beautiful "Morning Mood" from Norwegian composer Edvard Grieg's *Peer Gynt Suite No. 1* was heard around the world as the Nescafé coffee theme. Composed in 1875 as part of the incidental music of Henrik Ibsen's play *Peer Gynt*, Grieg later chose "Morning Mood" along with seven other pieces from the complete set of pieces that accompanied the play performances to form two suites. This is usually how the music is heard today on recordings and in concert.

Many people will instantly recognize the beautiful, peaceful melody and delicate orchestration of "Morning Mood" and associate it with sunrise, breakfast, and coffee because of its brilliant use by the producers of the Nescafé coffee series of television and radio commercials that ran in 2000. The music went so well with the images of a husband and wife waking up, sunrise, garden flowers, steaming hot cups of Nescafé coffee, and other scenes of domestic morning life that many thought the music was created specially for the ad campaign.

Other pop culture appearances by Grieg include the very famous piece "In the Hall of the Mountain King," which was heard in many films, including *Dead Snow* in 2009. Rock artist Rick Wakeman included the big theme in his *Journey to the Centre of the Earth* album and series of concerts in 1974, as did rock group Electric Light Orchestra on their *On the Third Day* album in 1973. Perhaps the most interesting interpretation is Duke Ellington's jazz version from 1960. —DD

Expressionism

OUT WITH CONVENTION, IN WITH INVENTION

Arnold Schoenberg is (once again!) the ringleader of this important musical period. Schoenberg himself went through many evolutions. As discussed on page 228, he began as a transitional figure between the Romantic and modern eras. This expressionism period is equivalent to Schoenberg's middle period, or the beginnings of atonality, before he developed the 12-tone compositional technique.

This free atonal music set out to ignore any and all bits of compositional convention. Traditional form? Cadence? Sequence? Repetition? All gone. The idea was a complete rejection of musical tradition in hopes of creating a blank slate on which music could begin to rebuild itself.

Schoenberg and his pupils (Alban Berg and Anton Webern) comprised the Second Viennese School, which had its start during expressionism but really came to full maturity slightly later in the century. Nevertheless, Berg, Webern, and—to some extent—Béla Bartók also contributed to expressionism.

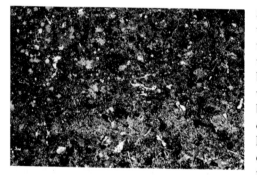

Schoenberg was good friends with the artist Kandinsky; they shared the similar view that the unconscious should be free to act on its own, without being influenced by the outwardly controlled conscious. Next time you listen to one of Schoenberg's early 20th-century works, flip through a book of Kandinsky's paintings—you'll undoubtedly better understand both the music and art of expressionism. —SL

LISTENING HOMEWORK

Schoenberg's Second String Quartet

Schoenberg's Erwartung

Schoenberg's Die Glückliche Hand

Chamber Music

FOR JUST A FEW CLOSE FRIENDS...

When discussing how many musicians are performing at a given time, we can generalize to three categories: solo, large ensemble, and chamber music. Chamber music covers a very big spread, anything from 2 violins to 20 percussionists. But they all share the same traits of collaboration, equality, and intimacy.

The term "chamber music" comes from *sonata da camera,* an Italian phrase used during the Renaissance to describe instrumental music composed for private parties at palaces or parlors. Today, chamber music can involve vocalists as well as instrumentalists.

One newer ensemble that has become popular is based on a specific piece: Schoenberg's *Pierrot Lunaire.* "Pierrot Plus" ensembles like eighth blackbird play the instruments used in Schoenberg's work (flute, clarinet, violin, cello, and piano), plus percussion.

Members of eighth blackbird. Back row, left to right: Nicholas Photinos, cello; Tim Munro, flutes; Matthew Duvall, percussion; and Lisa Kaplan, piano. Front row, left to right: Michael J. Maccaferri, clarinets; Matt Albert, violin and viola. Photo by Luke Ratray.

The compositional form of chamber music can vary, but the most common type is the multi movement sonata. The three or four movements will usually alternate two fast movements with one or two slow movements. These movements will have their own forms, from sonata-allegro to binary to minuet and trio. —SS

STANDARD CHAMBER ENSEMBLES

String Quartet: 2 violins, viola, 'cello

Woodwind Quintet: flute, oboe, clarinet, bassoon, horn

Brass Quintet: 2 trumpets, horn, trombone, tuba (or bass trombone)

Piano Trio: piano, violin, cello

Saxophone Quartet: soprano, alto, tenor, and baritone saxophones

Tuba Quartet: 2 euphoniums, 2 tubas

Percussion Ensemble: any number of percussionists, though 4 is common

Piano Four Hands: 1 piano with 2 players

Instrumental Sonatas: piano with another instrument (violin, 'cello, clarinet, trumpet, etc.)

Richard Strauss (1864-1949)

THE BALANCING ACT

Richard Strauss, a late Romantic German composer, drew his inspiration from two polar musical opposites: the Classicism of Mozart and the wild Romanticism of Wagner.[1] His compositions were a sort of balancing act between these poles, usually leaning toward one or the other.

In the prime of his career, Strauss leaned most toward Wagner in his compositions; these works proved to be his most controversial and influential. His symphonic poem *Don Juan* was met with equal parts cheering and booing at its debut; his operas *Salome* and *Elektra* drew riotous responses initially for their dark moral content and tonal dissonance.[2] Soon, almost inexplicably, Strauss shifted back toward Mozart with a series of lighter pieces that were well received but far less influential.

Unfortunately, the balancing act Strauss attempted in life ultimately worked against him. Although he didn't share their views, he accepted a musical position with the Nazi regime, believing he could influence German culture within it. The Nazis eventually dismissed him for collaborating with a Jewish lyricist.

While controversy was his ally musically, in life it was his enemy. Strauss's association with the Nazis proved more personally damaging than any provocative piece he wrote. Although his name was cleared after the war, his career never quite recovered from the blight. He died a few years later, unaware that he would one day be remembered as an icon alongside his beloved Mozart and Wagner. —JJM

The Nutcracker

BY PYOTR IL'YICH TCHAIKOVSKY, 1892

The holidays just wouldn't be the same without the magical music of *The Nutcracker*. Tchaikovsky is unsurpassed among composers for his ability to create memorable melodies, and the Christmas-themed ballet showcases his talent for both composition and orchestration. From the festive bombast of the "Russian Dance" to the twinkling chimes and famous clarinet dive of the "Dance of the Sugar Plum Fairy," the many imaginative themes in *The Nutcracker's* two acts offer a variety of moods and tempos that capture the holiday spirit.

The ballet's child-oriented subject matter was not created by Tchaikovsky. On the contrary, he was not fond of the story and struggled with the idea of composing a ballet that lacked realistic human drama.[1] Nevertheless, the surreal nature of *The Nutcracker's* storyline suited his gift for enchanted musical hooks. In the story, a girl named Clara gets a nutcracker toy for Christmas that comes to life. After Clara helps him defeat an army of mice, the nutcracker turns into a prince and invites Clara to his "Kingdom of Sweets," where she is treated to a variety of dessert-themed dances.

Just like a peppermint candy cane or gingerbread latte, *The Nutcracker* may be a tad sweet for year-round enjoyment, but indulging in such delicacies is ideal for once-a-year holiday celebration. —CKG

RECOMMENDED RECORDING

Tchaikovsky: The Nutcracker *(Complete Ballet),* Sleeping Beauty *(Highlights);*
Antal Dorati (conductor); Royal Concertgebouw Orchestra; Philips; 1994

Manon

JULES MASSENET (1842–1912)

A young girl's difficult journey from innocence to womanhood is chronicled in Jules Massenet's *Manon*, an opera in five acts. Based on the Abbé Prévost's novel *L'histoire du chevalier des Grieux et de Manon Lescaut*, the French libretto was written by Henri Meilhac and Philippe Gille. The piece is Massenet's most popular opera and includes the poignant soprano aria sung by Manon in Act II, "Adieu, notre petite table" ("Goodbye, our little table").

Fifteen-year-old Manon meets and falls in love with the Chevalier des Grieux while on her way to the convent. The two run away to Paris to live together. Des Grieux intends to ask Manon's father for her hand in marriage, but Manon is told by her cousin Lescaut and the nobleman de Brétigny that des Grieux is to be carried off according to her father's orders. De Brétigny becomes Manon's new protector, and she later learns that des Grieux is to be ordained a priest. When she sees him preach at St. Sulpice, Manon reminds des Grieux of his love for her, and he abandons the priesthood. The two then encounter problems, as des Grieux is arrested while gambling, having been accused of cheating. He is quickly released, but Manon has also been arrested as his accomplice and is not released, having been condemned for her immoral lifestyle. Lescaut eventually bribes the sergeant so Manon may have a final moment with des Grieux. Dying, she begs his forgiveness. —CCD

The Piano

300 YEARS OF TICKLING THE IVORIES

Bartolomeo Cristofori, keeper of the instruments at the Medici court in Florence, Italy, is credited with making the first working piano in 1700. Referred to as the pianoforte, it produced sound by way of strings struck by hammers, combining the expressiveness of the clavichord with the loudness of the harpsichord.

The piano became popular in the mid-1700s with composers like J. S. Bach, and by the late 1700s manufacturing had flourished in Austria. With a soft, clear tone and delicate action, the Viennese pianos of Mozart's era were made with wooden frames, used two strings per note struck by leather-covered hammers, and often employed black keys for natural notes and white for accidentals.

By the early 1800s the piano's popularity grew as composers like Haydn and Beethoven began to use this harpsichord alternative. The addition of strong cast-iron frames and felt hammers along with three strings per treble note and a seven-octave range culminated in a louder modern concert grand piano.

Foot pedals had been used since the earliest designs, and today's pianos now include three. The sustain pedal lifts the damper so the notes can naturally sustain; the una corda pedal shifts the keyboard to the right so only one of the three strings is played; and the sostenuto pedal allows for some notes to be sustained while others are dampened.

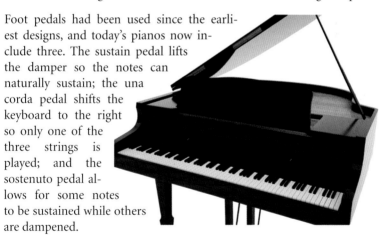

Composers of the Baroque, Classical, and early Romantic periods all wrote for a developing instrument quite different from the one we play today. —LMC

Contemporary Harmony and Polytonality
THE DEATH OF TONALITY

Having just surveyed the melodic, rhythmic, and harmonic foundations of Western classical tonal music, which took place over centuries, it's time to experience a cataclysmic shift in music: the use of several tonal centers at once (polytonality), and the complete loss of tonality.

Over the two generations of World Wars I and II, Western classical music underwent the same fragmentation, deconstruction, and loss of central focus in its tonal center as Western painting did within the visual compass—via cubism and other techniques—of its four-sided canvas.

Due to financial and spiritual pressures, both arguably resulting from and resulting in World Wars I and II, Germany and the rest of northern Europe suffered instability in the first half of the 20th century. On both the individual and collective levels, a sense of balanced inner wholeness disappeared from human life, and this was strongly marked by increasing fragmentation and dissonance in artistic expression. The soul center was damaged or completely gone in many people, and consequently in the arts too, a "leading indicator" of mental health.

In music, this meant that serene harmonies and melodies became tense, dissonant, and fragmented, with a loss of regular phrases, cadences, and rhythms. The tonic, the "heart center" of music, was obscured or disappeared completely.

True artists have always operated on a psychic or soul level, and, grasping the dark collective mood, they gave individual expression to the prevailing inner and outer crises of the times. —TH

La Scala

NOT FOR THE FAINT OF HEART

Italy certainly has its share of important venues, but La Scala in Milan holds a special place in the hierarchy of opera houses as the auditorium that inspires both greatness and fear in the performers who dare to brave its stage. Many singers have triumphs at La Scala, and others leave the stage in anger and humiliation, never to return.

The controversy stems from an institution known as the "loggione"—the upper galleries where inexpensive seats are located, or more specifically, the harsh public critics who populate those seats. In the Italian opera world, approval from the loggione is just about the highest praise a singer can receive. But nothing escapes their perceptive ears; they can sniff out a weak performance instantly. And they are vocal about their disapproval—singers as celebrated as Roberto Alagna have literally been booed off the stage mid performance.

Critics of La Scala's loggione insist that the booing and hissing amount to nothing more than childish hooliganism, keeping up a stale tradition that might best be retired in the interest of respect toward the performers. Others argue that opera is an art form in which high standards are essential, and that the role of the loggione rite of passage is to separate the wheat from the chaff.[1] Whatever your opinion, one thing is certain: Attending a performance at La Scala, with the palpable tension between singers and audience, is not something you're likely to forget! —MM

The Stradivari Museum and the Ancient Instruments Collection

BIRTHPLACE OF THE VIOLIN

Cremona, a charming northern Italian town in Lombardy that lies on a rise beside the Po River, boasts beautiful town squares and gastronomical specialties. But it is also considered the birthplace of the violin and the home of some of the greatest string instrument makers, including members of the Amati family, Giuseppe Guarneri del Gesù, and the town's most famous luthier, Antonio Stradivari (1644–1737).

At Cremona's Stradivari Museum, housed in the 16th-century rooms of the Palazzo Affaitati, visitors gain insight into the master's process. Donated to the town in 1930, the museum's collection includes the molds, patterns, and various tools that belonged to Stradivari and other Cremonese violin makers; in all there are some 700 artifacts.

An instrument in the shop window of a luthier in Cremona, Lombardy, Italy.

Across town visitors can find instruments made by Cremona's master lute makers at the "Gli Archi del Palazzo Communale di Cremona" collection. Located in the town's civic center, Piazza del Comune, the collection of ancient instruments includes a 1566 violin made by Andrea Amati that was part of a group of instruments constructed for the court of Charles IX of France; a 1689 violin made of maple and spruce woods by Guiseppe Guarneri; and one of Stradivari's earlier works, a 1669 violin that shows the influence of his teacher Nicolò Amati.[1] —KFG

Prokofiev and Lexus

MUSIC TO DODGE ORBS BY

Since the early days of radio and all through the days of television, Sergei Prokofiev's music has been broadcast. From 1944 to late 1958 the producers of the CBS Radio program *The FBI in Peace and War* used the "March" from *Love for Three Oranges* as the show's opening and closing theme. Also on the radio airwaves were various productions of *Peter and the Wolf*, which was a perfect choice for any children's radio show.

As television commercial production became more sophisticated with the use of special optical effects and bigger budgets, car manufacturer Lexus launched a campaign in 1989 entitled "The Relentless Pursuit of Perfection." The producers chose the orchestral piece from Prokofiev's *Romeo and Juliet* ballet entitled "The Montagues and Capulets" (also known as "Dance of the Knights") for one of its most memorable television commercials. The commercial shows a Lexus LE-series car perilously maneuvering a course of huge swinging silver orbs. With each pass of these big metal monsters, the Lexus responds perfectly, avoiding disaster. The music gives the audience a sense of danger and tension. —DD

Fun Fact

Peter and the Wolf *became more famous when various records featuring narration by film and television stars like Charlton Heston hit the stores. In recent years even rock stars like Sting and David Bowie have recorded the narration.*

Futurism (1910–1930)

WHEN MACHINES CALLED THE SHOTS

Have you ever seen Björk's movie *Dancer in the Dark?* It tells quite the depressing story, but it defines futurism perfectly. For one thing, throughout the movie the mechanical sounds coming from Björk's factory are turned into songs. Futurist composers were obsessed with music deriving from the mechanical age; they sought inspiration from factories, airplanes, and cars, all of which were developing in the early 1900s.

The futuristic manifesto very much revolved around the ideas of speed, efficiency, and violence. *Dancer in the Dark* is an extremely macabre story, incorporating the need and unfortunate result of all three.

Balilla Pratella's futuristic manifesto included these strictures:

- The young should stay away from conservatories and study independently
- There should be a public musical review, independent of academics and critics
- Any competition that is not completely open should be boycotted
- Previous "well-made" music should be ignored
- All period settings, ballads, "nauseating Neapolitan songs and sacred music" should be prohibited
- New works should be promoted in preference to the old[1]

Many composers over the course of the 20th century were influenced by this manifesto, most notably George Anthiel. His *Ballet Mechanique* and *Death of the Machines* are perfect examples, incorporating all of Pratella's preferences.
—SL

LISTENING HOMEWORK

Anthiel's Ballet Mechanique *and* Death of the Machines
Prokofiev's The Steel Trap

Symphony
ALL TOGETHER NOW!

While the chicken-or-the-egg problem still plagues us, we do know that symphonies came after (and from) operas. The opening overture to operas, often called a "sinfonia," began to be expanded, and orchestras started performing on their own, encouraging the development of a multi movement work.

Much like piano sonatas or concertos, the symphony alternates between fast and slow movements, typically four in number, although later symphonies sometimes had five movements. The first movement is usually in sonata form, often with a hefty, slow introduction. The second is something slow and lyrical, but can be any variety of forms. The third movement is the dance movement, a minuet and trio or scherzo and trio. The fourth movement is either another sonata form or a rondo.

The emphasis is on the unity of the whole orchestra, though solos are frequent. The symphonic orchestra started out as only strings in the 1750s, and gradually added more woodwinds, brass, and percussion, until the beginning of the 20th century with Mahler's  famous Symphony No. 8 ("Symphony of a Thousand") for 21 woodwinds, 24 brass (including seven off-stage), nine percussion, four separate keyboards (organ, piano, harmonium, and celesta), two harps, mandolins, three separate choirs, eight vocal soloists, and a bevy of violins, violas, cellos, and basses. With these huge numbers, the dynamic ranges are incredible, from a single harp being plucked quietly to the whole orchestra peeling the paint off the walls with mighty fortissimo chords. —SS

Claudio Monteverdi (1567–1643)

ROMANTIC BEFORE HIS TIME

Italian composer Claudio Monteverdi was a key figure in the transition between the Renaissance and Baroque periods—a time when not only the compositional styles were changing, but the very structures of tonality and harmony were changing as well. An innovator and revolutionary, Monteverdi challenged the accepted modes of composition and tone by writing in what he called the "seconda prattica" (second practice)—a term used to differentiate the progressive new style from the old *prima prattica.*

Beginning at an early age, Monteverdi primarily wrote madrigals (a cappella songs written for multiple voices) until the age of 40. From there he changed over to an emerging new art form, the opera. His first, *L'Orfeo,* is one of the earliest operas still performed today.[1] He also wrote sacred music and held musical positions in both church and court. His church pieces tended to remain in the prima prattica; his more groundbreaking works were secular pieces.

One remarkable characteristic of Monteverdi's compositional style was that he deliberately wrote his music to reflect the emotion of the lyric, not unlike the Romantics of the 1800s. This might explain his preference for the madrigal, in which the music followed the flow of thought rather than a set pattern.[2] In this respect, Claudio Monteverdi foreshadowed music written over 200 years later. Historians classify him as Renaissance or Baroque, but his innovative approach to music really made Monteverdi a Romantic ahead of his time. —JJM

Appalachian Spring

BY AARON COPLAND, 1943–1944

In the same way that a Rachmaninov piano concerto is uniquely Russian or a Puccini opera is unmistakably Italian, the music of Aaron Copland is infused with the spirit of his homeland. The bucolic *Appalachian Spring*, in particular, embodies a distinctly American atmosphere in its adventurous passages. Lively changes in tempo and mood give the piece an instant accessibility as it fluctuates between extremes of serene beauty and majestic power, while the skillful incorporation of the Shaker hymn "Simple Gifts" leads to an unforgettable high point.

Although it's tempting to assume that America's natural splendor inspired Copland to compose the work, it was actually written on commission as a ballet for the celebrated dancer and choreographer Martha Graham. The music tells the story of a newly wed American couple who meet the challenges of 19th-century pioneer living.[1] Copland's talent for conjuring rural imagery through music transports us to their place and time. —CKG

RECOMMENDED RECORDING

Bernstein Century-Copland: Appalachian Spring, Rodeo, *etc.; Leonard Bernstein; New York Philharmonic; Sony; 1997*

Boris Godunov

MODEST MUSSORGSKY (1839–1881)

A complex psychological tale of deception and vengeance unfolds in *Boris Godunov*, Modest Mussorgsky's only completed opera. With a libretto written by Mussorgsky himself, the piece is based on Alexander Pushkin's drama *Boris Godunov* and Nikolay Karamzin's *History of the Russian State*, a 12-volume national history. The story is set between 1598 and 1605 during the reign of Tsar Boris Godunov, with a war-torn Russia set as a backdrop.

Boris Godunov, the regent of the young Tsar Fyodor, becomes tsar of Russia after arranging the assassination of the tsar's half-brother, 10-year-old Dimitri, the rightful heir. Young monk Grigori vows to avenge the murdered Dimitri and, disguised as the dead tsarevich, crosses the border into Lithuania, where he meets and marries Marina, a Polish noblewoman who dreams of becoming tsarina. Grigori, still disguised as Dimitri, leads the Poles in an invasion of Russia. They claim power as Boris dies, shocked and guilt-ridden by Dimitri's mysterious resurrection.

Heidi Stober as Xenia, Samuel Ramey as Boris Godunov. Photo by Ted Washington; courtesy Houston Grand Opera.

Rejecting standard German and Italian approaches to style, Mussorgsky sought to compose a truly Russian opera, relying on folk music traditions, dramatic choral scenes, and intensely detailed characterizations. After he died, the piece was revised by several composers who thought Mussorgsky's compositional style was a bit too raw. A version by his friend Nikolay Rimsky-Korsakov was particularly well received, especially in opera houses throughout Europe. The latest trend, however, has been to return to Mussorgsky's original composition. —CCD

The Harpsichord
STRIKING A CHORD IN THE BAROQUE PERIOD

Although this plucked instrument has much in common with the piano, the harpsichord's ancestry is more aligned with the handheld psaltery of ancient Greece. When a keyboard was added to aid in striking the strings, what we now know as the harpsichord began its evolution, mostly in the region of Flanders. Many adaptations for centuries after continued to follow the Flemish design and look.

By the 1500s, Italy had become a prominent manufacturer and developed a small version called the spinet, made famous by Queen Elizabeth I. The Italian versions were so light they were considered portable, placed on a table and performed while standing up. The harpsichord provided accompaniment to special events in people's homes, its ornate craftsmanship confirming the owner's social status.

Originally a single-string-per-note instrument that sounded similar to a lute, the harpsichord evolved as makers continued to experiment. By the 1700s three strings per note were used with complicated levers, foot pedals, and additional keyboards (also called manuals), giving the musician considerable manipulation of tone.

The harpsichord reached the height of its popularity during the Baroque era, and many composers wrote specifically for this fashionable instrument. Masters like Johann Sebastian Bach, George Frideric Handel, Jean-Philippe Rameau, Louis Marchand, and Claudio Monteverdi developed new techniques in composition and performance using the harpsichord.

Its bright percussive tone can be heard in many 18th-century sinfonias, suites, fugues, arias, and inventions, as well as in 20th-century songs from the Beatles.
—LMC

Suspended Fourths and Quartal Harmony

THREE'S COMPANY, FOUR'S A NOISE

In music theory, one result of the aforementioned death of tonality in the early 20th century was the retooling of the musical technical vocabulary.

In polyphonic music, sometimes the interval of a perfect fourth wound up just before a cadence point. Since fourths were considered more dissonant than thirds, and a cadence was by definition a return to harmonic rest from tension, the fourth interval above the bass was suspended for a sweet instant of dissonance before it resolved down to the major third of the last chord of the piece:

SUSPENDED PERFECT FOURTH RESOLUTION TO MAJOR THIRD ON E-FLAT

The perfect fourth is a relatively mild dissonance, and outside of Germany, where the most painful crux of the World War II crisis lay, the use of *planing* perfect fourth chords was a great way to modernize the sound without sending human ears into fits of agony.[1]

Germany, arguably "classical music central," used far more dissonant devices than this one, which, along with other techniques, was favored by the French.

Like organum, there are no chord progressions here, just the modal scale:

PARALLEL "PLANING" OF 4TH CHORDS

The accidentals are used to keep the intervals "perfect" and avoid the sound of the major mode. —TH

FUN FACT

Thirds are major and minor, but fourths and fifths can be perfect, augmented (made larger), or diminished (made smaller).

Concertgebouw

CLASSICAL MUSIC ONLY—NOTHING ELSE SOUNDS AS GOOD

A favorite of music lovers everywhere, Amsterdam's Concertgebouw takes its place among the holy trinity of the world's finest venues, alongside the Musikverein in Vienna and Boston Symphony Hall. It is renowned for its first-rate acoustics, but here's the catch: The specific reverberant qualities of the venue perform well only with classical music, as failed experiments with pop performances have shown.

The superior acoustics of the Concertgebouw's two performance halls were mostly accidental. Designers did what they could to take ideas from previous structures, and the rest was mostly luck. The sound quality still remains a partial mystery, and great care has been taken during renovation projects to ensure that exactly the right materials and tools are used in order to keep the construction consistent. The acoustics in the Great Hall are perfect for large orchestral works, while the Small Hall is more readily suited for lieder recitals and chamber music. Amplified pop and rock music, however, are transformed into a muddy mess.

With an annual concert schedule of nearly 1,000 performances and almost 1,000,000 audience members visiting every year, the Concertgebouw has the second-highest rate of venue traffic in the world, after the Parco della Musica in Rome. In an effort to encourage the next generation to appreciate the value of classical music, the Concertgebouw hosts special performances and programs geared toward schoolchildren, and other programs for adults under the age of 30. —MM

Salzburg Festival

A FESTIVAL BRINGS RECONCILIATION

Inaugurated in August 1920 after the end of World War I, the Salzburg Festival was founded to bring reconciliation to "counteract…the crisis of meaning, the loss in values, the identity crisis of the individual, as well as of entire nations," festival organizers have said.[1]

Since its first event—the premiere of Hugo von Hofmannsthal's morality play *Jedermann* ("Everyman")—the festival has aimed to fulfill its mission of bringing enlightenment through opera, drama, and concerts. Throughout the 1920s and '30s the festival attracted the best directors, conductors, actors, and singers of the era. But the Nazi occupation of Austria proved a major blow; many artists were no longer welcome, and works were struck from the repertoire and replaced by "German art." Under the swastika, the festival drew mostly soldiers and Germans.

Cathedral Square, Salzburg. Copyright Tourismus Salzburg GmbH.

The programs were revived with the support of the American occupying forces just three months after the end of World War II. Over the remainder of the 20th century, the festival became more international, with a repertoire spanning Mozart to modern works.

In July and August, some 250,000 visitors flock to the Austrian city, whose baroque architecture and river Salzach provide a beautiful backdrop. They choose from 200 performances at 13 indoor and outdoor venues scattered throughout the city, including a temporary stage seating 2,500 outside Salzburg Cathedral; the Felsenreitschule, a former 17th-century riding school; the Grosses Festspielhaus (Large Festival Hall), which opened in 1960; and the smaller House for Mozart, which opened in 1925. —KFG

Classical Music in a Sitcom

THE ODD COUPLE BROUGHT CLASS TO THE GENRE

It is rare for a television comedy show to even refer to classical music, opera, or the ballet. Due to a very unique character named Felix Unger portrayed by the amazingly talented actor Tony Randall, *The Odd Couple* is the exception. Not only did the writers mention classical music in many of the episodes, but they actually dedicated four episodes to it.

The series was broadcast on CBS from September 1970 through July 1975. In season two, an episode entitled "Does Your Mother Know You're Out, Rigoletto?" features New York Metropolitan Opera baritone Richard Fredricks portraying himself and masterfully singing a number of highlights from Verdi's famous opera *Rigoletto*.

Season four delivered two more episodes devoted to classical music. "The Last Tango in Newark" features New York City Ballet star Edward Villella portraying himself and dancing throughout the episode to piano reductions of excerpts from Tchaikovsky's gorgeous *Swan Lake*. In "Vocal Girl Makes Good," opera star Marilyn Horne, cast as Jackie, beautifully sings excerpts from Bizet's opera *Carmen*.

Finally, in season five, "The Roy Clark Show" episode features Clark and Tony Randall playing an excerpt from Mozart's Piano Sonata No. 16 in C, as well as an adagio by Vivaldi.

Felix's love of classical music was enhanced by Tony Randall's own passion for the opera and ballet. His piano and singing talents greatly enhanced the show's authenticity and brilliant comedy. —DD

Second Viennese School
ARNOLD SCHOENBERG AND THE 12 TONES

If you remember way back to the Classical/Romantic eras, we talked a bit about the First Viennese School, which included Haydn, Mozart, and Beethoven. During the early 20th century, there was another round of strong Viennese influence led by Arnold Schoenberg. Schoenberg had two famous students named Anton Webern and Alban Berg; together, the three of them created the Second Viennese School. Their relationship was at times strained, but all in all they embodied the three musketeers of Berlin music and politics in the early 1900s. Many other composers followed in their footsteps, but these three were the definite founders.

The two main musical concepts of the Second Viennese School were atonality and 12-tone composition (see "Arnold Schoenberg and 12-Tone (Serial) Music," page 304). Atonality refers to music that lacks a tonal center. Twelve-tone composition is a type of atonality that creates a mathematical method of composing music, ensuring that all 12 notes are used with equal influence.

Schoenberg was really the ringleader of the group; however, Berg and Webern were not mere followers. They also had their own distinctive influence.

This movement has many different names; it seems each culture has titled it differently. Ranging from being called the "New Vienna School," the "Young Viennese," or even the "Schoenberg School," no one disputes the influence and importance these new German composers had on 20th-century music.
—SL

LISTENING HOMEWORK

Webern's String Quartet
Berg's Violin Concerto
Schoenberg's Pierrot Lunaire

March

HUP, TWO, THREE, FOUR!

You may think you know what a march is, with lots of brass and drums blasting to keep your feet moving in time with the sergeant as you wish you were back in bed. At least that's how I remember my time in marching band. But the march actually has its own form, thanks to the consistency of composers like John Philip Sousa and Henry Fillmore.

The march is usually in three sections, called "strains," with the last strain also called a trio like the minuet and trio; however, each strain has its own melody, and the trio is often in a separate key, a perfect fifth below the original key. It is quite common for the trombones to be given the melody in the second strain, and for the brass and woodwinds to alternate melodic lines in the trio. Each strain also repeats, and extra parts are often added in the repeat (obbligato).

Marches are always in meters of two or four beats, but the tempo varies depending on the nationality or purpose of the march. British marches are slower than French or American marches; circus marches are the fastest. Funeral marches were very popular as slow movements of Romantic symphonies such as Beethoven's Third Symphony and Gustav Mahler's First and Fifth Symphonies. The most famous funeral march is found not in a symphony but in the third movement of Chopin's Piano Sonata No. 2. —SS

Dmitri Shostakovich (1906–1975)

THE RELUCTANT SOVIET

Dmitri Shostakovich was a young musical genius who came of age shortly after the Russian Revolution. He was politicized for most of his life—not because of his political leanings (which are debated even today), but because of the highly charged environment that constantly surrounded him. Unlike other Russian composers who fled their homeland, Shostakovich engaged in a lifelong struggle to get along with the political system while being true to his gifts—a choice that landed him alternately in favor and disrepute with the Soviet regime multiple times.

Shostakovich wrote a total of 15 symphonies and 15 string quartets, as well as numerous other works for choir, orchestra, opera, and ballet. He incurred sharp criticism from the Soviets whenever he wrote something considered controversial; each time he was denounced, he was restored by writing something patriotic or favorable to the party. During one particularly difficult season, Shostakovich reportedly sat outside at night so his family wouldn't be disturbed if he were arrested or shot.[1]

It seems unfortunate that the life of Shostakovich was so clouded by politics. However, beyond the ongoing debate about whether he was a private dissident or a party man,[2] Shostakovich's life and music suggest he was at heart a composer attempting to express himself. The passionate and brilliant body of work he left behind speaks for itself. —JJM

A Midsummer Night's Dream

BY FELIX MENDELSSOHN, 1842

The long and lovely overture to *A Midsummer Night's Dream* was written when Mendelssohn was only 17 years old. It was a remarkable achievement, not only because of the composer's youth, but also because of the way it functioned as Romantic music while fitting neatly into classical sonata form. To this day, the overture is still a popular favorite as an isolated concert piece.

Nevertheless, when the King of Prussia asked him to write the incidental music for a stage production of the play in 1842—16 years after he had written the overture—Mendelssohn picked up right where he had left off and completed another 13 sections. As a lifelong lover of literature, and of *A Midsummer Night's Dream* in particular, the composer was able to conjure the spirit of the play and create a work that artistically reflects all the complexity and fanciful mischief of Shakespeare's script.

One section of the music is universally recognizable: the "Wedding March." We know the melody well from its regular use as a recessional in contemporary ceremonies, but Mendelssohn intended it to commemorate the magically arranged group wedding of Shakespeare's Athenian lovers. —CKG

RECOMMENDED RECORDING

Mendelssohn: A Midsummer Night's Dream; *Seiji Ozawa (conductor);*
Boston Symphony Orchestra; Deutsche Grammophon; 1995

Cavalleria Rusticana (Rustic Chivalry)

PIETRO MASCAGNI (1863–1945)

Easter dawns in a Sicilian village, and Turiddu's voice is heard in the distance singing about his mistress, Lola, the wife of the town's carter, Alfio. Later that morning, his wife, Santuzza, tells Turiddu's mother, Mamma Lucia, that she knows that Turiddu has left her to be with his old flame, Lola. Santuzza then confronts Turiddu, but he pushes her to the ground. Santuzza curses him and then tells Alfio that his wife has been cheating on him. Alfio vows revenge and challenges Turiddu to a duel. Though Turiddu confesses, he agrees to continue with the fight, asking his mother to care for Santuzza if he should lose. The opera ends as a woman runs in screaming that Turiddu has been killed.

Written in just one act, Pietro Mascagni's *Cavalleria Rusticana* is a suspenseful drama filled with some of opera's most beloved melodies, including the orchestral "Intermezzo," the Easter hymn "Regina Coeli" sung by Santuzza and the chorus, and her heartbreaking aria, "Voi lo sapete" ("You know it"). With an Italian libretto by Giovanni Targioni-Tozzetti and Guido Menasci, the story was adapted from a play based on a short story by Giovanni Verga. The opera premiered in 1890 at the Teatro Costanzi in Rome and was an instant success, making it the most popular of Mascagni's 16 operas. It is often performed as a double bill with Ruggero Leoncavallo's *Pagliacci.* —CCD

"Regina Coeli" chorus scene: Leann Pantaleo as Santuzza, Gioacchino Laura LiVigni as Turiddu, Margaret Yauger as Mamma Lucia. Photo by Martha Mickles (www.marthamickles.com); courtesy PORTopera (www.portopera.org).

The Clavichord

HARD TO HEAR, WORTH THE EFFORT

Popular between the 16th and 19th centuries, this simplest of keyboard instruments has been somewhat of a hidden jewel during most of its lifetime. Because of its low volume, the clavichord was not often used for large performances where instruments like the harpsichord could be better heard. The clavichord's softness, however, is accompanied by unrivaled subtlety and expressiveness.

Pressing a key causes a thin piece of metal, called a "tangent," to strike a pair of strings to create sound. For structural economy, two or more keys were often assigned to hit the same strings. The uniqueness of the clavichord is that the tangent must stay in touch with the string, much like a fret, to continue the sound, giving the player an extraordinary degree of control over the volume and color of the tone.

As a home instrument, the clavichord was used as an instrument for learning, practice, and composition. Organists could practice at home instead of in a cold, damp church and didn't require anyone to pump the bellows. It is said that Mozart and Chopin carried small clavichords with them on long journeys.

Clavichord. Bizzi Clavicembali, Italy. (www.bizzi.com)

During the 17th and 18th centuries, composers J. S., C. P. E., and W. F. Bach, Frobeger, Pachelbel, and Böhm were among many to write specifically for the clavichord. Modern uses include Paul McCartney's performance on the Beatles song "For No One" and the electric version, called a "clavinet," was very popular in 1970s funk and disco music. —LMC

Sounds Like Change

HOW THE ELEMENTS OF MUSIC DETERMINE STYLE

We've seen how the elements of music determine form. But there's something that music shares with the other arts—style. It's more elusive and harder to factually pin down than form; but form, melody, harmony, and rhythm contribute to style nonetheless.

Each composer is a product of his or her time; and in the 18th century, Bach and Handel expressed tonal music at what many today consider to be the height of its stylistic refinement and grace. (The Baroque period has close to a 50-50 balance of polyphony and homophony.)

The Classical period illustrates the continued prevalence of diatonic music. But by the end of the period, Mozart's melodies started to develop chromatic inflection, such as in his Concerto in C. And this chromaticism seems all the more striking as it often occurs above diatonic harmony.

Pushing the Classical envelope, Beethoven continued to stretch the existing harmonic vocabulary and promote the democratic artist, as well as continue to be a proponent of human freedom and brotherhood. His strong personality, as indicated by the emotional tone of his music, led to striking chord progressions, especially in his middle and late periods, which constitute the beginning of the Romantic period.

From this point through the late Romantic period, the sounds of European classical music become more rich and unfamiliar. There's more surprise and tension than tonal predictability and rest. There's more passion, more far-out use of all the musical elements. —TH

Berlin State Opera House

PERSEVERENCE THROUGH THE CENTURIES

The Berlin State Opera House is yet another venue marked by resilience in the face of disaster. Both fire and war tried to put an end to this remarkable and historic theater, but the determination of those involved in the repeated reconstruction has proven to be stronger than any destruction man or nature could concoct.

The Opera House was originally constructed in 1741, and within the first century quite a few prominent composers served as musical directors, most notably Giacomo Meyerbeer and Felix Mendelssohn. In 1843 the concert hall—which was then known as the Linden Opera—burned to the ground. Design and construction for a new building began immediately.

It was smooth sailing for nearly another century, and during the latter half of the 19th century a wealth of talented and historically important conductors graced the podium of the Opera House. World War II, however, spelled disaster for the venue not once, but twice. After a bomb caused significant damage in 1941, rebuilding began immediately, and performances resumed in December of that same year. A second bomb in 1945 destroyed the Opera House completely, though, and this time concerts had to be moved to another venue, as reconstruction took just over a decade.[1]

Today, the Berlin State Opera House stands as a reminder of the turmoil of the German nation and the strength of its people. Internationally acclaimed conductor Daniel Barenboim has stood as musical director since 1992. —MM

Staatsoper unter den Linden. *Photo courtesy Christopher McNulty.*

Tanglewood Music Festival

VIEW FROM THE SHED

The main concert venue of one of the most respected summer music festivals in the U.S. may be called a "shed," but don't be fooled. Grand sounds emerge from the permanent open-air structure, nestled in the Berkshires of western Massachusetts, that has hosted some of the finest musicians and conductors and attracts nearly 350,000 visitors during its summer season.

The shed is a big step up from the original venue—a large tent where the Boston Symphony Orchestra gave a three-concert series in August 1936. A 5,100-seat shed replaced the tent and was eventually rededicated as "The Serge Koussevitzky Music Shed," after the Boston Symphony Orchestra music director. The Boston Symphony Orchestra has performed in the shed every year since (except for several years during World War II).

Tanglewood shed at dusk. Photo by Stu Rosner.

Located on a large estate about a mile from the center of Lenox, Massachusetts, Tanglewood is the summer home of the Boston Symphony Orchestra. Festival attendees experience a range of music— piano concertos, chamber music, instrumental and vocal recitals, contemporary music, and performances by popular and jazz artists— in various venues on the sprawling 500-acre grounds, including a chamber music hall and the Seiji Ozawa Hall. Many people pack picnics and feast on the lawn to enjoy the stunning natural views before concerts or during a performance if they purchased lawn seats.

Committed to developing new talent, the Tanglewood Music Center, founded in 1940, is the Boston Symphony Orchestra summer academy for music study and performance for emerging artists. According to some estimates, 20 percent of the members of American symphony orchestras studied at Tanglewood Music Center.[1] —KFG

Orff and Old Spice®

SHAVING NEVER FELT SO TRIUMPHANT

Television commercials often use dramatic classical music to command fickle viewers' attention. Few pieces are better at this than "O Fortuna," from German composer Carl Orff's scenic cantata *Carmina Burana.*

The opening and closing movement to Orff's most famous work is instantly recognized by anyone who's ever been exposed to television shows and commercials, feature films, sporting events, and pop/rock concerts.

A British television ad campaign for Old Spice aftershave in the late 1970s and early '80s was one of the first to use this very powerful music. We see a man splashing on the aftershave in front of his bathroom mirror while nautical scenes of a sailing ship on a rough ocean play in his head. "O Fortuna" was used in another Old Spice commercial featuring a man daydreaming about conquering powerful surf atop his surfboard, again while splashing on Old Spice.

Pop star Michael Jackson used "O Fortuna" in three of his film shorts about his career in 1988, '93, and '95. Metal rock star Ozzy Osbourne also used "O Fortuna" as an opening for his concerts in the late '90s. Feature films
Excalibur, The Bachelor, The General's Daughter, as well as television
commercials made for Gatorade®
in 2007 and Pringles® in 2004 also
featured this movement. The New
England Patriots play the music
at all home games as a possible warning to the visiting
opposition. —DD

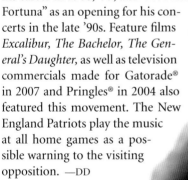

Neoclassicism

EVERYTHING IN MODERATION

The sequel is never as good as the original, right? With few noted examples (think *The Godfather*), we can all generally agree that sequels are little more than attempted moneymakers. I mean, other than your little niece or nephew, who really wants to see *The Lion King II: Simba's Pride?*

But when it comes to classical music, the second time around can actually be a welcome change. The Neoclassical time period refers to music written between the two World Wars (approximately 1920–1950), yet is musically reminiscent of compositions written in the early 1800s.

Neoclassicism started as a backlash of sorts—it was a knee-jerk reaction to the lushness and ambiguity of Romantic-era music. Marked by slight parody, irony, and distaste for authority, neoclassical music oftentimes sounds sarcastic and irate, like a roll of the eyes behind the general's back.

So while wartime officials were pushing the popularized "We need YOU!" slogan, musicians and composers were chanting "Back to Bach!" to urge along the call for suppressed emotion. After all, these neoclassical composers (the best examples are Sergei Prokofiev, Igor Stravinsky, and Paul Hindemith) weren't suggesting that music shouldn't portray sentiment—they just thought everything should be done in moderation, and with good taste. Preference and credit were given to the original, and the last four *Rocky* movies would have been skipped altogether. —SL

LISTENING HOMEWORK

Prokofiev's Symphony No. 1 "The Classical Symphony" *(aptly named, right?)*
Stravinsky's Pulcinella *(who else had a similarly titled piece?)*
Hindemith's Kammermusik

Mass

SINGING PRAISES TO GOD

The history of classical music is indelibly linked to the Christian church. Up through the 1700s, composers and musicians got their training in church choirs. Even after secular music began to grow, composers still wrote religious music, either intended for services or just as inspirational concert music.

The most common church music is found in the mass, which has been used in the Catholic Church since the 4th century. The type of music changed over time, but the biggest artistic contributions came in the Renaissance.

A mass is divided into two parts, the Ordinary and the Proper. The Ordinary are the parts that occur in every mass of the year: the Kyrie, Gloria, Credo, Sanctus, and Agnus Dei. Portions that vary depending on the season and feast day are called the Proper: Introit, Gradual, Alleluia, Offertory, Sequence, and Communion. Mostly polyphonic and choral, the sections of the mass often related to each other musically. These masses would use a single Gregorian chant as the basis for each office of the mass. The melody would be used as the tenor voice, with each note held out for long durations. The other voices would be written in counterpoint.

Great examples of Renaissance masses include versions of the *Missa L'homme armé* (based on the French secular song *L'homme armé*) by Guillaume Dufay, Josquin des Prez, and Giovanni di Palestrina; and the *Messe de Notre Dame* by Guillaume de Machaut (the first known ordinary mass by a single composer). —SS

Jean Sibelius (1865-1957)

THE NOT-QUITE-FINNISH COMPOSER

As Edvard Greig was associated with Norway, so was Jean Sibelius with Finland. The music of Sibelius, written in the late Romantic tradition, was destined to become indelibly associated with Finnish nationalism.

Ironically, Sibelius was actually Swedish by nationality. Born Johan Christian Julius Sibbe when Finland was under Swedish control, he learned Finnish as a second language, and took the name Jean Sibelius as an adult. However, Finland was always home to him, and Finnish folklore deeply affected his work. One song in particular, "Aténarnes sang" ("The War Song of the Tyrtaeus"), was an outcry against the policies of the Russian czar, galvanizing Sibelius's reputation as a Finnish nationalist.[1]

Beginning with piano as a child, Sibelius switched to violin, and eventually discovered his true talent was composition. He was best known for his orchestral works, which included symphonic poems and seven symphonies (plus an eighth that he reportedly destroyed). By far his most famous works were the *Valse Triste* and his symphonic poem *Finlandia*.

Uncomfortable with modern compositional styles, Sibelius composed little in his latter years; however, he lived to see his work become immensely popular, and was deemed by many to be the world's greatest living symphonic composer.[2] Today, Sibelius—the not-quite-Finnish composer—is celebrated as one of Finland's great historic icons. —JJM

FACT

Alcoholism and unruly spending plagued Sibelius at various times in life; at one low point, he sold the rights to Valse Triste *quite cheaply. It became his most popular piece not long afterward.*

Music for 18 Musicians

BY STEVE REICH, 1976

When most people think of classical music, they envision the powdered wigs and horse-drawn carriages of centuries past. It may surprise some to discover that even since the advent of jazz and rock and roll, groundbreaking innovations have continued to appear in music considered "classical." The inventive creations of American composer Steve Reich, for example, prove that concert halls maintain a relevance to modern culture that is anything but outdated.

Reich's percussive *Music for 18 Musicians* was a major landmark in 20th-century music for the way it explored new sonic and structural territories. Many of the 18 performers involved in the work play percussive instruments such as xylophones, marimbas, and pianos, while clarinets and female voices also make major contributions to the 11 sections bookended by "Pulses." Each section explores the harmonic possibilities found within a single chord while an endlessly stimulating array of syncopated rhythmic patterns emerges from the brilliantly arranged score. Like the radiating ripples of raindrops in a pond, the effect is both infinite and immediate, hypnotic and exhilarating. —CKG

RECOMMENDED RECORDING

Steve Reich: **Music for 18 Musicians**; *ECM; 2000*

I Pagliacci (Clowns)

RUGGIERO LEONCAVALLO (1857–1919)

"Si puo? Signore e Signori" ("Excuse me, ladies and gentlemen"), sings the hunchback Tonio, peeking out at the audience during the prologue of Ruggiero Leoncavallo's short opera *I Pagliacci*. He reminds the audience that actors have feelings and the following show is about real people.

Canio, head of the commedia troupe, is suspicious of his wife, Nedda, when someone jokes that Tonio is in love with her. Alarmed by her husband's suspicion, Nedda decides to run away with her real lover, Silvio. Tonio, who secretly witnesses the lovers planning their escape,

Todd Geer as Canio in I Pagliacci (Clowns). *Photo courtesy Opera Carolina (Charlotte, North Carolina, www.operacarolina.org).*

tells Canio, who catches the guilty couple. Silvio manages to get away without being identified. Nedda refuses to reveal who her lover is. Tonio suggests Canio wait until that night's performance to catch his wife's lover. Left alone, Canio sings the famous tenor aria, "Vesti la Giubba" ("Put on the costume"), and weeps that he is forced to now play the clown, even though he is heartbroken.

The villagers, including Silvio, gather to watch the troupe perform the play *Pagliaccio e Colombina*. Colombina, played by Nedda, is cheating on her husband, Pagliaccio, played by Canio. Disregarding the script, Canio demands to know the name of his wife's real lover. Nedda attempts to continue with the play, which drives him to stab Nedda and then Silvio, who has come to her aid. Tonio cries that the comedy is finished. —CCD

The Celesta

GENTLE TONES FROM A HEAVENLY INSTRUMENT

Patented by Parisian Auguste Mustel in 1886, the celesta is an orchestral percussion instrument known for its soft, tinkling, ethereal sound. Although it is categorized as an idiophone, its uniqueness lies in the fact that it is housed in an upright piano-like enclosure and a keyboard is used to operate it. In orchestral terms, it is generally considered a member of the keyboard family and played by a keyboardist. Its name comes from the heavenly sound it produces.

Depending on the model, a celesta has a range of three to five octaves above middle C. When a key is depressed, a small metal bar attached to a wooden resonator box is struck by a small felt hammer and a gentle metallic sound is produced. A foot pedal is used to lift a felt damper pad to allow the player to create sustained or dampened notes.

Ernest Chausson was one of the first composers to call into play this modern striker, and Pyotr Tchaikovsky is generally considered the first major composer to use it in a symphony orchestra. His ballet *The Nutcracker* features one of the most notable uses during Dance of the Sugar Plum Fairy. Béla Bartók also highlights this angelic instrument in his *Music for Strings, Percussion and Celesta,* as does Gustav Mahler in Symphony No. 6 and Gustav Holst in *The Planets.* —LMC

Getting Lost In Opera

THE WAGNERIANS AND ULTIMATE CHROMATICISM

The Romantic sounds found in the works of Beethoven (middle to late periods), Brahms, Tchaikovsky, Wagner, and Mahler show much more emotionalism than previously. All this overfilling of the old containers (operatic forms, songs, symphonies, and sonatas) with stark, dramatic feeling resulted in a gradual loss of the old tonality.

The prevailing social taste for music as a pleasure that would not let us down had been replaced by a music expressing loss and need in the form of longing and yearning. The psychosociological reasons for this are fascinating, but our object is to understand the intimate connection between sharps, flats, and accidentals with feeling.

For raw feeling in classical music, most musicians agree the first place to listen is opera. More sharps and flats were added to operatic melodies, in particular in the later operas of Richard Wagner. Chord progressions followed suit. This led to changing, obscuring, and dispensing with those little reminders of where we are in tonality, the cadences. It also led to "endless melodies" of chromatic inflection, supported by more augmented and diminished chords (which really don't serve a tonal function).

These devices led to long, long buildups ending in enormous crashing climaxes—and, surely, the axiom, "It ain't over till the fat lady sings." —TH

LISTENING HOMEWORK

Play a chromatic scale, then listen for chromaticism in any opera by
Richard Wagner, and Schoenberg's Verklärte Nacht.

Eszterhaza

WHERE HAYDN FELT RIGHT AT HOME

For a venue to boast that famous composers have conducted or premiered there is one thing; Eszterhaza in Fertod, Hungary, is unique in that composer Joseph Haydn was actually in residence there for nearly a quarter of a century. In fact, Eszterhaza was so significant in Haydn's life that he composed and premiered most of his symphonies there, performed with the help of the in-house orchestra.

This grand palace had quite murky beginnings, literally. In 1762, Prince Nikolaus Esterhazy, a renowned lover of the arts, set about to begin construction of the complex on swampland near the Hungarian border with Austria. The location was remote and isolated, and the prince took the opportunity to create a sprawling series of rooms and halls, many of which were dedicated to the creation and promotion of music. In 1766, Haydn was given living quarters in a large building behind the palace.

This setup proved to be a mixed blessing for Haydn. Unlike many composers of the time, the very existence of this venue meant Haydn had a job and a place to live, as well as unlimited access to musicians. On the other hand, his workload was immense, and the isolation of the palace led to unhappiness for both him and the musicians.

In 1790, a new prince ascended the Hungarian throne, and Haydn and the musicians were summarily dismissed, turning this once incomparable venue into a mere monument to a glorious musical past. —MM

Eszterhaza. Photo © Civertan Grafikai Stúdió.

Marlboro

COMMUNAL ARTISTRY IN SOUTHERN VERMONT

To get to what has been called a musical oasis, visitors travel a winding country road in the rolling foothills of southern Vermont. When they arrive at the small town of Marlboro, they find white barns, historic houses, and preeminent chamber music.

Founded in 1951, the Marlboro Music School and Festival is where the concept of having master artists play with emerging talent was born. Every summer, under the artistic direction of pianists Richard Goode and Mitsuko Uchida, about 60 talented young professional musicians and 30 highly experienced master artists live and work together, share insights, try new approaches, and refine their interpretations. The Pulitzer Prize-winning critic Alex Ross described Marlboro in a June 29, 2009 *New Yorker* article as "classical music's most coveted retreat."[1]

For nearly a month in the summer, artists rehearse some 230 works of their own choosing—from masterworks to rarely heard pieces and new music—but perform only the pieces they feel have achieved especially satisfying results. For that reason, concert repertoire are released only a week or so in advance.

Photo by Allen Cohen.

The musicians, festival staff, and their families share daily meals, social events and seminars, and even dining hall chores—in a warm community setting. Indeed, it was not unusual to see one of the founders of the festival and its first, longtime director, the eminent pianist Rudolf Serkin, "sharing the dining room cleanup duties or lining up, plastic tray in hand, at the cafeteria!"[2] On some "lazy days," wrote Ross, "it becomes a high-brow summer camp, where brainy musicians go swimming in the local pond."[3] —KFG

The Barber of Seville and Ragú®

ROSSINI AND VERDI SELL THE SAUCE

When Ragú pasta sauce began its television and radio commercial campaign back in the 1970s, people couldn't resist singing along with the music even though they often had no idea what they were singing. The fun, uplifting aria was *Largo al factotum* from Gioachino Rossini's most famous opera, *The Barber of Seville*. The opera is sung in Italian, and this aria in particular is sung very fast. "The Ragú Sauce Song" became very familiar to many and was often heard performed in domestic kitchens across the country (at least the wordless and humming versions were).

An aria that's much easier to sing and even more popular than Rossini's is *La donna e mobile,* composed by Giusseppe Verdi for his opera *Rigoletto.* This aria was used in the Leggo's Pasta Sauce commercial as well as in a number of other Italian food commercials both on television and radio. The spirit and zest of the melody captures the special love, excitement, and care that goes into preparing meals in the Italian culture. Even though the song within the context of the opera is about the fickleness of a certain woman, no matter: The tune is joyous and bounces along in an almost harmless kind of way. The melody is so catchy, in fact, that gondoliers in Venice often sing it in the canals and waterways. —DD

Electronic Music/Music Concrète

PLUGGING INTO THE FUTURE

In the 1950s, the technological world was exploding and the arts were determined to keep up.

Composers started to use electronic mediums to record acoustic instruments and then manipulate the sounds in ways previously impossible. This type of composition was aptly titled electronic music (see page 344).

When electronic generators produced the original sound bytes (and no "live" musicians were utilized), the music was called music concrète.

In the decades that followed, composers began to merge the two types of electronic music, using both synthesizers and instrumentalists in the same piece. Stockhausen and Davidovsky were two composers who used this blended compositional technique. As the two types of electronic music merged together, "electronic music" became an all-inclusive term.

On the American compositional front, the Music for Magnetic Tape Project paved the way. John Cage led the pack of New York composers, who begged and borrowed studio time in order to further the movement of electronic music.[1]

Because it developed around the globe concurrently, the music itself varies tremendously. Electronic music is consequently more of a definition of sound production rather than a description of what you'll actually hear in a composition. It can all be kind of overwhelmingly "out there," but give it a shot; this music is certainly bursting with creative possibility and compositional enjoyment. —SL

LISTENING HOMEWORK

Varèse's Déserts
Cage's Williams Mix
Davidovsky's Synchronisms

Trio Sonata

GOOD THINGS COME IN THREES...OR FOURS

One very popular form of chamber music in the Baroque period was the trio sonata, for two soloists with accompaniment. This accompaniment, called the "continuo," consisted of a harmony instrument—organ, harpsichord, or lute—and a bass instrument—cello, trombone, bass viol or double bass, bassoon, or viola da gamba—reinforcing the harmonies. The two solo instruments were usually violins, though flutes, cornetti, oboes, and recorders were also used.

Occasionally an organ trio sonata would be composed with the two solo parts on two different types of pipes. The two melody instruments often imitated each other as a fugue, like C. P. E. Bach's Trio Sonata in B flat major. Sometimes the continuo would also imitate the melodic subject, such as the first movement of Guiseppe Torelli's Trio Sonata No. 1 in G major. But the instruments were considered equal, and were usually in the exact same range of notes. One exception is Vivaldi's Trio Sonata in A minor, RV 86 for recorder and bassoon. The sonatas were in multiple movements, and were either in binary or ternary form, or were fugues with no overarching form to the episodes and statements of the subject.

The best-known composer of trio sonatas was Arcangelo Corelli, who wrote 48 trio sonatas for two violins and continuo. The trio sonata was the most popular type of chamber music in the 17th century, but died out with the continuo in the Classical era. —SS

George Frideric Handel (1685–1759)

THE "WORLDLY" CHURCH MUSICIAN

A product of classical music's Baroque period, Handel was born in Germany and eventually settled in England. While his father wanted him to be a lawyer, Handel's early aptitude for music dictated another path. His first love was opera, which led him to Italy as a young adult, where he gained acclaim as an operatic composer. His relocation to London likely had political underpinnings; he was sent there in the employ of a German elector who later became King George I of England.[1]

Handel's first London opera, *Rinaldo*, was a great success, and from that point, Handel spent various seasons composing for the public, the royal court, and the church. The eventual failure of his operas and other setbacks sent Handel into crisis; it was at this point he was commissioned to write an oratorio, *Messiah*. Deeply inspired, he wrote the three-hour piece in only 24 days.[2] A year later, when the king heard it performed in London, he stood spontaneously at the opening bars of the now famous "Hallelujah Chorus." Centuries later, it remains customary to stand whenever the "Hallelujah Chorus" is performed.

In a time when most composers had to choose between sacred and secular paths, Handel was an anomaly, transitioning smoothly in and out of church settings, and even across denominational lines. It was just such a man who wrote what has become one of history's most beloved sacred works.[3] —JJM

Symphony No. 40

BY WOLFGANG AMADEUS MOZART, 1788

At the age of 32, just a few years before his untimely death, Mozart wrote his last three symphonies—Nos. 39, 40, and 41. Amazingly, the works were all composed in about two months during the summer of 1788. Of the three, Symphony No. 40 in G minor stands out partly because of its unsettled mood. Its minor key contributes to a feeling of restlessness and lends the piece a shadowy gloom.

Most of Mozart's symphonies begin with an authoritative and enthusiastic hook, but Symphony No. 40's opening movement cautiously sneaks up on us with its familiar main theme. The furtive approach is as alluring as any bombastic introduction could be, creating a sense of eager anticipation in the listener that persists throughout the following three movements.

In contrast to the tympani-filled bravado of Mozart's 41st and final symphony, "Jupiter," the troubled nature of Symphony No. 40 is undeniable. There is profundity embedded in its internal distress, though, and that is precisely what makes his penultimate symphony so affecting. —CKG

RECOMMENDED RECORDING

Mozart: Symphonies Nos. 40 & 41; Charles Mackerras (conductor);
Prague Chamber Orchestra; Telarc; 2003

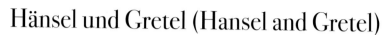

Hänsel und Gretel (Hansel and Gretel)

ENGELBERT HUMPERDINCK (1854–1921)

Hänsel und Gretel is a *Märchenoper* (fairy tale opera) written in three acts by Engelbert Humperdinck. The German libretto was written by Humperdinck's sister, Adelheid Wette, who was also the originator of the idea of the opera. She had written several songs for her children for Christmas based on the Grimm brothers' fairy tale *Hänsel und Gretel* and asked her brother to set them to music. Humperdinck used the songs as the basis for a full-scale opera, and it premiered on December 23, 1893, conducted by Richard Strauss.

As the opera begins, Hansel and Gretel have been sent into the forest to find strawberries, since their mother has just accidentally knocked over the milk, their only source of nutrition left in the house. In the forest, Hansel and Gretel are lost, but manage to fall asleep guarded by angels.

When they wake in the morning, they find a gingerbread house and its owner, the witch. She takes the children in, making Gretel her servant and fattening Hansel up to be eaten. Just as she readies the oven for him, the children manage to push her inside instead. They then release the other children whom the witch had turned into gingerbread boys and girls. Their parents arrive, and they all sing a hymn of thanksgiving. —CCD

Victoria Livengood as the Witch, Leah Wool as Hansel, Anya Matanovic as Gretel. Photo by J. David Levy; courtesy Kentucky Opera.

The Harp

HARP STRINGS TOUCH OUR HEARTSTRINGS

An instrument of antiquity dating back to ancient Egypt, the harp has been a beloved part of myths, legends, and daily life for 4,500 years.

Comprised of strings, a neck, and a resonator to amplify the sound, this finger-plucked chordophone differs from most stringed instruments in that the plane of the strings is perpendicular to the soundboard. Early, simple open harps with bowed or angular designs were able to accommodate a limited string tension.

Sometime after the 8th century, the frame harp appeared, using a fore-pillar to connect the top of the neck to the lower end of the resonator for additional support. Development of this new triangular harp facilitated two and even three ranks of strings, strategically tuned, to allow the harp to play in different keys.

Around the turn of the 18th century, pedals were introduced to alter the tuning of the strings, and by the early 1800s the double pedal system was able to efficiently shift the tuning up or down one semitone. Today's full-size chromatic concert harp has a breadth of six-and-a-half octaves; employs seven pedals, one for each note in the scale; and is a member of the symphony orchestra.

In addition to works by Handel, J. C. Bach, Mozart, Liszt, Puccini, Debussy, and Tchaikovsky, the harp can be heard in Marx Brothers' movies, played by Harpo Marx; the Beatles song "She's Leaving Home"; and on recordings by renowned Celtic harpist Alan Stivell. —LMC

Atonality and German Expressionism
THE AGONY AND THE ECSTASY

The road to German expressionism is one of ever increasing atonality and dissonance. Older music has more harmonic rest (consonance) than tension (dissonance). Newer music has more tension than rest.

In classical music, the tonic is often repeated to "pin it down." Melodies might only have the notes of the tonic and dominant chords for measures on end. Harmonies are consonant, hardly ever clashing.

In 18th-century Baroque, the great emotions of joy and sorrow are controlled by a knowing and tonally based chromaticism employed by Bach, Handel, and Vivaldi; consequently, a height of tonal expression is reached.

In the Classical period, comforting diatonic music continues. There is comparatively little dissonance, but this makes every little B-flat and F-sharp of Mozart and Haydn extremely important in conveying emotion, whether broad or subtle.

With the end of Romanticism, when creeping chromaticism starts to "take out" the tonal center, the polarities of consonance and dissonance become obvious.

Here's an example of two aspects of dissonance (and consonance) you can play for yourself:

"NAKED" AND "PADDED" DISSONANCE

"Naked" Dissonance (Less Consonant)   "Padded" Dissonance (More Consonant)

The *naked* interval of a major seventh is one of the harsher intervals. But as soon as you insert a couple of notes into the sandwich, three intervals of a third result, thus "mellowing it out."

Add this increased harmonic tension to atonality, mix well, and you have the recipe for expressing the fear and anguish of German expressionism. —TH

LISTENING HOMEWORK
Alban Berg, "Three Excerpts for Voice and Orchestra" from Wozzeck
(or complete opera)

Walt Disney Concert Hall

RAISING THE BAR FOR AMERICAN VENUES

Walt Disney was a known patron of the arts, and in 1987, when his widow, Lillian, gave $50 million to the city of Los Angeles, she had a vision for continuing that patronage. She wanted to create a venue in the downtown area that would be a fitting tribute to her late husband, and that would serve as an architectural and artistic triumph in a city where performing arts already reign supreme.[1]

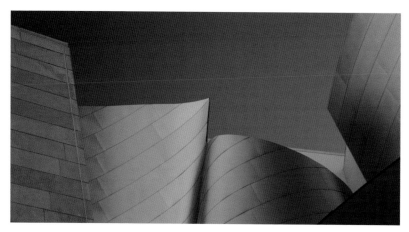

Sixteen years after the idea was born, the Walt Disney Concert Hall opened to the public. There is no doubt that it is a masterpiece of modern architecture, but the real achievement is that it sounds as good on the inside as it looks on the outside.[2] With acoustics that can be described as warm and intimate, it is shocking that a venue with more than 2,000 seats can provide an agreeable listening environment for every member of the audience.[3] As the Los Angeles Philharmonic prepared to move into their permanent new home at the Walt Disney Concert Hall, then director Esa-Pekka Salonen boasted, "Everyone can now hear what the L.A. Phil is supposed to sound like." —MM

> ### Fun Fact
> *After a long process of reconciling the experimental tastes of architect Frank Gehry with the practical limits of organ-building, the Walt Disney Concert Hall boasts perhaps the most unusual-looking pipe organ in the world.*

Lucerne Festival

A BIT OF SWISS MAGIC

August 1938. As Germany and Austria become tainted by the Nazi cloud, some musicians refused to perform there. Independent Switzerland provided the staging ground for a new classical music festival. On a beautiful afternoon in Lucerne, Italian conductor Arturo Toscanini lifted his baton to conduct Richard Wagner's *Siegfried-Idyll*, a symphonic poem for chamber orchestra.

To ensure the nervous Toscanini would not be disturbed during the dress rehearsal and concert, city officials enacted extreme measures to reduce noise: all boat traffic, except regular transport boats, was prohibited; parents of young children were encouraged to take them on walks away from the concert site; and all dogs at the surrounding farms were herded into soundproof kennels.

Among Europe's oldest and most distinguished music locales, Lucerne is situated on picturesque Lake Lucerne and attracts some 120,000 people every year to its three festivals: the largest one in August and September; the 10-day Easter festival devoted to sacred music (founded in 1988); and the weeklong November Lucerne Festival at the Piano (founded in 1998).

Every year since 2003 Lucerne's summer season has opened with a concert by the Lucerne Festival Orchestra—founded that year by famed Italian conductor Claudio Abbado and Lucerne's artistic director, Michael Haefliger. It has been called "the greatest orchestra in the world," and its rendition of Mahler's Symphony No. 4 in G major in 2009 was called "achingly beautiful" by the *New York Times*.[1] —KFG

Conductor Claudio Abbado and the Lucerne Festival Orchestra get a standing ovation at the 2009 Lucerne Festival. Photo by Priska Ketterer.

Turning Classical Into Rock

EMERSON, LAKE & PALMER TAKE THE CHALLENGE

While some rock and pop artists incorporate classical themes or melodies into their songs (like Rufus Wainwright's brilliant inclusion of an excerpt from Ravel's *Boléro* into his song "What A World"), the critically acclaimed rock group Emerson, Lake & Palmer took it a giant step further. They arranged, recorded, and performed a number of full classical compositions and complete movements as a rock band. The most notable is their amazing interpretation of Modest Mussorgsky's 1874 piano composition, *Pictures at an Exhibition.*

Based on Mussorgsky's original piano composition and composer Maurice Ravel's very popular orchestration of the work in 1922, pianist, organist, and composer Keith Emerson; vocalist, guitarist, bassist, and composer Greg Lake; and drummer, percussionist, and composer Carl Palmer created a dynamic and colorful arrangement for performance and recording. The group toured

with this powerhouse piece and recorded it for album release in 1971. No other rock band has taken on creating and playing their own arrangement and interpretation of a full-length classical work in this depth. —DD

Fun Fact

Be sure to explore E. L. P.'s other recordings of classical composition interpretations and arrangements for rock trio, including "Dances With the Black Spirits—The Enemy God" from Sergei Prokofiev's Scythian Suite, "Toccata," an interpretation of Alberto Ginastera's 4th Movement of his Piano Concerto No. 1, as well as a very interesting fusion of original lyric and vocal by Greg Lake on Leos Janecek's composition known as "Sinfonietta."

Contemporary Music (1945–1970)

THE NEW GENERATION

There are so many different names and subdivisions for recent music, it can all start to sound pretty darn arbitrary.

And you know what? You're right. As much as musicologists and music historians try to define and categorize our musical timeline, it is all done after the fact; so strict rules are hard to come by, and exact timing is almost impossible.

By now, we've talked a lot about 20th-century music, and it's totally understandable to ask how this so-called contemporary music is any different.

Generally speaking, contemporary music refers to *art music*, with the death of Anton Webern in 1945 creating the division between 20th-century and contemporary music.

Okay, fine, you say. But what exactly is art music, then?

Well, once again, art music can be a lot of things, including, but certainly not limited to: serial music, experimental music, minimalist music, conceptualist music, and art rock-influenced music.

Basically, contemporary music refers to anything written after 1945 (although some put the line as late as 1970) that is experimental in nature. This experimental nature could refer to the inclusion of new instruments, a sharing of the stage with visual representation, a strong sense of improvisation, or a heavy dose of extended techniques.

Contemporary music is what you make it. It can be frustrating because it is hard to understand, or it can be wonderfully challenging and exciting because it is so fresh and new. The choice is up to you. —SL

LISTENING HOMEWORK

Schoenberg's Pierrot Lunaire
Cage's 4'33" No. 2 (also known as 0'00")
Carter's Scrivo in Vento (Written in the Wind)

Rotational Form

WHAT GOES AROUND, COMES AROUND

Rotational form is a new idea formulated by Warren Darcy and James Hepokoski to explain the compositional strategies in very late Romantic and 20th-century tonal works by composers such as Richard Wagner, Gustav Mahler, Jean Sibelius, and Anton Bruckner.[1]

The form is based on a series of themes or motives that is constantly repeated in order, but each new rotation develops the motivic ideas, so it is a combination of repetition and development. The first rotation of the themes is taken as a reference point, both structurally and rhetorically, for the rest of the piece. The number of themes in the rotation can vary, from two themes in the first movement of Mahler's Sixth Symphony to three themes in the first movement of Sibelius's Fifth Symphony to four motives in a complex series of 12 iterations in the beginning of Act II of *Parsifal*.[2] The number of rotations also varies, and can be overlaid on a more traditional form like the sonata or scherzo-trio.

What makes the rotational form special is the way it reveals more about the themes or motives with each rotation, creating a feeling of fulfillment when the final rotation unveils the ultimate realization of the motives. This organic means of developing motives, rotating as much as is necessary to get to that final goal, is more natural than the formal strictures of sonata and rondo forms, but also very difficult to carry out successfully. —SS

Franz Joseph Haydn (1732–1809)

THE "PAPA" OF CLASSICAL MUSIC

Few composers (if any) could be credited for single-handedly shaping the music of a generation, but Joseph Haydn came close. An extremely prolific composer, Haydn's work was a key influence in the evolution of numerous musical forms of the Classical period, including the sonata, the string quartet, and the symphony (of which Haydn himself wrote over 100).[1]

Haydn was fortunate enough to have the patronage of nobility, working as music director for the Esterházy family for most of his career. Their summer palace was far from the musical center of Vienna, which proved both a blessing and a curse for Haydn. He missed the interaction, but the isolated environment served to fuel his creativity. Despite the distance, Haydn managed to maintain connections with Vienna, and his fame as a composer spread far beyond. An incurable joker, he often laced his pieces with subtle humor, the most famous example being his "Surprise" Symphony (No. 94), into which he inserted a sudden fortissimo in the slow second movement to wake up the audience.

Haydn's mastery of composition influenced such greats as his friend Mozart and his student Ludwig van Beethoven. In his old age, his broad influence and his good humor garnered him the affectionate term "Papa Haydn." By the time of his death, Haydn was recognized as the greatest living composer of his time; today, he is remembered as one of the greatest composers of *all* time. —JJM

Meditation

BY JULES MASSENET, 1892

Here is another brief piece of music that, like Debussy's "Clair de Lune" or Saint-Saens's "The Swan," is so captivating that listeners welcome it in any setting. In its original context, though—as an interlude in the opera *Thaïs*—"Meditation" is especially poignant. As its name suggests, the melody accompanies a period of deep reflection for the title character, and the resulting decision is life-changing for her. Later in the opera, the theme recurs in a tragic story of love lost.

Today the interlude's title has conveniently taken on new meaning as it is enjoyed as a complement to yoga-style meditation, and it naturally functions quite well as the soundtrack to any kind of tranquil rumination. When performed according to the intended score, solo violin carries the quaint melody above soft layers of harp and orchestra. Its dreamy warmth recalls, once more, "Clair de Lune" and "The Swan," which were created by Massenet's French contemporaries in the Romantic era. Clearly their sense of abstract beauty was not confined to that time or place. —CKG

RECOMMENDED RECORDING

Massenet: Thaïs; *Renee Fleming; Thomas Hampson; Yves Abel (conductor); Bordeaux Aquitaine National Orchestra; Decca; 2000*

La Bohème (The Bohemian)

GIACOMO PUCCINI (1858–1924)

Arguably the most famous opera in history, *La Bohème* includes many favorite pieces, including Rodolfo's aria, "Che gelida manina" ("What a cold little hand") and Musetta's waltz, "Quando me n'vò" ("When I go along"). The Italian libretto was written by Luigi Illica and Giuseppe Giacosa, based on Henri Murger's *Scènes de la vie de bohème*.

The story takes place in Paris circa 1830. Four bohemians—Rodolfo, a poet; Marcello, a painter; Colline, a philosopher; and Schaunard, a musician—live together in the Latin Quarter, barely able to afford rent. It is Christmas Eve, and they depart to celebrate. When Rodolfo stays behind to finish writing, he meets Mimì, a neighbor who stops by when her candle goes out. They are instantly drawn together, as he confides his dreams and she tells of her solitary life. They leave together to join the celebration. The group is entertained by Musetta, Marcello's former lover, who is attempting to make Marcello jealous. They reunite, only to part ways later.

Meanwhile, Mimì and Rodolfo's love blossoms. But Mimì's health is failing, and Rodolfo decides it would be best to split up, as the poverty in which they live can only make her sickness worse.

Months later, Musetta arrives to bring Rodolfo to Mimì, who is near death. The bohemians sell their belongings for medicine as Rodolfo stays by her side, but Mimì dies. Devastated, Rodolfo cries out her name. —CCD

Photo © Carol Rosegg; courtesy New York City Opera.

The Classical Guitar
FROM EVOLUTION TO REVOLUTION

A plucked string instrument and member of the lute family, the classical guitar is comprised of a resonating body with a sound hole, a neck with a fretted fingerboard, and a set of strings stretched across the two. It has as much in common with the violin as it does with its rock 'n roll grandson, the electric guitar.

Coming into its own in the Renaissance period, this guitar was small and paired strings together like today's 12-string model. A four-course treble version was common then, featuring two strings per note (course) for the lower three and a single string for the high note.

During the Baroque period, the guitar grew in size, and five-course instruments fitted with ornate inlays and woodwork became popular, using different stringing and tuning techniques.

By the turn of the 19th century the Baroque five-course gave way to a six-string standard and the introduction of single strings. It was during this time that virtuosos Fernando Sor, Dionysio Aguado, and Federico Moretti, along with composers Paganini and Berlioz, brought this new instrument into the limelight.

Late 19th-century Spanish maker Antonio de Torres Jurado standardized the instrument; by 1946, when traditional gut strings were replaced with nylon, today's axe emerged.

Although not composed for the guitar, J. S. Bach's works have been the most adaptable and can be enjoyed on recordings by Andrés Segovia and Christopher Parkening. —LMC

Arnold Schoenberg and 12-Tone Music
GOTTA GET THROUGH 'EM, ALL 12 OF 'EM

Expressionism is "a style striving to penetrate to the very essence of a subject by expressing it in abstract terms, as in atonality."[1] Composers now felt freer to impose their own personal terms upon creation. Romanticism began it, but the arts now made the creative personality of the individual artist of paramount value.[1]

The formerly arch-Romantic Viennese composer Arnold Schoenberg formulated a composing method that guaranteed atonality in any musical work. It amounts to "total chromaticism, totally fragmented." All 12 pitches of the scale are set up in a "tone row."

None of the 12 notes may be returned to, in any voice or instrument, until all 12 have been played:

TWELVE-TONE ROW

Tone Row Serial Number:

The note choices are completely arbitrary.

Here's a musical setting for piano:

12-TONE THEME

Travers Huff

The figures above each note are the row numbers. The treble clef has the tone row in *retrograde,* or backward, while the left hand has the original row. —TH

Opernhaus, Zurich

WHAT WILL THEY THINK OF NEXT?

Opernhaus is the name of the theater that replaced Zurich's Aktientheater after the latter burned down near the end of the 19th century. Originally called the Stadtheater, the venue staged spoken dramas as well as operas and orchestral works, until a separate playhouse was built in 1926, allowing the newly renamed Opernhaus to concentrate on its musical productions.

Right from the beginning, the Opernhaus was a leader and innovator. It was the first opera house in Europe to be lit electrically, greatly reducing the risk of deadly fires that frequently destroyed theaters and concert halls. The history of the Opernhaus is equally bright in terms of artistic merit; Arnold Schoenberg, Alban Berg, and Paul Hindemith have all had world premieres there. Today, audiences at the Opernhaus are treated to more than 270 performances each season, and artists like Anna Netrebko and Cecilia Bartoli are frequent visitors to the stage.[1]

Even now, the Opernhaus exercises its dedication to forward thinking and modernization in its management style. Recently it achieved yet another first among opera houses in Europe: the distinction of offering complete packaged international trips, including round-trip train or airfare to Zurich, a stay in a hotel, and, of course, tickets to the opera.[2] It will certainly be interesting to see what surprises the Opernhaus has in store for the rest of the 21st century. —MM

Photo by Gina Jen.

American Classical Music Hall of Fame

HONORING AMERICA'S CONTRIBUTIONS

Europe abounds in shrines to classical music masters. The houses where composers such as Beethoven, Handel, and Puccini were born or lived have been turned into museums that honor the men and their music. Thanks to Cincinnati, Ohio, the United States, also, has an organization devoted to celebrating classical music: the American Classical Music Hall of Fame.

Founded in 1996 by Cincinnati businessman and civic leader David A. Klingshirm, the Hall of Fame recognizes America's contribution to the field of classical music. Since its first induction in May 1998, the nonprofit organization has recognized about 100 individuals and organizations that have created American symphonies and songs, built orchestras, and developed schools and conservatories—from composer Elliott Carter to conductor Leonard Bernstein to the Cleveland Orchestra.

Located in Cincinnati Memorial Hall (built in 1908) in the historic Over-the-Rhine neighborhood, the Hall of Fame features biographical plaques for each inductee, two interactive listening kiosks to hear samples of each inductee's work, and a 45-minute video presentation tracing the history of classical music from the Renaissance to today.

A 500-seat auditorium in Memorial Hall is home to the Cincinnati Chamber Orchestra. Next door to the Hall of Fame is Music Hall, where the Cincinnati Symphony Orchestra (established in 1896, it is the fifth-oldest symphony orchestra in the U.S.), the Cincinnati Pops, and the Cincinnati Opera (America's second-oldest opera company) perform. —KFG

Rock Band Yes and Classical Music

A VERY GRAND ENTRANCE

The band members of Yes—the legendary progressive rock band of such hits as "Roundabout" and "Owner of a Lonely Heart"—owe much of their success to their love of classical music. Formed in London in the late 1960s by co-founders Jon Anderson (vocalist and composer) and Chris Squire (bassist, vocalist, and composer), the band achieved stardom in the early 1970s and are still popular today.

Though the band had a number of member changes over the years, the core players were either classically trained like Rick Wakeman (pianist, organist, multikeyboardist) or very heavily influenced by classical music, like Steve Howe (electric and acoustic guitarist). Perhaps the biggest tribute given to the world of classical music was their use of a recording of "The Finale" from Igor Stravinsky's *Firebird Ballet* as their opening to each concert beginning in 1972.

The hushed notes of the finale theme played by the French horn would begin without much notice from the audience. As the theme continued with strings and harp, it picked up power and speed. When the orchestra burst into the fanfare itself, the house lights went out to the cheers of thousands of fans. The climax of the finale was accompanied by the band itself as they segued into their opening song. It was a powerful and unique, wordless introduction that became a tradition for the group and their fans. —DD

Rock band Yes performs in Warsaw in 2004. Photo by Zbigniew Lewandowski.

Postmodern Music

THE SOUNDS OF SILENCE AND RANDOMNESS

A generic definition of music might be simply "organized sound."

This definition is generally correct... at least it was until the mid-20th century. At that point, composers began experimenting by composing pieces that included elements of chance and environmental influence. This music, called postmodern, was largely invented and pursued by American composer John Cage. He wrote a piece for 12 radio receivers entitled *Imaginary Landscape No. 4,* where each radio was to be set to different random radio stations, and the resulting music and noise created the piece of music. Perhaps even more extreme is his 4'33", in which the pianist is instructed to go on stage and not play a thing for precisely 4 minutes and 33 seconds (see "'Chance,' 'Aleatory,' or 'Stochastic' Music," page 324).

This may sound ridiculous, but think of it like this: The silence, the noises of the audience, the birds chirping nearby, the airplane flying overhead, and the cars honking from miles away—all these sounds we each hear every day and largely ignore—contributed to create a piece of music. John Cage enabled, even *forced,* his audiences to open their ears and hear the world around them.

Nowadays, Postmodern music refers to everything after these initial breakthroughs by Cage. Without him, music today (composers and audiences alike) would be completely different. —SL

LISTENING HOMEWORK

John Cage's 4'33", Imaginary Landscape No. 4, *and* Music of Changes

---

Prelude

HEY! I'M STARTING NOW!

The prelude started life as a short, improvised instrumental piece meant to introduce the key and mood of the composed piece that was to follow, and to get the attention of the unruly audience. Eventually composers began writing down preludes, initially to introduce church chorales, called "organ preludes" or "chorale preludes." These preludes would take the choral melody as the basis for extended counterpoint, much like masses did with chant melodies.

In the Baroque era composers like Arcangelo Corelli and J. S. Bach also started writing preludes to introduce their instrumental suites, though Bach still wrote spectacular organ preludes. He also wrote a prelude for every one of his fugues in *The Well-Tempered Clavier*, his matchless collection of preludes and fugues in every possible key.

Preludes are polyphonic, but maintain an improvisational feel, with no clear overall form. One particular type of prelude that Bach used was the figured prelude, such as the "Prelude in C major" from Book I of *The Well-Tempered Clavier*. As you can see from the example, a repeated arpeggio—the figure—is used throughout the piece. It is not truly polyphonic, but multiple voices are suggested.

In the Romantic period, "prelude" began to indicate short keyboard works, like character pieces, collected in a wide variety of keys, such as Chopin's 24 Preludes op. 28 or Debussy's *Préludes*. These tend to be in binary or ternary form, but often with small twists. —SS

Sir Edward Elgar (1857–1934)

OVERCOMING THE ODDS

Edward Elgar's journey from village piano tuner's son to the preeminent English composer of his generation is a story worth telling. A self-taught composer, a minority Roman Catholic, a member of the working class in a culture where social standing determined nearly everything—by all accounts, Elgar should have spent his life in obscurity. Instead, hard work and the support of key individuals helped him overcome the odds.

At age 16, Elgar began earning his keep with freelance music assignments.[1] He eked out a meager existence for well over a decade, with little success. At this point, two key relationships gave Elgar a huge boost. The first was Caroline Alice Roberts, a novelist who elevated his social status when she married him in 1889, and whose confidence in him gave him the courage to keep writing. The second was publisher August Jaeger, who published Elgar's *Enigma* Variations in 1899, propelling him to international fame. During the next 10 years, Elgar wrote his best-known works, including the famed *Pomp and Circumstance* marches.

A man given to melancholy, Elgar lost momentum as he lost his support system—first with the death of Jaeger in 1909, then with his beloved wife's death in 1920. Still, before he died, Elgar managed to provide posterity with audio recordings of many of his pieces. He is remembered today as one of England's icons, his face appearing on the British 20-pound note. —JJM

Hungarian Rhapsody No. 2

BY FRANZ LISZT, 1847

Liszt was not known for subtlety. On the contrary, the Hungarian-born composer was an unparalleled virtuoso and a flamboyant showman, and many of his keyboard compositions were tailor-made to display a combination of dexterity and flashiness. His *Hungarian Rhapsody No. 2* is no exception, requiring technical wizardry from the performing pianist. Along with the other *Hungarian Rhapsodies* that Liszt composed between 1846 and 1885, it tests the limits of what is possible from both a pianist and a piano. In later years, Liszt rearranged this work for full orchestra, and that version is not uncommon today.

Like all 19 of the *Hungarian Rhapsodies,* the second pays homage to traditional Hungarian gypsy music and follows the basic form of 19th-century dances called "verbunkos." After a short, pensive introduction, it contains a slow movement called a "lassu" and then a fast "friss" section.[1] The vivacious friss in *Hungarian Rhapsody No. 2* will be immediately familiar to any aficionado of Saturday-morning cartoons, having been performed by such entertainers as Bugs Bunny and Woody Woodpecker. —CKG

RECOMMENDED RECORDING

Liszt: Hungarian Rhapsodies; *Georges Cziffra (piano); EMI Classics; 2001*

Tosca

GIACOMO PUCCINI (1858-1924)

Known for its tense drama and poignant melodies, Puccini's *Tosca* is one of the most performed operas today. With an Italian libretto by Luigi Illica and Giuseppe Giacosa, the piece was based on Victorien Sardou's drama, *La Tosca*. The opera includes the beloved arias, "Vissi d'arte" ("I lived on art") and "E lucevan le stele" ("And the stars were shining").

The story takes place in Rome in 1800. The fugitive Angelotti has taken refuge in a chapel of Sant'Andrea della Valle, where his political ally, the painter Cavaradossi, is working on a picture of Mary Magdalene. Cavaradossi promises to help him escape from Rome. Angelotti hides again when he hears the voice of Cavaradossi's lover, Tosca, a famous singer. Baron Scarpia enters the church to look for signs of Angelotti and suspects Cavaradossi is his accomplice.

Cavaradossi is arrested and sentenced to death, but Tosca is told she can save him if she submits to Scarpia. She agrees, and once Scarpia has written a note guaranteeing Cavaradossi's safety through a fake execution, she kills Scarpia. As Cavaradossi prepares to die, Tosca explains that it will be a mock execution and then they will escape together.

After shots are fired and everyone is gone, Tosca tells him it is safe to get up. When he does not respond, she realizes that Scarpia has had his final revenge. Tosca jumps from the battlements to join her lover in death. —CCD

Photo courtesy Festival Puccini.

The Pipe Organ
KING OF THE INSTRUMENTS

Rivaling the clock as one of the most complex of all mechanical instruments developed before the Industrial Revolution, the organ may be the oldest instrument still in use today and affords the largest repertory in existence.

This keyboard wind instrument consists of four main components: a wind source; a box to collect the wind, called a chest; a multitude of pipes in graduated sizes; and a keyboard and valve system to control the flow of wind to the pipes. Invented in the 3rd century BCE by Greek engineer Ctesibius, the first organs used water pressure and the *hydraulis* to provide wind to the pipes. Eventually, weighted bellows were used instead.

The Renaissance was a great time of development for the organ. Pipes producing different octaves and harmonics were used together to create a wider tonal range, whereas a complex switching system, referred to as stops and employing multiple chests and sliders, was developed to control their use. Three or four keyboards, called "manuals," became common to allow the organist to have immediate access to these different sounds.

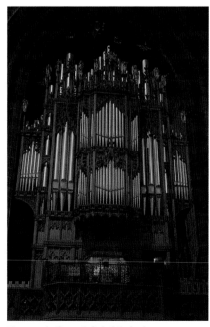

During the Baroque period refinement was at its peak, and permanent installations exemplifying ornate, masterful craftsmanship filled cathedrals and churches with resplendent sound. The repertoire was primarily liturgical: composers Georg Böhm and Johann Pachelbel created chorale partitas; Johann Sebastian Bach contributed many preludes, fugues, and chorale works; and George Frideric Handel composed the first organ concertos. —LMC

Pipe organ in Chester Cathedral, England.

Bloop! Bleep! Every Element Can Be Serialized!

FOR WHEN YOU WANT TOTAL CONTROL

Serializing pitches obliterated tonality. This serialization was extended to octave displacement: each note had to be in a different octave than its predecessor. Also, a stricter application of serialization dictated that no single note could *ever* be repeated before using all 12. Serializing also controlled rhythm and silence.

Here's the same 12-tone theme with the stricter pitch application, arbitrary octave displacement, and rhythmic duration serialization (first note has 4 beats; the second has 3, 2, 1, ½, etc., also used in retrograde):

12-TONE THEME VARIATION

SHOWING ARBITRARY OCTAVE DISPLACEMENT AND RHYTHM SERIALIZATION

These last factors make it sound more "bloop-bleep" than it otherwise would.

Note the lack of octave displacement in the faster figures for playability's sake. The lines that connect notes of the same pitch are *ties*; they make the note longer because the second (tied) note is not sounded. The "little" notes with lines through them in measures one and five are *grace* notes. They're so fast that their duration doesn't greatly influence the rhythm. —TH

LISTENING HOMEWORK

Schoenberg: A Survivor From Warsaw; *or Webern, Anton:* Variations for Orchestra

---

Teatro Carlo Felice

THE PRIDE OF GENOA

At the end of the 18th century, Genoa was feeling left out of the music game. They did not have an adequate opera house to host major productions, and there was some discussion in the community about constructing a theater to alleviate this problem. The idea was to have a venue appropriate for large-scale operas, orchestral concerts, and recitals.

In 1828, the Teatro Carlo Felice was built. The new venue was the pride of the local people, and even though construction on it had not been completely finished, that did not stop the inaugural season, which kicked off in April of the same year with Bellini's *Bianca e Fernando*.

During the great majority of World War II, Genoa's favorite theater managed to avoid major damage, but in 1942 it was finally hit by a bomb. The damage was patched up and performances continued, but when the theater took a second direct hit in 1943, the structure was destroyed.

Although the city seemed eager to rebuild as soon as possible, a series of delays and mishaps held up the process, and the actual construction of the new theater was not begun until 1987.[1] The venue is now officially called the Municipal Opera House, but the classical music world will probably always know it as the Teatro Carlo Felice. —MM

Monteverdi Festival

HAIL TO THE GODFATHER OF OPERA

With the resurgence of Baroque music in the late 20th century, operas and other works by early music composers increasingly have been programmed in concert halls and opera houses. It's only natural that one of Italy's famous sons, the early Baroque composer Claudio Monteverdi, who wrote such masterpieces as the operas *The Return of Ulysses* and *The Coronation of Poppea*, has been the focus of a major European festival in his hometown in northern Italy since 1982.

Often recognized as the "godfather" of Italian opera (though he did not invent it), Monteverdi wrote *L'Orfeo*, his first opera, in 1607, and helped shape the musical form.

For three weeks in May and June 5,000 to 6,000 people head to Cremona to listen to Monteverdi's works and those of the composers he inspired. A recent festival looked at how the early Baroque Italian school of music—of which Monteverdi was a central figure—led to the works of George Frideric Handel, and focused on those pieces where the influence of the Italian school is most evident.

The concerts take place in local historic churches, in Baroque mansions and courtyards, and at Teatro Ponchielli, which also manages the festival.
—KFG

Production of Orfeo *at the 2007 Monteverdi Festival. Photo by Federico Zovadelli.*

FUN FACT

Cremona is also renowned as a center of violin making—
Andrea Amati developed the modern violin here.

Classical Melodies in Rock Music

RUFUS WAINWRIGHT PAYS HOMAGE TO MAURICE RAVEL

It's difficult to categorize or put into any one genre the music, recordings, and performances of Rufus Wainwright. His music is daring, pop, operatic, rock, fun, dramatic, folksy, orchestral, intimate, outrageously over-the-top, dark, romantic, and extremely innovative; still, all of it is brilliant and inspired.

When he released two of his masterpiece albums in 2003 and 2004, *Want One* and *Want Two*, he delivered many surprises and took his listeners and fans on a wonderful and very personal journey. From the beginning, during the first song entitled "Oh What A World," we hear Rufus's love of classical music come through loud and clear in the form of excerpts from the big melody of *Boléro* by composer Maurice Ravel. The song builds from a lone tuba accompanying Rufus's voice to an amazingly big sound of orchestra and chorus. During this glorious buildup and as the song peacefully comes to a close, we hear Ravel's most famous theme woven in and out of Rufus's song seamlessly.

While other pop/rock artists took a classical piece or theme and turned it into something easily consumed by the popular market, Rufus worked his tribute to Ravel into "Oh What A World" as if it were an extension of his vocal melody. It sounds like the two composers collaborated on the song. —DD

Minimalism (1960s AND '70s)

ON AGAIN, OFF AGAIN

Every fall and spring you have to reset your clocks. You meander around the house, comparing timepieces and trying to coordinate them all to the correct time. But inevitably the clocks become further and further apart throughout the year, until you reset them again.

This is the concept upon which minimalism is built. The idea of gradual change and rhythmic continuity was first substantially introduced by Terry Riley with his early *In C*. In this piece, there is a set list of slight rhythmic iterations. The performers are instructed to play each cell for an indeterminate amount of time. Throughout the piece, the note "C" is repeated at a steady eighth-note pulse.

Steve Reich was also a formative composer in this movement. He required performers to play the same rhythmic/melodic cell repeatedly at slightly different tempi. Thus the players would slowly ease out of sync with each other, and the performance would go on until the performers once again achieved synchronization.

Philip Glass is still composing minimalist pieces today; he writes for many movie soundtracks, especially high-intensity suspense scenes. He uses the idea of beginning with a short phrase and slowly, almost imperceptibly adding to it.[1]

All of these techniques are based on the idea of breaking the music down to its most fundamental aspect; then expanding upon that element. —SL

LISTENING HOMEWORK

Riley's In C

Reich's Piano Phase and Drumming

Glass's 1+1

Chaconne

LOVE THAT PROGRESSION!

In the Baroque era, musicians enjoyed composing a series of variations on a particular chord progression. This progression, called "chaconne," came from a late-16th-century Latin American dance made popular in Spain through guitar books. The actual progression changed over time, but the concept of repeating four to six chords over and over again stayed consistent through the Baroque era. Because the progression is so short, the melodic themes often stretched out across two or more iterations of the chord pattern, and the chord progression repeated up to 100 times. Eventually the chaconne was associated with slow triple meters and major keys. The first chaconnes were written for guitar or keyboard, but soon were composed for other instruments or as vocal pieces.

Theorists distinguish between the chaconne (repeated chord progression) and the passacaglia (repeated bass line), but composers in the 18th century would often use the terms interchangeably to indicate any continuous-variation form, such as Wenzel Raimond Pirck's passacaglia in his G major Trio.[1]

The most famous chaconne is from Bach's *Partita No. 2 in D minor* for solo violin. This beautiful piece is quite long for a Baroque work, and also one of the most difficult works composed for violin in that period. It was one of the pieces Joshua Bell played in 2007 in a Washington, D.C., subway station as part of a social experiment led by journalist Gene Weingarten. The idea was to see how a piece of beautiful but lesser-known music would be received by passersby out of context, even though performed by a world-class violinist. —SS

Joshua Bell played a Bach chaconne in a subway station one day to see if anyone would stop to listen. Photo by Marc Hom; courtesy Sony Music Entertainment.

François Couperin "le Grand" (1668-1733)

A QUIET INFLUENCE

Although François Couperin's name is not the most widely known among the great composers, in his day he was considered the foremost composer of the French Baroque period. His was a lineage of noted musicians; in fact, on his 18th birthday Couperin inherited his father's post as organist at St. Gervais, a post he held his entire life. He was often referred to as Francois Couperin *le Grand* (the Great) to differentiate him from another relative who shared his name.

Couperin's first published work was *Piéces d'orgue,* a collection of organ masses; however, he was most widely known as a master of the harpsichord, publishing a four-volume collection of 220 pieces known simply as *Piéces de clevicin.* His compositional style successfully combined elements of the Italian school with French Baroque style. Couperin also published an extensive treatise on harpsichord keyboard technique, and his keyboarding style would be a major influence on one Johann Sebastian Bach.[1]

Sadly, none of Couperin's manuscripts survived him, and today we remember only a fraction of what he wrote.[2] However, from what we know of his life and music, it is apparent that his influence upon the future direction of music was quiet yet unmistakable. —JJM

Fun Fact

François Couperin was actually born more into a musical dynasty than a musical family. Several Couperins had held the organist post at St. Gervais before François, and after his death the post remained in the family until the French Revolution.

Messiah

BY GEORGE FRIDERIC HANDEL, 1741

For English-speaking audiences, Handel's monumental oratorio *Messiah* is a perennial favorite. Handel composed the music for his collaborator, Charles Jennens, who wrote the religiously themed text for the work. Astonishingly, it took Handel less than a month to complete the score.[1]

Since the libretto recounts the biblical story and message of Jesus Christ, *Messiah* is most commonly heard around the Christian holidays of Christmas and Easter. As an oratorio, it is structurally similar to an opera (with arias, recitative, choruses, and an overture), but without the acted-out drama.

Messiah's choruses are especially memorable, the most famous of which being the triumphant "Hallelujah" chorus. If you've ever attended a performance of *Messiah,* you probably saw the entire audience stand during the "Hallelujah" chorus. Legend has it that King George II of England once stood up as the chorus began, and out of respect for national custom, everybody else stood also.[2]

To this day, listeners are routinely moved by the inspiring majesty of Handel's masterpiece, *Messiah.* —CKG

RECOMMENDED RECORDING

Handel: Messiah; *Academy of Ancient Music; Christopher Hogwood (conductor); Emma Kirkby, Paul Elliott, et al.; Decca; 1991*

Madama Butterfly (Madame Butterfly)

GIACOMO PUCCINI (1858-1924)

Another great Puccini tragedy emerges in *Madama Butterfly,* an opera originally written in two acts, but later revised to three acts. Like *La Bohème* and *Tosca,* the Italian libretto was written by Luigi Illica and Giuseppe Giacosa. The composer based the opera on David Belasco's dramatized version of John Luther Long's short story *Madame Butterfly,* as well as on Pierre Loti's novel *Madame Chrysanthème.*

The simple plot begins in Nagasaki circa 1900, as U.S. Navy Lieutenant B. F. Pinkerton weds Cio-Cio-San, a 15-year-old geisha. Taking the marriage more seriously than he does, she adopts his religion, but is consequently denounced by her family. Three years later, Pinkerton leaves for America, but Cio-Cio-San refuses to believe that her husband has abandoned her for good. Sharpless, the U.S. Consul in Nagasaki, cannot bring himself to tell her the truth. Eventually Lt. Pinkerton and his new American wife return to Nagasaki, having heard that Cio-Cio-San is the mother of Pinkerton's son, Dolore (Sorrow). When Cio-Cio-San realizes they have come prepared to take the child, she is completely heartbroken and kills herself.

Considered to be the greatest opera in history, *Madama Butterfly* is a stunning theatrical experience, both visually and musically. Audiences will find Butterfly's aria, "Un bel dì" ("One beautiful day"), as well as the "Flower Duet" between Butterfly and her maid Suzuki, to be particularly exquisite. —CCD

Cynthia Lawrence as Cio-Cio-San. Photo courtesy Opera Carolina (Charlotte, North Carolina, www.operacarolina.org).

The Bagpipe
SWEET NOTES FROM A WINDBAG

The modern history of the bagpipe is rooted in Western Europe during the early Middle Ages. This reed pipe aerophone exists regionally in many different designs, but in its simplest form consists of an air source, an air bag and chanter, and drone pipes.

Air is driven into the bag through a single or double reed blowpipe, which employs a flap over the end inside the bag to keep air from escaping. Air can be supplied by the player's lungs or by bellows operated with the player's arm.

The drone pipes typically incorporate a single reed and produce a fixed note. Most bagpipes consist of one to four drones worn over the shoulder, across the arms, or down alongside the chanter.

While the drones sustain seemingly endless legato notes, the sound of the bagpipe is completed as the melody is played on the finger holes of the chanter pipe. The end of the chanter is open, and once music begins, there is no easy way for the player to stop the sound until the bag is nearly depleted of air.

The bagpipe enjoyed popularity in liturgical music and during the Renaissance with King Henry VIII. The Scottish Highland and the Irish Uilleann are the most well known today, and are still popular in traditional music and with pop artists like Paul Mc-Cartney, Peter Gabriel, and Van Morrison. —LMC

"Chance," "Aleatory," or "Stochastic" Music

IN OTHER WORDS, ANYTHING GOES

After such tightly circumscribed serialization of not only the parameters of music, but of sound itself, it's not surprising that polarities reversed and that "chance" choices of sound and silence became a temporary fashion.

Traditional melody and tonality were now completely gone, and methods for choosing notes, rests, and loudness ranged from tossing coins or dice to simply choosing at random without regard for the consequences.

Traditional notation is often forsaken. One system called the "toothbrush-splatter" method has the composer dipping a toothbrush in ink and flipping it at the lined score paper, letting the notes fall where they may.

In 1952, the iconoclastic modernist/postmodern composer John Cage produced a work entitled 4'33" (four minutes, 33 seconds). It is for any instrument, although it is most commonly performed (or non-performed, in this case) in a piano version, *with no sounds intentionally made.* In other words, 4'33" is 4 minutes, 33 seconds of silence. The only criterion is that the span of silence must last exactly 4 minutes, 33 seconds.

These two extremes of "tight control" and "no control" often produced competitions for extremities of controlling or not controlling timbre or tone-color (Anton Webern's "tone-color melody") as well as dynamics (loud and soft volume) and parameters both musical and acoustical, with introductions of East Indian ragas and variants in tuning systems.

These last variants include experiments with the physical, acoustical, and sonic propensities of *well temperament, equal temperament,* and *just intonation.* —TH

Mozarteum

WHERE EDUCATION AND PERFORMANCE MEET

Salzburg's music and arts university, the Mozarteum, shares a name with its modest concert hall, known to students as the Great Hall. This venue may not seem so "great" in terms of size, but it has a spotless reputation for quality performances both within and outside the realm of the music of Mozart.

The Great Hall at the Mozarteum University may only be a century old, but its roots can be traced right back to Mozart himself. Constanze, the composer's widow, formed the Cathedral Music Association and Mozarteum in 1841. Its purpose was to encourage artistic excellence for musicians and students of music within the context of honoring Mozart's body of work. The Mozarteum thrived as an academy of music, and in 1910 construction began on a complex of official educational buildings, including the Great Hall, which was completed in 1914. The hall is often used for student recitals, and with the Mozarteum boasting graduates as distinguished as Herbert von Karajan, Thomas Bernhard, and the Hagen Quartet, audiences are treated to an incredibly high standard of performance.

The Mozarteum became an official university in 1998, and currently offers courses in many different areas of classical music and performing arts. Performances at the Great Hall are often budget-priced or even free, and up until 2008 the hall also featured concerts performed on the in-house organ. The organ is currently being replaced with a newer instrument, and is due to be back in operation for the 2010 festival season. —MM

Bachfest Leipzig and Bach Museum

TWO GREAT REASONS TO VISIT GERMANY

Bach festivals abound in Germany. There are some 30 celebrations honoring Johann Sebastian Bach, the German composer and organist who wrote both secular and sacred works for choirs, orchestras, and solo instruments. Home of the Bach Archives and a Bach museum, Leipzig also celebrates the master who lived and worked in the city for 27 years with its own 10-day June festival.

In 1723 Bach was appointed cantor of St. Thomas Church in Leipzig, Germany, a post he held until his death in 1750. Bach is so tied to the city that his grave is in the choir of the church and a monument stands outside.

Held at historic venues in Leipzig including some where Bach performed, Bachfest Leipzig aims to present the breadth of his sacred and secular music and integrate composers and works influenced by him. Although festivals honoring Bach have been held in Leipzig from time to time since 1904, it wasn't until 1999 that the city resolved to establish an annual Bachfest.

Next to St. Thomas Church stands Bosehaus, which houses the Bach Museum and Archive. The former residence of Bach's friend, the merchant Georg Heinrich Bose, the house was built in 1586 and converted to Baroque style in 1711. After a period of extensive restoration and renovation in 2008–09, the museum is reopening with a new design and interactive elements. Visitors will be able to arrange the instrumental parts of a Bach hymn and examine original Bach manuscripts in the treasure chamber. —KFG

The 2009 opening concert of Bachfest Leipzig in St. Thomas Church.
Photo by Gert Mothes.

The Beatles

CLASSICAL MUSIC INFLUENCE FROM THE OTHER GEORGE

Sir George Martin's long association with the Beatles resulted in many brilliant arrangements, voicings, and instrumentation taken directly from the world of classical music. Sir George, a trained classical musician and conductor, has often composed for the full symphony orchestra. Along with Sir Paul McCartney, he was responsible for the innovative and inspiring sounds that pushed the boundaries of rock and pop music to new places.

Rather than sugarcoat the love song "Yesterday" with lush strings, a spare string quartet arrangement was created and recorded as the sole accompaniment to Sir Paul's voice and guitar. "Eleanor Rigby" was constructed around a more dramatic string arrangement played by a slightly larger string ensemble, giving the song a wonderful urgency. The use of the high-pitched Bach trumpet on "Penny Lane" made the song ring with yet another new sound. Whenever Sir George and the Beatles used a symphony orchestra, the effect was always powerful. Think of "A Day In the Life," in which the orchestra is used in an unconventional and random way to create a most dramatic crescendo.

Sir George Martin also brought classical composition styles to many of the Beatles' songs. The baroque piano passage in "In My Life" and the French horn solo arrangement in "For No One" deliver a gentle beauty and create a perfect balance to the vocals. —DD

Neoromanticism (1930s, 1950s, AND NOW)

THIS TIME WITH FEELING

W e've talked a lot about the 20th century and all the different aleatoric aspects of modern music. It can start to sound like all contemporary music is based on mathematical endeavors. However, throughout the 20th century, there have been several returns to compositions with a melodic and emotional emphasis.

The first such return was in the 1930s with the founding of La Jeune France, a group of French composers, including Andrè Jolivet and Olivier Messiaen, who concentrated heavily on the mystic, a concept that is a massive departure from modernist tendencies.

Neoromanticism also includes the mid-20th-century enclosure of folk melodies in classical music. Ralph Vaughan Williams and Gustav Holst are appropriate examples of this type of Neoromanticism.

Contemporary composers that fit within the framework of Neoromanticism include John Corigliano, Ellen Taaffe Zwilich, and James MacMillian.

Obviously this type of music is far-reaching, applying to music written throughout the entire century and many different countries. The main thing to remember is that Neoromanticism takes the traits of other current musical movements (minimalism, futurism, and even electronic music) and re-inserts the emotional aspects, thus bringing the music back to a Schumann level of heartthrob prominence. —SL

LISTENING HOMEWORK

Jolivet's Chant de Linos
Vaughan William's Fantasia on a Theme by Thomas Tallis
MacMillian's Veni, Veni, Emmanuel

Fantasia

I'M MAKING THIS UP AS I GO ALONG!

Many famous composers were also well known as performers, especially for their skills in improvising. J. S. Bach and George Frideric Handel could make up complex fugues on the organ, Mozart could quickly whip off a series of variations on a theme sung to him, and contemporaries raved about Chopin's effortless improvisations.

One of the things so appealing about improvisation is the spontaneous energy, often accompanied by reckless abandonment of rules. Composers have attempted to re-create this spontaneity with keyboard compositions that don't follow any standard forms. These are called "fantasias" or "fantasies," "impromptus," "intermezzi," or even "improvisations." In the Baroque era these pieces usually alternated between fast technical sections and slower lyrical sections, such as Bach's Chromatic *Fantasia and Fugue*. Mozart composed his Fantasia in C minor in four sections of varying tempi, with none of the normal key relationships of traditional forms.

In the Romantic era hybrid forms were created that maintained the improvisatory nature, but wedded them to elements of sonata or binary forms, such as Chopin's Fantasy in F minor or Liszt's Impromptu in F sharp. The phrase lengths and tempi would shift unpredictably, but larger key relationships and thematic designs would follow historic plans. The improvisatory form has remained popular through current times, including pieces by Donald Martino, Lowell Liebermann, John Corigliano, and Frederic Rzewski. —SS

Robert Schumann (1810–1856)

A FINE LINE

One of the most prominent Romantic composers, Robert Schumann's life and art easily embody the pathos of the age in which he lived. He walked a fine line between the artist and the critic, between unbridled emotion and self-restraint, between (in today's vernacular) the right brain and the left. Yet through this lifelong inner conflict, he created some of the most moving music ever written.

Schumann began studying law, but eventually forsook his studies for a career in music. A physical disability in his hand cut short his dreams of being a concert pianist, so he became a composer and music journalist; his wife, Clara, a great pianist and composer herself, often premiered his works (see "Clara Schumann," page 340). In his writings, Schumann endorsed a controlled compositional style, openly opposing the popular flamboyant approach. However, Schumann's own music exhibits deep emotion and melodic innovation. Two of his piano pieces, *Floristan* and *Eusebius,* are musical depictions of two pseudonyms he wrote under in his music journal, representing the conflicting poles of his personality—a haunting incarnation of the manic depression from which he likely suffered,[1] and a precursor, perhaps, of what was to come.

Over time, the fine line seemed to be too much for Schumann; mental illness took over, and after attempting suicide, he spent his final two years in an asylum.[2] Despite his personal tragedy, the genius of Schumann's music has been deeply felt, shaping the musical landscape for generations to come. —JJM

Träumerei

BY ROBERT SCHUMANN, 1838

Being a grown-up isn't easy, and sometimes it's beneficial to take a moment and reminisce about simpler times. Robert Schumann seemed to understand this, as much of his music is tailor-made for wistful remembrance.

One such work was composed when Schumann's fiancée, Clara, was away, touring as a concert pianist. He was feeling lonely, and during that time he remembered that Clara had once said that he often seemed like a child. Inspired by the comparison, Schumann wrote about 30 short, impressionistic piano pieces, picked 13 of his favorites, and called them *Kinderszenen*, which means "Scenes from Childhood."[1]

By far the most cherished of the imaginative little pieces is the seventh scene, "Träumerei," which means "reverie." The brief sketch is appropriately infused with a feeling of naïve innocence, creating in the listener an evocative nostalgia for the simple joys of childhood.

Schumann had a tremendous gift for this kind of lyrical intimacy in his short piano works, of which he wrote many. Because of its calming, comforting appeal, "Träumerei" has become a perennial favorite as a solo piano encore piece. —CKG

RECOMMENDED RECORDING

Schumann: Kinderszenen; Kreisleriana; Martha Argerich (piano);
Deutsche Grammophon; 1990

Turandot

GIACOMO PUCCINI (1858-1924)

*T*urandot was incomplete at the time of Puccini's death, and was later finished by Franco Alfano. Based on Carlo Gozzi's commedia dell'arte *Turandot*, the Italian libretto was written by Giuseppe Adami and Renato Simoni. The opera is best known for the tenor aria "Nessun dorma" ("Nobody shall sleep").

Turandot is set in ancient Peking (now Beijing). Princess Turandot vows to marry a prince capable of answering three riddles. Calaf, the long-lost son of Timur, the former king of Tartary, has fallen in love with Turandot and vows to win her heart, despite warnings from three imperial ministers, Ping, Pang, and Pong. Calaf answers all three of Turandot's riddles correctly. Shocked, she begs her father to release her from her oath. Calaf then offers his own riddle: If she can discover his name by dawn, she may kill him.

As all Peking is trying to discover the suitor's name, Timur and his slave Liù are captured. Liù, who is secretly in love with Calaf, confesses she knows his

name, but will not divulge it. Liù is then sentenced to execution, but commits suicide before it is carried out. Calaf declares his love for Turandot and reveals his name. The princess is moved and tells her father she finally knows the suitor's name: Love. —CCD

Eric Greene as Ping, Robert Mack as Pang, Daniel Ross Hinson as Pong in Turandot. *Photo courtesy Opera Carolina (Charlotte, North Carolina, www. operacarolina.org).*

The Human Voice

OUR OWN BUILT-IN INSTRUMENTS

Quite possibly the oldest and most natural of all instruments, the human voice has for millennia celebrated, mourned, worshiped, and documented history in song. There is evidence of choral repertory dating back to the Delphic hymns of ancient Greece, and a chorus of human voices has always offered the composer a varied and unique medium.

Led by a choirmaster, choirs are technically divided into four sections performing in four-part harmony: sopranos, altos, tenors, and basses. Many combinations of male, female, boys, and girls have been written for and enjoyed but four- and eight-part mixed choirs are the most common.

European choirs have long had a connection to and primarily evolved through the church, beginning with the all-male Medieval monophonic Gregorian chants and liturgical plainchant.

The early Renaissance choirs were greatly skilled and also performed a capella. The choral music of this period featured an abundance of masses and motets written by composers like Dufay, William Byrd, and Giovanni Pierluigi da Palestrina.

As accompanying instruments emerged and church choirs became even more proficient during the Baroque period, composers like Monteverdi, Bach, and Handel created great choral works to magnificently fill large churches and cathedrals with their heavenly sound.

In addition to liturgical uses, the nonsecular choral section played a strong supporting role in opera and is movingly exemplified by Mozart, Rossini, and Verdi. —LMC

The Sensuous, Whole-Tone French

MUSIC WITH MYSTERY

While the Germans fragmented, the French sought to soar free of earthly bonds and boundaries through techniques such as the whole-tone scale and the *planing* of seventh chords.

WHOLE-TONE SCALES
TWO HEXACHORDS

The first measure is constructed on one whole-tone hexachord, the second on the other:

"PLANING" 7TH CHORDS

Strings

At first sensuously used by Ravel and Debussy, the sounds of whole-tone scales quickly became commercialized, consequently overused in the public ear, and discarded.[1] In film and dramatic scoring from the '50s, their sounds frequently signaled "a mysterious, unaccounted-for passage of time," or "oblivion." Completely lacking in the modality-defining characteristic placements of half steps, they seem weirdly faceless.

Using nonresolving sequences of seventh and ninth chords on a whole-tone scale is a characteristic Impressionistic sound. In tonal music V[7] resolves to I, but not here. —TH

Großes Festspielhaus

THE MUSE'S HOLY HOUSE

The magnificent entrance to the Großes Festspielhaus in Salzburg bears the following inscription: "The Muse's holy house is open to those moved by song; divine power bears us up who are inspired."[1] This bit of wisdom may seem lofty or over-the-top at first glance, but given the astoundingly high caliber of performances that have occurred at the venue since its opening in 1960, even the most extravagant characterizations of this festival hall seem well warranted.

The Großes Festspielhaus is one of the chief venues for several of Salzburg's annual and periodic music festivals, and was specifically designed for hosting festival performances. With a stage measuring nearly 300 feet wide, it is known as one of the largest opera houses in the world. The famed Salzburg Festival occurs there (see "Salzburg Festival," page 266) every July, and spin-off events such as the Easter Festival and the Whitsun Festival attract a respectable number of visitors as well. The Easter Festival in particular, founded by late Herbert von Karajan, frequently features the most exclusive artists in classical music, and is currently organized by Sir Simon Rattle.[2]

Aside from musical excellence, the Großes Festspielhaus is known for its equally impressive art collection. Many famous sculptors, painters, and other artists have contributed works to decorate the interior of the building,[3] making any visit to this venue an event in its own right. —MM

Verdi Festival

CELEBRATING ITALY'S NATIVE SON

Italy pays homage to its native son, Giuseppe Verdi, the great Romantic composer known for dramatic melody and passion, every October. For the entire month, Verdi, who grew up in Busseto close to Parma, is the star of Parma and the surrounding area. The Verdi Festival honors him with operas, concerts, recitals, conferences, exhibitions, readings from the masterpieces of literature that inspired his opera libretti, and other events held at locations from Milan to Bologna—along the great road that Rome built more than 2,000 years ago.

The sights, sounds, and even tastes of the composer envelop the region. In many store windows in Parma—a small town with cafes, a compact historic center, and magnificent frescoes in its cathedral—visitors might see costumes from Verdi operas.

The two main venues for performances are the 19th-century opera house Teatro Regio di Parma and the tiny yet splendid Teatro Verdi di Busseto. Verdi Festival attendees step back in time when they enter Teatro Regio di Parma: In its foyer is a grand staircase that leads to the vast and elegant "ridotto" salon, with its high ceilings decorated with frescoes, huge windows, and chandeliers. In the salon visitors can enjoy dishes from Verdi household recipe books at after-theater dinners.

In 2013, in anticipation of the 200th anniversary of Verdi's birth, the theater plans to perform the whole corpus of his work and to record it live in high definition. —KFG

View of the crowded hall central of Teatro Regio di Parma. Photo by Roberto Ricci.

The More, the Merrier

ROCK GROUPS ACCOMPANIED BY SYMPHONY ORCHESTRA

A number of pop/rock artists and groups have performed accompanied by a full symphony orchestra for a single performance or a series of performances at one venue, such as Elton John's famous concert in Melbourne with the Melbourne Symphony. Many have recorded entire albums accompanied by a full symphony orchestra, like the Moody Blues on their album *Days of Future Past*. Yet rarely has anyone taken on the expense and complicated logistics of having an entire orchestra travel and perform on a lengthy concert tour.

In 1974, international superstar keyboardist/composer Rick Wakeman (known mostly as a member of the group Yes and from recording with artists like David Bowie) took his mammoth *Journey to the Centre of the Earth* production on a concert tour in North America, during which he was accompanied by an entire orchestra, narrator, rock band, and choir. It was an unbelievable undertaking, and ultimately all the money earned was spent to cover the massive expenses.

Emerson, Lake & Palmer took on the same challenge to support their double album *Works, Volume One*. Halfway through the tour, however, the orchestra had to be let go, as the band was going broke. The musical arrangements were reworked and the tour carried on, with Emerson, Lake & Palmer playing once again as a trio. —DD

FUN FACT

The standard for most artists who require an orchestra for their concerts, like Sarah Brightman, is to use pick-up musicians from each city in which the concerts are scheduled.

Postminimalism/Totalism

A LITTLE BIT OF EVERYTHING

As the 20th century reached its conclusion, composers again experimented with the time-continuum as a musical starting point. But this time, all the other elements of music were included as well.

To put it in list form, postminimalism includes the following attributes:

- a steady pulse, either throughout the movement or the whole piece
- a tonal framework consisting of a few different pitches—rhythm is the concentrated aspect of this music
- even dynamics; music lacks loud/soft climaxes or nuances
- no linear formal framework, which makes postminimalism different from minimalism
- the influence of world and popular music (such as bluegrass or Jewish themes)[1]

This music was very similar to minimalism, but it sought to include other aspects as well, which made it more complex and led to the synonymous name totalism.

John Adams and Arvo Pärt are definitely considered some of the foremost composers in this genre.

As with many musical time periods, postminimalism is a movement within the visual arts as well. The postminimalist artist seeks to show essential elements of time through handmade works that usually incorporate grids through simplistic means. Architects also followed suit, showing the all-inclusive influence that the postminimalist held, and in fact still holds today. —SL

Postminimalist/totalist art by Natasha Ann Loewy.

LISTENING HOMEWORK

Adam's Nixon in China

Pärt's Credo

Character Piece

SONGS WITH PERSONALITY

In the 19th century, composers became interested in wedding instrumental music with art forms, particularly literature. This resulted in the birth of the art song and the rise of the character piece.

Composed for solo piano, these works were meant to evoke the same images, moods, or characters for which 19th-century poetry was known. The character was usually determined through particular combinations of rhythms, tempi, and modes (major or minor). Thus a piece in a minor key that alternated between fast yet simple rhythms and slower, stretched-out durations could portray the alternating energy and sadness of a lonely orphan. These short pieces would usually be collected into a large album, such as Schumann's *Carnaval* or Debussy's *Préludes*.

Robert Schumann was especially fond of the character piece. His contributions include *Kreisleriana* op. 16, eight pieces intended to represent a fictional character created by E. T. A. Hoffmann. *Carnaval* Op. 9 consists of 20 pieces that portray the different aspects of Schumann's personality (Eusebius and Florestan), stock comedy characters (Pierrot, Arlequin, Coquette, Pantalon, and Columbine), or people in his life (Chopin, Clara Schumann, Paganini, and Ernestine von Fricken). Two of his collections are focused on children, *Kinderszenen* Op. 15, "Scenes from Childhood," and *The Album for the Young,* Op. 68.

Carnavale by Daniel Wynn (www.wynn-art.com).

Modern composers have created character pieces for any type of instrumentation, from Carl Nielsen's two *Character Pieces* for oboe and piano to Eric Ewazen's portrayal of four different English pubs in his *Colchester Fantasy* for brass quintet. —SS

Clara Schumann (1819–1896)

WRITING IN THE SHADOWS

Clara Wieck Schumann, born into a musical family in Germany and trained by her father, was known first as a brilliant concert pianist and later as the wife of composer Robert Schumann. But she was also an accomplished composer in her own right.

Clara first met Schumann, one of her father's students, when she was 11 years old (about the same time she began composing);[1] eventually, she married him against her father's wishes. As a performer, she wrote numerous compositions for her own repertoire; when she married Robert, she began expanding into German *lieder*. She and Robert jointly published a series of 12 songs, and she went on to write at least 50 others.[2] However, her composing ability went largely unrecognized—partly due to her husband's high profile, and partly because of her own categorization as a performer.

When Robert became mentally ill, Clara focused on touring and performing to pay the bills; after Robert passed away, Clara stopped composing altogether, choosing instead to promote her late husband's works. Despite Robert's encouragement, Clara believed her own compositional abilities to be inferior, although her pieces demonstrate great technical ability and depth of feeling. Not until this century have her compositions—and talent—been recognized for what they truly were. As a composer, she wrote in the shadows—not just of her husband, but of her culture. Not even Clara Schumann knew how good she really was. —JJM

Symphony No. 9 in D minor ("Choral")

BY LUDWIG VAN BEETHOVEN, 1824

It's hard for most of us to fathom, but Beethoven was almost completely deaf when he wrote his magnificent Ninth Symphony. As the story goes, while he was directing the symphony's tempo at its premiere, Beethoven could not hear the performance and, having lost his place in the movement, continued to wave his baton even after the musicians had stopped playing. It wasn't until a singer turned him around and he saw the sea of clapping hands that he knew the performance was a monumental success.[1]

The work is cherished for its contagious jubilance and vigor, but it is also renowned for what it meant. Especially noteworthy is the powerful chorus in the final movement. As the first choral section ever incorporated into a major composer's symphony, it permanently transformed the landscape of Western music. Perhaps even more significant, though, is the particular message that Beethoven communicates through the singers. Based on Friedrich von Schiller's poem "Ode to Joy," the words are an urgent plea for exultation and brotherly love. Coming from a man who was all too familiar with human suffering, it is an all the more touching finale. —CKG

RECOMMENDED RECORDING

Beethoven: Symphony No. 9; Herbert von Karajan;
Berlin Philharmonic Orchestra; Deutsch Grammophon; 1996

Salome

RICHARD STRAUSS (1864–1949)

The ultimate example of operatic decadence can be found in Richard Strauss's *Salome,* a drama in one act. Based on Hedwig Lachmann's German translation of Oscar Wilde's French play *Salomé,* the German libretto was written by the composer. The opera is best known for its "Dance of the Seven Veils."

The story begins in the palace of Herod, the tetrarch of Judaea and Perea. Salome, Herod's stepdaughter and great-niece, demands that the prophet Jokanaan be brought to her from where he is imprisoned in the palace cis-

tern. Enamored with Salome, Narraboth, captain of Herod's guard, complies. Jokanaan denounces the incestuous marriage of Herod and Herodias, Herod's niece and Salome's mother. He then demands that Salome follow Christ. Though appalled, she is drawn to Jokanaan even more.

Herod has emerged from the palace seeking relief from his nightmare visions. Herodias demands that Jokanaan be delivered to the Jews. Herod, however, is now focused on Salome, promising her any wish if she will dance for him. She then performs the Dance of the Seven Veils and, upon completion, demands the head of Jokanaan as her wish. After the executioner delivers his head on a silver platter, Salome kisses the prophet's lips. Shocked, Herod orders her death. —CCD

Linda Roark Strummer as Herodias, Eilana Lappalainen as Salome, Robert Brubaker as Herod in Salome. *Photo by John Fitzgerald; courtesy Kentucky Opera.*

The Serpent

EASY ON THE EARS, HARD ON THE LIPS

Often considered half brass and half woodwind, the serpent is a unique brass instrument invented in 1590. It has historically been made of wood and covered in leather. It is considered a member of the brass family because it produces sound via a player's lips vibrating into a mouthpiece shaped similar to that of a trombone.

Because of its conical bore, the serpent has a mellow but firm timbre similar to that of a bassoon or French horn and can articulate equally well at low and medium dynamics. When played loudly, it is powerful and crisp. Using six finger holes, it is very difficult to play and relies heavily on the player's lip abilities to provide adequate intonation for all the notes of the scale.

The instrument's double-S shape is where the serpent derives its name. The unusual look was created out of the necessity to bring the finger holes of this nearly 8-foot instrument to a comfortable position for the player. A bent metal crook is used to connect the mouthpiece to the instrument's body.

The serpent is a bass apparatus and was originally used to accompany plainsong in the church, adding strength to the low voices. It found favor in 18th-century England as the bass for the military wind band.

Rossini's *Siege of Corinth*, Verdi's *Sicilian Vespers,* and Wagner's *Rienzi* are wonderful examples of its use in operas. —LMC

FUN FACT

A late-20th-century revival includes a newly penned concerto for the serpent by Simon Proctor that can be heard in a recording by Douglas Yeo.

Musique Concrète and "Found Objects"

MAKING JOYFUL NOISES

If 12-tone or serial music was an overthrowing of the old form of music theory, a further redefinition of parameters was advocated by Pierre Schaeffer in 1940s France. Schaeffer was in the vanguard of newly emerging electronic music, predating digital recording by approximately four decades. With good financial and business connections, he was able to set up one of the first music lab/recording studios.

Schaeffer's medium was tape. His method: to record raw sound (a hammer breaking a rock, footsteps on pavement) and subject it to feedback, reverberation, and other alterations before placing it in sequence with other sounds. Schaeffer founded a "school" of music and proclaimed it *Musique Concrète,* which translates into English as "real" music, in the sense of "actual."*

This extends us back into "music as organized sound," using sound, the most fundamental base of the art form, as a building block. The Dadaists were making art out of "found objects," such as collar buttons, bicycle wheels, and toilet seats, in the decade following 1910. More than 30 years later, Schaeffer compiled "found" sounds, made art from them in 1948, and helped pave the way for electronic music. This style needed electronics to get started and was dependent on the technology for the timing of its emergence. —TH

National Theater and Concert Hall

A MEMORIAL FOR A CONTROVERSIAL LEADER

The death of Chiang Kai-shek in 1975 brought forth a wave of mixed emotions about one of the most controversial leaders Taiwan had ever known. Nonetheless, the Taiwanese government authorized a major memorial complex to be built in Taipei, including a theater, a concert hall, and a park containing a monument. The resulting venues became the National Theater and Concert Hall, and combined they represent one of the foremost performing arts centers in all Asia.

The complex opened to the public in 1987, and it instantly became a magnet for international dignitaries and figures of political importance. The following year, the National Concert Hall established its place on the world map of classical music with a concert featuring Placido Domingo. In 1990 Pavarotti performed on the same stage with a public simulcast in the plaza, an event that drew an audience of well over 10,000 opera fans.[1]

The NTCH, as it is commonly referred to, contains a total of four performance areas that host events ranging from chamber music to orchestral concerts and operas.[2] In addition to an impressive list of Western classical artists, the Theater and Concert Hall also promote the Chinese and Taiwanese traditions of classical music. Both the Theater and Concert Hall are known for their superior sound isolation qualities, keeping outside noise to a minimum so that even the subtlest nuances in the music come across beautifully.[3] —MM

Beethoven-Haus Bonn Museum

BITS AND PIECES FROM THE GREAT COMPOSER

In the attic room where the great composer was born in December 1770 stands only a bust—a fitting silent memorial to one of the greatest composers who ever lived. Thanks to 12 wealthy residents of Bonn, who in 1889 bought Beethoven's birthplace and converted it to a museum, music lovers can make pilgrimages to the row house, located in the city's center not far from the Rhine River.

Beethoven lived in his family's house in Bonn, Germany, for just a few years, but it is filled with treasures that span his lifetime and provide insight into his genius. The most famous portrait of the composer (the 1820

An 1820 portrait of Beethoven by Joseph Karl Stieler; courtesy Beethoven-Haus Bonn Museum.

painting by Joseph Karl Stieler), his last grand piano, and the original handwritten manuscript of "Moonlight Sonata" are among the many mementos at the museum. Home to the largest and most diverse Beethoven collection in the world, the museum holds letters, manuscripts, coins, instruments, furniture, and everyday items—from a shopping invoice to his ear trumpets.

Beethoven's parents, the electoral court tenor Johann van Beethoven and his wife, Maria Magdalena, moved into the garden wing of the house at Bonngasse 20 in November 1767. As the family grew, they were forced to look for larger lodgings and moved to an apartment in Rheingasse.

If you aren't planning a visit to Bonn anytime soon, you can take a virtual tour (accessible through the museum Web site) of the museum's 12 rooms, garden, and courtyard. —KFG

Sarah Brightman

BRINGING CLASSICAL AND OPERA TO THE MASSES

Pop music and show vocalist Sarah Brightman has been singing pop songs, Broadway show songs, and folk songs for years on stage and in her many recordings. Her soprano voice has allowed her to include classical songs and opera arias in her recorded and performance repertoire. With the help of her creative partner and producer Frank Peterson, Brightman paved the way for similar artists like Andrea Bocelli, Josh Groban, and il Divo, who often sing classical songs or opera arias with popular music sound arrangements and voicings.

Brightman has recorded works by Puccini, Beethoven, Bach, Schubert, Catalani, Chopin, Rachmaninov, Dvořák, and Canteloube. Many were produced with contemporary arrangements using electronic instruments. When performing these classical and opera pieces in concert, Brightman applies her often dramatic theatricality to create a memorable visual effect. She has sold millions of records all around the world and performs in some of the biggest theaters, concert halls, and even sports arenas.

Opinions are mixed on Brightman. Some feel she successfully brings classical music and opera to those who have not been exposed to it before. Other classical music experts and enthusiasts disapprove of the classics making their way into pop culture. They feel that when the music is performed and recorded with pop music sensibilities and qualities, it is diminished. Nevertheless, performers like Sarah are certainly opening up more ears to the classics. —DD

New Simplicity and New Complexity

HERE IS WHERE IT GETS CONFUSING, AND VERY EXCITING

As we've been discussing music history, you may have noticed a major trend: many of these musical time periods came into existence as a reaction to the previous type of music. It's as though composers are a bunch of rebellious teenagers, all striving to do their own thing and adamantly ignoring their parents.

New Simplicity, originating mainly in Germany, came about as a reaction to neoromanticism. Composers wanted to express themselves, but they didn't want to use the complicated harmonic language of the Romantic era. Instead, they strived for impersonal simplicity, harkening back to the harmonies of the Renaissance.

Then, as I'm sure you could guess, New Complexity arose as a reaction to New Simplicity, and is actually a current method of composition. Basically, this music is what any of us would consider "new" music—highly complicated scores with unusual notational methods, extended techniques, and quarter-tone microtuning.

But whether simple or complicated, composers in the late 20th century all have common goals. They each want to push the envelope in classical music; they want to challenge their audiences' ears and brains so that they are open to just about anything. We might not understand their music—we might truly dislike it—but we must appreciate their altruistic ideals. —SL

LISTENING HOMEWORK

Wolfgang Rihm's Ins Offene
James Dillon's helle Nacht

Cyclic Form

WAIT, DIDN'T I ALREADY HEAR THAT?

While composers have always wanted to make the different movements of suites, sonatas, symphonies, concertos, and chamber pieces sound like they belong together, most of these pieces have completely different themes for each of the movements. But sometimes composers will use a specific musical idea in each of the movements, creating a cyclic form.

This is most often associated with the Romantic era, starting with the *Symphonie Fantastique* by Hector Berlioz. Berlioz composed a melody that he meant to haunt the autobiographical artist as he pursues an unattainable love. This melody occurs in all five movements of the symphony in differing contexts, yet it is always recognizable. Cesar Franck composed his Symphony in D in a cyclic form.

Many scholars associate the cyclic form with the French style, including Camille Saint-Saëns, Vincent D'Indy, and Édouard Lalo. However, composers in other countries also used cyclic form, such as the German pianist Franz Liszt and the Czech composer Antonin Dvořák in his famous "From the New World" Symphony.

Tying together various musical movements with a recurring idea was not new to the 19th century. One type of Renaissance mass used a single plainsong chant as the basis for each movement, and some Baroque dance suites had the same theme in each dance movement. In all cases, the recurring theme is intended to create a sense of familiarity, though often the return of the melody is in an entirely new context. —SS

Amy Beach (1867–1944)

THE LIGHT THAT COULDN'T BE HIDDEN

Amy Marcy Cheney Beach, who became the first internationally acclaimed American female composer, demonstrated an amazing capacity for music at an early age. She reportedly had perfect pitch, could recall over 40 songs by age two, and composed her first pieces on the piano by age four.[1]

Social attitudes toward women were changing at the time, but were still restrictive. Beach's parents wouldn't permit her to study music abroad, and also limited her public performance opportunities until age 16—at which time she quickly gained a name for herself as a pianist. At 18, she married the older Dr. Henry Beach, who frowned on the idea of his wife having a public career, so she only played publicly for charity events once a year. Developing her skills privately, Beach dove into composing, writing mostly vocal songs, but also more elaborate works such as her Mass in E-flat and the "Gaelic" Symphony.

After her husband's death, Beach revived her performing career, this time without restraint—first in Europe, then in the United States. She continued to compose, though not as prolifically as before. After her death, Beach was all but forgotten until the latter part of the 20th century, when several recordings of her compositions acquainted the public with her music.

Amy Beach never openly defied the conventions of her day, but ultimately the light of her talent could not be hidden. Her genius gained her a place among the masters of composition. —JJM

The Swan

BY CAMILLE SAINT-SAËNS, 1886

In Prokofiev's *Peter and the Wolf*, the composer illustrated the animal characters of a children's story by identifying each with a specific orchestral instrument. Decades before that, the French composer Saint-Saëns undertook a similar project when he penned *Carnival of the Animals*, which he called a "zoological fantasy."[1] In it, the characteristics of animals like lions, elephants, and kangaroos are portrayed musically through an imaginative application of instrumentation and structural composition.

The most celebrated movement of the work is "The Swan," or "Le Cygne." The three-minute composition floats by just as gracefully as you would expect as a solo cello carries the flowing melody over the backing ensemble. Around the time *Carnival of the Animals* was completed, Saint-Saëns was battling the belief that his works were frivolous, so he prohibited the work from being published during his lifetime. "The Swan," however, he recognized as something special and therefore permitted its release.[2] In 1905, a short ballet called "The Dying Swan" was choreographed for the legendary ballerina Anna Pavlova based on this lovely piece. —CKG

RECOMMENDED RECORDING

Saint-Saëns: Carnival of the Animals; *Christopher van Kampen (performer); Charles Dutoit (conductor); London Sinfonietta; Decca; 1990*

Elektra

RICHARD STRAUSS (1864–1949)

Based on Sophocles's Greek tragedy of the same name, Richard Strauss's one-act opera *Elektra* was adapted from the 1903 drama written by Hugo von Hofmannsthal, who also wrote the German libretto.

As the action begins, Princess Elektra swears vengeance for the murder of her father, Amamemnon, by his wife, Klytemnestra, and her lover, Aegisth. Her sister, Chrysothemis, warns her that Klytemnestra and Aegisth have plotted to imprison her. Elektra plans for her brother, Orest, to assassinate the couple upon his return, but learns from two strangers that Orest has also been killed. Elektra then insists that she and her sister carry out the murders themselves, but Chrysothemis refuses. Elektra then digs up the axe used to murder her father. Orest then reveals himself as one of the strangers, and he enters the palace and murders Klytemnestra and Aegisth. As Elekra dances to celebrate the return of her brother to court, she suddenly falls dead.

Somewhat similar to Strauss's *Salome, Elektra* offers audiences a tense theatrical experience. Strauss took modernism a step further in this piece through his use of dissonance, sounds that may seem unstable to the listener and in need of resolution. He also used chromaticism, a compositional technique based on nonharmonic tones. Just as Wagner used leitmotifs, Strauss also used motives and chords to identify characters in *Elektra*. The most famous of these is the "Elektra chord," a highly dissonant polychord. —CCD

Photo © Carol Rosegg; courtesy New York City Opera.

The Glass Armonica

SIMPLY STUNNING SOUND

The phenomenon of rubbing wet fingers on the rim of a water-filled glass to produce sound waves has caught the attention of many, including Galileo. It was in London in 1761 that Benjamin Franklin heard a musical performance on a system of water-tuned glasses. Delighted and intrigued by the sound, the inventor set out to build a better instrument.

Franklin mounted 37 glass bowls horizontally on an iron rod, which was turned using a foot pedal system similar to that of a sewing machine. Sound was made by lightly touching the rims of the rotating bowls with wet fingers.

The first armonica was built with the aid of London glass blower Charles James, and with Franklin's design influence and performance style it was now possible to play 10 glasses at once. In 1762, a premiere performance by Marianne Davies introduced this new instrument to the world.

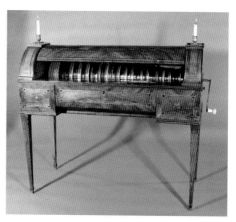

The enchanting sound of this glass device became very popular, especially in Germany. Many composers, including Mozart, Hasse, and C. P. E. Bach, created works for it. But as performance venues became larger and instruments became louder, use of the quiet, soothing armonica lessened.

National Music Museum, The University of South Dakota. Photo by Simon Spicer.

Also known as the glass harmonica, popular 20th century recording artists Pink Floyd, Tom Waits, and Linda Ronstadt have incorporated its magical tone. An original Franklin glass armonica can be seen at the Franklin Museum in Philadelphia, Pennsylvania. —LMC

American Jazz and Rock

WHERE CLASSICAL MUSIC HAS COME

The sound of tonality continued to reign in American folk and commercial music throughout the 20th century and the first decade of the 21st, despite all the foregoing intellectual "formulas" of classical musical composition.

The most agreeable syntheses of musical styles in the 20th century were tonal jazz and rock 'n' roll, composed of propulsive African rhythm and 19th-century European-American hymn-tune homophony, soulful blues and gospel music. The blues' vocal form is 12 measures using the chords I, IV, V, and I. Melodically, it uses a jazz scale with a lowered third and seventh.

From the 1920s through the '70s, songwriters from New York and Hollywood, such as Rodgers and Hart (and Hammerstein), George and Ira Gershwin, and Cole Porter, were masters at crafting single, beautiful melodies above a series of sometimes impressionistic chords, bringing homophony to heights practiced by great classical melodists like Tchaikovsky, Verdi, Ravel, and Debussy.

Jazz artists sought these songs and blues to use as forms for improvisation. Their eloquent melodies and beautifully structured chord progressions were inspiration for playing them "straight," as well as for improvisation.

In the 1960s rediscovered folk music brought the rise of the guitar, fostering a broader knowledge of harmony and melody among the public. A new "do-it-yourself" era of music had begun, which seemed to rebel against stuffy academicism. And it was all tonal. Even spoken rap and hip-hop often have a single subwoofer tonal bass line under the words. —TH

Festspielhaus

GOVERNMENT INTERVENTION SAVES THE DAY

The Festspielhaus in Baden-Baden, currently the largest concert hall and opera house in Germany, began its young life with a much different distinction. Opened in 1998 as a privately financed venue, it was originally a disaster of near comic proportions. Rife with mismanagement, lack of funds, and public disapproval, the Festspielhaus faced closure only three months after opening.

In order to turn the Festspielhaus from a catastrophe into something resembling a viable undertaking, the city of Baden-Baden injected public funds into the project and replaced the managing and artistic directors. Things began to turn around the following year, and by the end of 1999 the venue was enjoying increasing public approval and artistic growth. The real goal was finally met in 2002, when the Festspielhaus had reached a level of private sponsorship that allowed it to operate with no help at all from public funding.[1]

The Festspielhaus has truly gone from strength to strength, and today hosts some of the most renowned performers and conductors in the world. Soloists like Cecilia Bartoli, Anne-Sophie Mutter, and Renée Fleming are listed on the roster alongside conductors like Sir Simon Rattle and Valery Gergiev.[2] In fact, Gergiev has such strong ties to the Festspielhaus that his Mariinsky Theatre Orchestra has adopted the venue as its unofficial second home. In just over a decade, the Festspielhaus has gone from a public embarrassment to a triumph of private enterprise. —MM

Festival of the Sound

CHAMBER MUSIC ON THE WATER

Many a summer evening in Ontario's Parry Sound, people head to the waterfront to listen to works by Mozart, Haydn, Liszt, and Mendelssohn. As the sun sets on Georgian Bay, festivalgoers enter the new Charles W. Stockey Centre for the Performing Arts or board a cruise ship and listen as international and Canadian musicians take turns playing solos, duets, and ensembles. The cruises, a mainstay of the Festival of the Sound, are informal; in between sets the musicians mingle with an appreciative audience.

Located about two hours north of Toronto, Parry Sound has been home to the Festival of the Sound since 1979, when renowned pianist Anton Kuerti purchased a summer house near town and organized three concerts by Canadian musicians. Internationally preeminent clarinetist James Campbell has been artistic director of Ontario's oldest annual international summer classical music festival since 1985.

Today the festival offers some 60 events over a three-week period in July and August. Focused on chamber music, the repertoire ranges from Baroque works to premieres of pieces by Canadian composers. —KFG

Audience members enjoying intermission on the deck of the Charles W. Stockey Centre for the Performing Arts. Photo by Sarah Boyd.

Classical Crossover

JOHN BAYLESS MAKES CLASSICAL ROCK

Many of our classical superstar instrumentalists like Itzhak Perlman, Nadja Salerno-Sonnenberg, Manuel Barrueco, Joshua Bell, James Galway, Yo-Yo Ma, and Gabriela Montero perform and record other styles of music, bringing their virtuosity to create something difficult to define and definitely new. Occasionally these artists will perform or record pop/rock music, but none have so completely embraced the combination of pop and classical music with the devotion and passion of pianist/arranger/composer John Bayless.

Bayless's illustrious performance career includes playing with major symphony orchestras around the world and working with great artists like maestro Leonard Bernstein. His recording career has mostly been devoted to his special re-creations of pop music in the style of the famous classical composers. Beginning in 1989 with his groundbreaking recording *Bach Meets the Beatles* and followed by *Bach on Abbey Road*, Bayless's virtuosity and composing/arranging talents brought a very unique fusion to a new emerging musical genre eventually called "classical crossover."

John Bayless, 2005. Photo by Mark Leet.

His studies and work with Maestro Bernstein led him to record a special arrangement of excerpts from Bernstein's *West Side Story* played in a classical style. His love of Puccini's operas resulted in a 1993 solo piano recording of beautiful interpretations of the famous arias. Bayless also recorded an album devoted to the music of Elton John (released in 2008), again played in the style of the great composers. —DD

Art Rock Influence

FEELING THE BEAT, AND PROUD OF IT

As the 20th century progressed, musicians realized that in order to continue to appeal to the general population, they were going to have to broaden their base a bit. If they continued only playing the old standards (Mozart, Beethoven, Bach) or forcing atonal music down the throats of unwelcome receivers, the orchestras were going to end up playing to empty concert halls.

So it could certainly be considered a good thing when a movement of composers began using popular music as the starting point for classical composition. Of course, other composers scoffed at the "cheesy movie music" and the cross-culture pop influence. It wasn't *real* music, they argued.

However, the movement took off, and now you'd be hard-pressed to find a composer who considers him/herself exempt from rock influence. Some of these first art rock composers actually started out as rock musicians, and only later turned to writing scored music. Others started out in the midst of postmodernism, moving from futurism to minimalism and later writing in a more easy-on-the-ear style.

Regardless of how each art rock composer came to be, one thing is certain: It's a good thing they existed. Say what you will about the quality of the music; all in all, they attracted a younger audience of classical concertgoers and created an energy that otherwise might never have existed. —SL

LISTENING HOMEWORK

Scott Johnson's **Stalking Horse**
Christopher Rouse's **Symphony No. 1**

Tone Poem

EVERY PIECE TELLS A STORY

Remember how Romantic composers were inspired to portray literary scenes or characters with short character pieces? These composers also composed larger orchestral works based on literature, called "tone poems." There had been earlier symphonies based on literary programs, most notably Berlioz's *Symphonie Fantastique*. But those programmatic symphonies were still based on traditional symphonic forms.

Tone poems are not based on sonata, binary, ternary, or other standard forms. Rather, the form is determined by the literary model, with references to other musical works or representations of sounds like bird calls.

Richard Strauss is well known for his many tone poems, such as *Till Eulenspiegel, Ein Heldenleben,* and *Also sprach Zaruthustra,* made famous by the movie *2001: A Space Odyssey. Till Eulenspiegel's Merry Pranks* is about the trickster and folk hero as he laughs, plots, and eventually ends up being executed. *Also sprach Zaruthustra (Thus Spoke Zaruthustra)* is based on the treatise by philosopher Frederick Nietzsche, in which he declares that "God is dead." Strauss labeled nine sections, but they mostly flow right into each other. *Ein Heldenleben (A Hero's Life)* sets up Strauss himself as the hero, using leitmotifs to signify himself, his wife, and his enemies (critics). He even quotes from his other tone poems—*Till Eulenspiegel, Macbeth, Also sprach Zarathustra,* and *Don Quixote*—to represent "The Hero's Works of Peace."

Pick a tone poem by Liszt, Strauss, or Sibelius, and see if you can figure out the story without reading the liner notes. —SS

Maurice Ravel (1875–1937)

BEYOND IMPRESSIONISM

French composer Maurice Ravel is often associated with Debussy and the impressionist movement in music; yet while Ravel admired Debussy, the two actually had vastly different approaches. While Debussy seemed mainly sensory and experimental, Ravel was more methodical, writing every single note on purpose.[1]

Entering the Paris Conservatory at age 14, Ravel studied under composer Gabriel Fauré, writing mainly in the impressionist vein. As he grew musically, by far his greatest contribution to music became his unmatched ability to orchestrate. He was known for taking his own piano compositions and re-writing them for orchestra—and sometimes adapting the works of others for orchestra, as he did with Mussorgsky's *Pictures at an Exhibition*.

Eventually Ravel became intrigued by the music of Igor Stravinsky and other neoclassicists, and his compositions began drawing from that influence. He also drew from Asian music, European folk influences, and eventually even American jazz. His most famous work, *Boléro*, is a repetitive theme-and-variation piece with a distinct Spanish flavor. Ravel was able to assimilate all these streams into a building-block–style of composition that prompted Stravinsky to label Ravel "the Swiss watchmaker" of music.[2] Ravel's beginnings were in impressionism, but he moved well beyond it, creating a form that was unmistakably his own. —JJM

FUN FACT

Ravel failed to win the famed Prix de Rome competition after five attempts, likely due to ideological differences with the conservatory administration. The suspected bias against Ravel caused the resignation of the conservatory director in 1905.[3]

Mass in B minor

BY JOHANN SEBASTIAN BACH, CA. 1733–1748

Bach's compositions are known for their brilliant intricacy and sublime beauty, but his prolific rate of creative output is equally impressive. He worked tirelessly to earn his place in the uppermost echelon of the classical music pantheon, producing an abundance of work every year for decades on end. That is why it is so intriguing to consider that he spent at least 15 years crafting the glorious *Mass in B minor*.

The magnum opus was written toward the end of Bach's life and is considered by many to be the culmination of his entire life's work. It combines the best elements of his vast repertoire—alluring melodies, ornate counterpoint, and graceful arrangement—into a comprehensive whole. Furthermore, it draws on his mastery of sacred forms and fervent personal faith to create a potent spiritual effect.

Still, the *Mass in B minor* is shrouded in mystery. It is too long for actual liturgical use, and it is doubtful that Bach ever planned on hearing it performed.[1] It would seem, instead, that he was determined to leave behind a masterpiece—one that would encompass his tremendous range of talents and skills while simultaneously conveying his deepest convictions. If that was in fact his intention, it's safe to say that, as usual, he thoroughly succeeded. —CKG

RECOMMENDED RECORDING

Bach: Mass in B minor; *John Eliot Gardiner (conductor);*
The English Baroque Soloists; Archiv Produktion; 1990

The Consul

GIAN CARLO MENOTTI (1911–2007)

The Consul was Gian Carlo Menotti's first full-length opera and later won him the Pulitzer Prize and New York Drama Critics' Circle Award. Composed in three acts, the English libretto was written by the composer. The opera premiered at the Schubert Theater in Philadelphia in 1950. Sir Lawrence Olivier first brought *The Consul* to England. After making its Italian premiere at La Scala, the piece was then translated into 14 languages.[1]

Menotti was inspired to write the piece after reading an article dated February 12, 1947, regarding the tragic fate of a real-life Magda Sorel, a Polish woman who was refused admission to the United States and later hanged herself at Ellis Island.[2]

Set in Europe, the opera revolves around political dissident John Sorel. He has fled his country, which is under a dictatorship, to save his life and wants his wife, Magda, his baby, and his mother to join him. Magda is frustrated by the red tape at the consul's office and her inability to see her husband. When John returns home, he discovers that Magda is dead, and he is arrested by the secret police.[3]

Musical highlights of the opera include Mother's Act II "Lullaby," a sweet and deeply rich contralto aria, and Magda's famous Act II "Papers" aria, "To This We've Come," a showcase for a dramatic soprano both theatrically and vocally. —CCD

Lina Tetriani as Magda Sorel. Photo by Katie Roupe; courtesy Chautauqua Opera (www.ciweb.org).

The Vibraphone

ALMOST HUMAN

One of the youngest members of the symphony orchestra, the vibraphone was born in 1916 at the Leedy Drum Company. There, in an attempt to create a quirky new instrument for the vaudeville community, Hermann Winterhoff applied a mechanical vibrato to a steel marimba to create a human voice effect.

Its popularity grew quickly, and within a decade the instrument we now refer to as "vibes" was established.

A sibling to the marimba, this American-made instrument uses tuned bars struck with mallets to produce its sound and employs metal resonator tubes under each bar for amplification. It differs primarily in that it utilizes aluminum bars instead of wood, and the long sustain of the metal bars calls for a damper pedal so the player can control the length of the decay. The incidental bars remain on the same horizontal plane as the fundamentals to allow for easier playing with multiple mallets.

The most unique feature of the vibraphone is its vibrato. This is accomplished by the use of revolving vanes installed in the top of the resonators. The vanes, attached to a motor-driven axle, cause a pulsating effect when rotated.

Although the vibraphone initially found a comfortable home in jazz with players like Lionel Hampton and Gary Burton, you can hear it in Berg's opera *Lulu*, Britten's "Spring" Symphony, Maderna's Serenata No. 2 for 11 Instruments, and Vaughan Williams's *Sinfonia Antartica* and Symphony No. 8.
—LMC

Music Theory and You

SCIENCE THAT JUST SOUNDS GOOD

Learning the elements of music theory makes you a more aware listener, capable of digging more deeply into the music you listen to. Theory tells you what is going on. This can transform a piece from what was a merely exciting musical experience into a musical friend, both now and in the future.

Before reading these pages, you might have known you liked or disliked certain kinds of music, but didn't know why. Now you know: The music is tonal or modal, or not; the rhythms are jagged or uniform; the harmonies are consonant or dissonant; the melodies have a certain degree of chromaticism or lack it; and so on.

Theory enables you to define what you have been hearing as succinctly as you can define the elements of visual or graphic arts. In music, much of this is done by using notation as a metaphor for the sounds and silences. But the final judge is the ear, and the ear alone.

Listen to the recordings that go with this book, and to the listening suggestions. Hopefully these scientific notes on music will lead you to more exciting, enduring, and enchanting experiences in the vast world of organized sound.

—TH

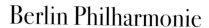

Berlin Philharmonie

BEAUTY AND BRAINS ALL IN ONE PLACE

I t's not often that a concert hall sounds as good as it looks, but the Berlin Philharmonie enjoys nearly universal acclaim for being outstanding on both accounts. Its modern, asymmetrical design and bold architectural statements make a stunning visual impression, and inside the hall, many wonderful surprises await audiences.

The pentagonal auditorium features a stage in the center, with seats arranged in a "vineyard" configuration. This layout, introduced by Hans Scharoun, set a trend from which other architects would base their own venue designs. Aside from contributing to the astonishingly clear sound in the hall, the design of the auditorium also affords a fantastic view for the audience.

The Philharmonie and its orchestra have hosted three stellar principal conductors since opening in 1963: Herbert von Karajan, Claudio Abbado, and Simon Rattle. Von Karajan was responsible for countless memorable performances and recordings in the concert hall. Abbado introduced more innovative and modern works into the orchestra's repertoire, bringing new sounds to audiences. Rattle has been the principal conductor since 2002, and has proven so popular both with the musicians and the public that his contract has been extended to 2020.

The Berlin Philharmonie is one of the first classical music venues in the world to embrace the Internet, and their new Digital Concert Hall now brings performances from the stage of this spectacular venue directly to a computer near you.[1] —MM

Spoleto Festival
A BIT OF ITALY IN CHARLESTON, SOUTH CAROLINA

For 18 years, Pulitzer Prize–winning Italian composer Gian Carlo Menotti searched for a site in the United States to host the American counterpart of the arts festival, Festival of Two Worlds that he founded in 1958 in Spoleto, Italy. He searched for a location that would provide the charm of Spoleto, a small and picturesque town in the hills north of Rome, as well as its wealth of theaters, churches, and other performance spaces. He finally found it in Charleston, South Carolina, a beautifully preserved 18th-century city. In 1977, Spoleto Festival USA was born.

When Menotti was asked why he had chosen Charleston, he replied, "It is a much needed sign of hope in this age of suspicion and mistrust when two beautiful towns so different and so far away from each other, through the common quest for beauty, unfurl the flag of friendship."[1]

For more than two weeks during May and June, emerging and renowned artists from around the world in the fields of chamber, symphonic, choral, and jazz music as well as opera, theater, musical theater, dance, and the visual arts perform in Charleston. Among the venues is the Dock Street Theatre, one of America's oldest theaters. —KFG

The Dock Street Theatre, one of America's oldest theaters, and one of the venues for Spoleto Festival USA. Photo by Doug Hickok.

Classical Music's Influence on Film and Television Composers

BLAME IT ON THEIR TRAINING

For those of you beginning and those continuing to learn about and enjoy classical music, you may often take notice of strong similarities between the classic works you're now discovering and your favorite movie and television scores. This is mostly due to the classical history, performance, and composition training that many successful film/television composers have had. In fact, it has been said that today's film and television composers, especially those who write for the symphony orchestra, are the new classical composers.

John Williams, Bernard Hermann, Miklos Rosza, James Horner, Jerry Goldsmith, Patrick Doyle, George Fenton, and Maurice Jarre, to name a few, have all enhanced their work for film and television with reflections of the great composers' works. The innovative and dramatic orchestrations created by Shostakovich, Prokofiev, Ravel, and Stravinsky; the style of the grand and often romantic melodies of Tchaikovsky, Holst, and Rachmaninov; and the unique, adventurous sound design of Bartók and Messiaen are all present and easy to recognize.

Because the scope of classical music covers such a vast section of our history (and often incorporated folk and sacred music), you may hear many familiar periods of time (such as Baroque or Renaissance) when today's composers write for a project with a story that takes place deep in our past. —DD

World Music Influence

THE GLOBAL SYMPHONY

Just as composers toward the end of the 20th century began to use rock as an avid influence in their classical compositions, they also began to use world music as a source for inspiration. Actually, this trend was already present as early as the 1920s and '30s when composers such as Béla Bartók used folk songs from around the world as part of their music.

There are two trends in world-music influence. In one, Western composers used instruments from other cultures; some examples are Chinese traditional instruments, Indian ragas, and the Indonesian gamelan. These exotic instruments were added alongside our typical orchestral instruments, creating a new flavor in the music.

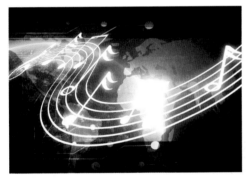

In the other method, composers used the tonalities of Eastern-European music in our Western context; within the structure of a symphony, for example, you might hear suggestions of a Chinese pentatonic scale.

Of course, with the increasing links in our global community, the reverse influence was also popular. Japanese composer Toru Takemitsu added a Western influence to his otherwise Eastern compositions.

Just like many of the other modern time periods, world music's influence has encompassed a large genre of classical compositions. Really, this trend simply acknowledges the fact that we, as musicians and as a global society, are coming together to create something that can be understood by everyone. —SL

LISTENING HOMEWORK

Bartók's Romanian Folk Dances
Takemitsu's Requiem for strings

Invention

A MUSICAL CONVERSATION THAT'S HARD TO FOLLOW

In the 1980s, Apple used a particular keyboard piece for all its advertising, something that motivated me to learn what the piece was and how to play it. The music was J. S. Bach's Invention No. 13 in A minor.

Bach composed 15 inventions as keyboard exercises for his son, Wilhelm Friedrich Bach. They were called inventions after the rhetorical idea of discovery or novelty, perhaps inspired by the Italian composer Bonporti. Every Renaissance and Baroque composer who used the term "invention" had their own idiosyncratic form, but Bach's inventions became so well known as pedagogical tools for young pianists that his style has become firmly associated with the term.

All Bach inventions are in counterpoint for two voices. Similar to fugues, inventions are based on a theme in one voice that is answered in the other voice. But unlike fugues, inventions can have both voices start at the beginning with

two different themes (double counterpoint), or even in loose imitation like No. 13. And the difference between the *exposition* (the introduction of the theme in each of the voices) and the *episodes* (free counterpoint that develops the themes) is much less obvious. The episodes develop the themes through methods similar to canons: augmentation, diminution, inversion, retrograde, and transposition. —SS

> ## Fun Fact
> *Bach also composed 15 three-voice counterpoint pieces for keyboard, but he called these "sinfonias" instead of inventions.*

Pyotr Ilyich Tchaikovsky (1840–1893)

MUSIC OF THE SOUL

O f the numerous prominent Russian composers who emerged in the late 19th century, Tchaikovsky stands head and shoulders above the rest. Musically speaking, he was not a groundbreaker,[1] and rarely did he impress the critics of his day. Yet his music was always popular with the public, his gift for melody infused with the deep, raw emotion that flooded his colorful personal life.

Tchaikovsky showed an early propensity for music but didn't train formally until adulthood, when he was admitted as the first student to the newly formed St. Petersburg Conservatory.[2] His early works are generally considered mediocre, but eventually he found his stride, gaining acclaim throughout Europe and the United States. He found his greatest successes in orchestral and ballet works, Piano Concerto No. 1, "Swan Lake," and *The Nutcracker* being standouts.

Tchaikovsky's reserved appearance and demeanor concealed a life of turbulence and deep inner struggles—including depression, suicidal tendencies, alcoholism, and a homosexual urge that conflicted with social norms at the time.[3] He desperately tried to fight the latter through an ill-fated marriage to an admirer, from whom he fled weeks after marrying her. Speculation still surrounds his sudden death, explanations ranging from cholera to suicide. Yet it seems Tchaikovsky's inner battles fueled the deep emotional nature of his music. To this day, some of the best-loved melodies in history have come from Tchaikovsky. —JJM

Wiegenlied (Lullaby)

BY JOHANNES BRAHMS, 1868

Pieces of classical music are not usually called "songs" unless they belong to a specific compositional form from 19th-century Germany called "lieder." Literally meaning "song," a lied is an arrangement for solo voice and piano whose words come directly from German folk poetry. Brahms wrote over 200 songs during his illustrious career, but by far the most recognized is his ubiquitous "Lullaby," which has been endlessly altered and marketed in modern contexts.

Properly titled "Wiegenlied," which means "cradle song," the work was indeed written as a lullaby—Brahms wrote it to honor the birth of his friend's son.[1] With its gentle piano undulations, sedative vocal melody, and comforting 3/4 sway, "Wiegenlied" is truly the perfect pacifier, and the poetic lyrics only enhance the effect. The first lines translated from German mean:

Good evening, and good night, with roses adorned,
With carnations covered, slip under the covers.
Early tomorrow, God willing, you will wake once again.

Tonight, experience it as Brahms intended it, and let the soothing soprano lull you to sleep. —CKG

Amahl and the Night Visitors

GIAN CARLO MENOTTI (1911–2007)

One of the most popular Christmas traditions, *Amahl and the Night Visitors* by Gian Carlo Menotti, was actually commissioned by NBC television to be broadcast live as the debut production of their *Hallmark Hall of Fame* on December 24, 1951. The original English libretto was written by the composer for this one-act opera.

The action is set in Bethlehem in the first century. Amahl, a disabled 12-year-old boy, is attempting to explain to his mother that he has seen a star with a long tail. Accustomed to her son's usual lies, she does not believe him. There is a knock at the door, and Amahl insists that three kings have come to visit them. This angers his mother even further until the kings greet them at the door, saying they have come to find a king and give him gifts. That night, Amahl's mother attempts to steal some of the kings' gold to help her crippled child. She returns it, however, when they explain that the king they seek will only need love to rule his kingdom. When Amahl offers the staff he uses as a gift to this king, he suddenly discovers he can walk without it. The opera ends as Amahl goes to see for himself this child king who has healed him. —CCD

Dale C. Bryant, Daniel M. Boye, George Washington III in Amahl and the Night Visitors. *Photo by Gregory Cable; courtesy Opera Carolina (Charlotte, North Carolina, www.operacarolina.org).*

SOURCES CITED

Page 6
1. David Ewen; *Encyclopedia of Concert Music.* New York: Hill and Wang, 1959.

Page 10
1. Cooper, Barry. *Beethoven.* Oxford University Press, 2000, 1.
2. Prevot, Dominique. "Beethoven: Biography." LvBeethoven. http://www.lvbeethoven.com/Bio/BiographyLudwig.html (accessed December 2009)
3. Encyclopedia of World Biography. "Ludwig van Beethoven." http://www.notablebiographies.com/Ba-Be/Beethoven-Ludwig-van.html (accessed December 2009)

Page 16
1. Mozarthaus. http://www.mozarthausvienna.at/en/ (accessed October 2009)

Page 20
1. Encyclopedia of World Biography. "Johannes Brahms." http://www.notablebiographies.com/Be-Br/Brahms-Johannes.html (accessed November 2009)
2. Biography. "Johannes Brahms." http://www.biography.com/articles/Johannes-Brahms-9223886?part=2 (accessed November 2009)

Page 26
1. The Fryderyk Chopin Institute. http://en.chopin.nifc.pl/chopin/places/poland/id/579 (accessed January 2010)
2. Chopin Festival. http://www.chopin.festival.pl/?lang=en (accessed January 2010)

Page 30
1. Felixmendelssohn.com. "Felix Mendelssohn (Bartholdy)." http://www.felixmendelssohn.com/felix_mendelssohn_bio_002.htm (accessed January 2010)
2. Steen, Michael. *The Lives & Times of the Great Composers.* Oxford University Press, 2004, 346.

Page 31
1. Encyclopedia Britannica. "August Wilhelmj." www.britannica.com. (accessed October 2009)

Page 36
1. The New York Times. Jones, Finn-Olaf. "Bayreuth Without a Ticket; Opera-less in the Realm of Wagner." July 1, 2007. http://travel.nytimes.com/2007/07/01/travel/01journeys.html (accessed November 2009)

Page 40
1. Ramos, Paul-John. "Sergei Vassilievich Rachmaninoff." Classical Net. http://www.classical.net/music/comp.lst/rachmaninoff.php (accessed October 2009)
2. Gifford, Katya. "Sergei Rachmaninov-Biography." Humanities Web. http://www.humanitiesweb.org/human.php?s=c&p=a&a=i&ID=751 (accessed October 2009)

Page 41
1. Libbey, Ted. *The NPR Listener's Encyclopedia of Classical Music.* New York: Workman Publishing, 2006, 3-4.
2. Ibid.

Page 46
1. 5280 Magazine. Dugdale, Julie. "Natural Composition: Slickrock be damned — the Moab Music Festival showcases southern Utah's spectacular canyonlands in ways mountain biking never could." August 2009. http://www.5280.com/issues/2009/0908/feature.php?PageID=1858 (accessed February 2010)

Page 50
1. Encyclopedia of World Biography. "Richard Wagner." Advameg, Inc. http://www.notablebiographies.com/Tu-We/Wagner-Richard.html (accessed October 2009)
2. Elyon, Lili. "The Controversy over Richard Wagner." Jewish Virtual Library. The American-Israeli Cooperative Enterprise, 2009. http://www.jewishvirtuallibrary.org/jsource/anti-semitism/Wagner.html (accessed October 2009)
3. Evenson, Kristian. "Leitmotifs in Der Ring des Nibelungen - an introduction." http://www.trell.org/wagner/motifs.html (accessed October 2009)

Page 56
1. London Handel Festival. http://www.handel.cswebsites.org/ (accessed January 2010)

Page 61
1. Old Poetry. "Clair de Lune." http://oldpoetry.com/opoem/show/29816-Paul-Verlaine-Clair-De-Lune (accessed December 2009)
2. *All Music Guide to Classical Music,* All Media Guide, LLC, Ann Arbor, MI, 2005, 355.

Page 66
1. Verbier Festival. www.verbierfestival.com (accessed November 2009)

Page 70
1. Steen, Michael. *The Lives & Times of the Great Composers.* Oxford University Press, 2004, 163.
2. Encyclopedia of World Biography. "Wolfgang Amadeus Mozart." http://www.notablebiographies.com/Mo-Ni/Mozart-Wolfgang-Amadeus.html (accessed January 2010)

Page 71
1. *All Music Guide to Classical Music,* All Media Guide, LLC, Ann Arbor, MI, 2005, 1057.
2. Ibid

Page 76
1. Aspen Daily News Online. Williamson, Damien, Time Out Staff Writer. "60 Years of Aspen Music Festival and School." July 3, 2009 (accessed November 2009) http://www.aspendailynews.com/section/entertainment/135294 (accessed November 2009)
2. Aspen Music Festival. http://www.aspenmusicfestival.com/ (accessed November 2009)

Page 80
1. Allmusic.com. Schrott, Allen. "Claude Debussy." http://www.allmusic.com/cg/amg.dll?p=amg&sql=41:7223~T1 (accessed December 2009)
2. mhhe.com. "Claude Debussy (1862-1918)." McGraw-Hill Companies, Inc., 1998. http://www.allmusic.com/cg/amg.dll?p=amg&sql=41:7223~T1 (accessed December 2009)

Page 81
1. Libbey, Ted. *The NPR Listener's Encyclopedia of Classical Music,* Workman Publishing, New York, NY, 2006, 676-677.

Page 86
1. The Boston Globe. Eichler, Jeremy. "Monteverdi's Romans, speaking to the present." June 9, 2009. http://www.boston.com/ae/theater_arts/articles/2009/06/09/boston_early_music_festival_stages_a_monteverdi_masterpiece/ (accessed January 2010)
2. Boston Early Music Festival. www.bemf.org (accessed January 2010)
3. Ibid.

Page 90
1. Rollinat, Charles. "Liszt and Chopin: A Chapter of Remembrances." *The New York Times,* 1874. (Translated from French for *The New York Times.*) http://query.nytimes.com/gst/abstract.html?res=9F0DE3DD173DE43BBC4C53DFB667838F669FDE (accessed October 2009)
2. Walker, Alan. *Franz Liszt: v.1, The Virtuoso years, 1811-1847.* Cornell, 1987. http://www.materialized.com/liszt/ (accessed October 2009)

Page 91
1. *All Music Guide to Classical Music,* All Media Guide, LLC, Ann Arbor, MI, 2005, 286.

Page 96
1. Mendelssohn 2009. http://www.men-delssohn-2009.org/index.php?option=com_content&task=view&id=598Itemid=55&lang=en (accessed November 2009)

Page 100
1. Allmusic.com. Rodman, Michael. "Franz Liszt." http://www.allmusic.com/cg/amg.dll?p=amg&sql=41:7627~T1 (accessed February 2010)
2. Steen, Michael. *The Lives & Times of the Great Composers.* Oxford University Press, 2004, 426.

Page 108
1. Palisca, Claude V.. "Baroque." In *Grove Music Online. Oxford Music Online,* http://www.oxfordmusiconline.proxy.libraries.rutgers.edu/subscriber/article/grove/music/02097 (accessed January 2010)

Page 110
1. Guffman, Peter. "Hector Berlioz: Symphonie Fantastique." ClassicalNotes.net, 2002. http://www.classicalnotes.net/classics/berliozsym.html (accessed October 2009)
2. Steen, Michael. *The Lives & Times of the Great Composers.* Oxford University Press, 2004.

Page 111
1. *All Music Guide to Classical Music,* All Media Guide, LLC, Ann Arbor, MI, 2005, 1162.

Page 112
1. "Il dolce suono" Lyrics and Text Translation The "Mad Scene" from Donizetti's Lucia di Lammermoor By Aaron Green, About.com Guide, Translation by Ilya Speranza

Page 115
1. The Japanese TImes Online. Iuchi, Chiho. "Suntory Hall in 'ruins' for Mozart production." 6 March, 2009. http://search.japantimes.co.jp/cgi-bin/fm20090306a1.html (accessed February 2010)
2. Adam Fischer & Haydn Orchestra Fan Club. "Concert Halls of the World." http://www.haydnphil.org/en/newsletter/hallwrld.htm#SUNTORYHALL (accessed February 2010)
3. Suntory. "Facilities: Main Hall." http://www.suntory.com/culture-sports/suntoryhall/facilities/index.html (accessed February 2010)
4. Suntory. "Facilites: Karajan Platz in ARK Hills Corner." http://www.suntory.com/culture-sports/suntoryhall/facilities/hallmap08.html#here (accessed February 2010)

Page 116
1. Puccini Festival. www.puccinifestival.it (accessed October 2009)
2. Ibid.

Page 120
1. Gifford, Katya. "Antonin Dvorák-Biography." http://www.humanitiesweb.org/human.

php?s=r&p=a&a=i&ID=745 (accessed January 2010)
2. WWNorton.com. "Antonin Dvorak." http://www.wwnorton.com/college/music/enj9/shorter/composers/dvorak.htm#bio (accessed January 2010)

Page 126
1. Bernheimer, Martin. *The Financial Times.* Aug. 24, 2005.

Page 128
1. Downs, Philip G. (1992). *Classical Music: The Era of Haydn, Mozart, and Beethoven,* Norton Introduction to Music History, Volume 4. W.W. Norton & Company. ISBN 039395191X (hardcover).

Page 130
1. Giuseppe-Verdi.net. "Giuseppe Verdi Biography." Nov. 12, 2007. http://www.giuseppe-verdi.net/giuseppe-verdi-biography/ (accessed October 2009)
2. Music Academy Online. "Giuseppe Verdi." http://www.musicacademyonline.com/composer/biographies.php?bid=55 (accessed November 2009)

Page 131
1. "Ave Maria." www.carols.org.uk/ave-maria.htm (accessed December 2009)

Page 135
1. Musikverein. "The Musikverein." http://www.musikverein.at/dermusikverein/dermusikverein.asp (accessed November 2009)
2. Musikverein. "A Golden Sound in the Golden Hall." http://www.musikverein.at/dermusikverein/goldenerklang.asp (accessed November 2009)
3. WeinTourismus. "Haydn exhibitions in the Musikverein." 2009. http://www.wien.info/en/music-stage-shows/city-of-music/exhibitions-in-musikverein (accessed November 2009)

Page 140
1. Cummings, Robert. "Johann Sebastian Bach." Allmusic.com. http://www.allmusic.com/cg/amg.dll?p=amg&sql=41:6980~T1 (accessed December 2009)
2. Baroquemusic.com. "Johann Sebastian Bach." http://www.baroquemusic.org/bqxjsbach.html (accessed December 2009)
3. Encyclopedia of World Biography. "Johann Sebastian Bach." http://www.notablebiographies.com/Ba-Be/Bach-Johann-Sebastian.html (accessed December 2009)
4. Eidam, Klaus. *The True Life of J.S. Bach.* Basic Books, 2001, 118.

Page 145
1. Place des Arts. "History of Place des Arts." http://www.pda.qc.ca/infos/rensgeneraux/historique.en.html (accessed February 2010)

Page 146
1. Dresden Music Festival. http://www.musikfestspiele.com/cms/en/home/ (accessed January 2010)

Page 148
1. Downs, Philip G. *Classical Music: The Era of Haydn, Mozart, and Beethoven,* Norton Introduction to Music History, Volume 4. W.W. Norton & Company, 1992.

Page 150
1. Perlis, Vivian and Van Cleve, Libby. *Composers' Voices from Ives to Ellington: An Oral History of American Music.* Yale University Press, 2005, 285, 287.
2. Encyclopedia of World Biography. "Aaron Copland." http://www.notablebiographies.com/Co-Da/Copland-Aaron.html (accessed

November 2009)
3. 1. Perlis, Vivian and Van Cleve, Libby. *Composers' Voices from Ives to Ellington: An Oral History of American Music.* Yale University Press, 2005, 285, 287.

Page 151
1. Libbey, Ted. *The NPR Listener's Encyclopedia of Classical Music.* New York: Workman Publishing, 2006, 613.

Page 155
1. Royal Opera House. "Our History." http://www.roh.org.uk/discover/royaloperahouse/history.aspx (accessed December 2009)

Page 156
1. Times Online. Morrison, Richard. "The Joys of Glyndebourne: As the family-run festival turns 75, Richard Morrison examines the magic of Glyndebourne." May 9, 2009. http://entertainment.timesonline.co.uk/tol/arts_and_entertainment/music/classical/article6248616.ece (accessed October 2009)
2. Glyndeybourne Festival. http://www.glyndebourne.com (accessed October 2009)
3. Ibid, Times Online.

Page 160
1. Schirmer.com. "Charles Ives." G. Shirmer, Inc. and Associated Music Publishers, Inc., 2009. http://www.schirmer.com/default.aspx?TabId=2419&State_2872=2&ComposerId_2872=764 (accessed November 2009)
2. Encyclopaedia Britannica Online. "Charles Ives." http://www.britannica.com/EBchecked/topic/298255/Charles-Edward-Ives (accessed November 2009)
3. Perlis, Vivian and Van Cleve, Libby. *Composers' Voices from Ives to Ellington: An Oral History of American Music.* Yale University Press, 2005, 8.

Page 161
1. Jones, David Wyn. Decca [Liner Notes] # 289 473 846-2, 2003.

Page 165
1. Budapest.com. "Pesti Vigado." http://www.budapest.com/protected_monuments/pesti_vigado.en.html (accessed February 2010)
2. Tabula S. Kiado. "History of the Vigado." http://www.tabulas.hu/vigado/english/history.html (accessed February 2010)
3. Tabula S. Kiado. "Foundation for Art and Community Culture." http://www.tabulas.hu/vigado/english/foundat.html (accessed February 2010)
4. Tabula S. Kiado. "Present of the Pesti Vigado." http://www.tabulas.hu/vigado/english/present.html (accessed February 2010)

Page 166
1. Oregon Bach Festival. www.oregonbachfestival.com (accessed January 2010)

Page 168
1. Downs, Philip G. *Classical Music: The Era of Haydn, Mozart, and Beethoven,* Norton Introduction to Music History, Volume 4. W.W. Norton & Company, 1992.

Page 170
1. Humanities Web.com. Gifford, Katya. "Igor Stravinsky-Biography." http://www.humanitiesweb.org/human.php?s=c&p=a&a=i&ID=756 (accessed November 2009)
2. Stravinsky, Igor and Craft, Robert. *Memories and Commentaries,* new one-volume edition, Faber & Faber, 2002, 91.

Page 171
1. *All Music Guide to Classical Music.* Ann Arbor,

MI: All Media Guide, LLC, 2005, 1314.

Page 172
1. Met Opera Family. http://www.metoperafamily.org/metopera/season/production.aspx?id=8106 (accessed November 2009)

Page 176
1. Rossini Opera Festival. http://www.rossinioperafestival.it/index.php?id=42&L=1 (accessed December 2009)
2. The Telegraph. Allison, John. "Italy's annual Rossini festival celebrates its 30th birthday in style." Aug. 14, 2009. http://www.telegraph.co.uk/culture/music/classicalconcertreviews/6029603/Rossini-Opera-Festival-review.html (accessed December 2009)

Page 179
1. Lamb, Andrew. "Waltz (i)." Oxford Music Online (accessed January 2010).

Page 180
1. Gillies, Malcolm. *Bartók Remembered.* New York: W.W. Norton & Company, 1990, 3, 33.
2. Activemusician. "Belá Bartók." 2000-2009 http://www.activemusician.com/Bela-Bartok-Biography--t8i255 (accessed October 2009)

Page 186
1. Edinburgh International Festival. http://www.eif.co.uk/ (accessed December 2009)
2. Ibid.

Page 190
1. Gifford, Katya. "Gustav Holst-Biography." 1998-2007. Humanities Web. http://www.humanitiesweb.org/human.php?s=c&p=a&a=i&ID=754 (accessed October 2009)
2. Lace, Ian. "A Biography of Gustav Holst." 1995. Gustav Holst. http://www.gustavholst.info/biography/index.php?chapter=5 (accessed October 2009)

Page 191
1. Horton, John. "Ibsen, Grieg, and 'Peer Gynt.'" Oxford Journals: Music and Letters. Oxford University Press, 1945. http://ml.oxfordjournals.org/cgi/pdf_extract/XXVI/2/66 (accessed February 2010)

Page 192
1. Faust Programme Note Synopsis. G. Schirmer, Inc. http://www.schirmer.com/Default.aspx?TabId=2420&State_2874=2&workId_2874=28419

Page 195
1. TourMyCountry.com. "Wiener Konzerthaus: Vienna Concert Hall and Akademietheater Theatre." http://www.tourmycountry.com/austria/wiener-konzerthaus.htm (accessed November 2009)

Page 196
1. Calgary's News and Entertainment Weekly. Lafortune, Wes. "Banff arts fest planning a culture spree." May 13, 2004. www.ffwdweekly.com/Issues/2004/0513/festival.htm (accessed November 2009)

Page 200
1. Brown, Maurice J.E. "Franz Schubert Biography." Encyclopaedia Brittanica, 1994-2009. http://www.biography.com/articles/Franz-Schubert-9475558?part=0 (accessed October 2009)

Page 201
1. *All Music Guide to Classical Music.* Ann Arbor, MI: All Media Guide, LLC, 2005, 1340.

Page 202
1. The Metropolitan Opera International

Radio Broadcast Information Center, Opera Background, Gounod's Romeo et Juliette. http://archive.operainfo.org/broadcast/opera-Background.cgi?id=114&language=1 (accessed December 2009)

Page 205
1. Budapest Tourist Guide. "Budapest Opera House Great Architecture and Performances." http://www.budapest-tourist-guide.com/budapest-opera.html (accessed November 2009)

Page 210
1. Metropolitan News Company (MNC.net). Herresthal, Harald. "Edvard Grieg." http://www.mnc.net/norway/GRIEG.HTM (accessed November 2009)
2. Ibid.

Page 215
1. PBS. "Stravinsky's The Rite of Spring." http://www.pbs.org/keepingscore/stravinsky-rite-of-spring.html (accessed November 2009)
2. Cityvox.co.uk. "Theatre des Champs-Elysees." http://www.eng.cityvox.fr/shows_paris/theatre-des-champs-elysees-paris_103100005/profile-place (accessed November 2009)

Page 220
1. Glickman, Sylvia and Scleifer, Martha. *From Convent to Concert Hall: A Guide to Women Composers*. Greenwood Press, 2003, 228-229.
2. MusicianGuide.com. "Nadia Boulanger Biography." http://www.musicianguide.com/biographies/1608004698/Nadia-Boulanger.html (accessed November 2009)
3. Ibid.

Page 221
1. Kavanaugh, Patrick. "Orchestra Music." *Music of the Great Composers: A Listener's Guide to the Best of Classical Music*. Zondervan: Grand Rapids, MI, 1996, 56.

Page 224
1. Appel, Willi. *Harvard Dictionary of Music*. Cambridge, MA: Harvard University Press, 1965, 593.

Page 225
1. Gewandhaus zu Leipzig. "The Gewandhaus Orchestra." 11 November 2009. http://www.gewandhaus.de/gwh.site,postext,history-gewandhausorchester.html (accessed November 2009)

Page 228
1. Grout, Donald J., and Claude V. Palisca. *A History of Western Music*, 4th ed. New York: W.W. Norton & Company, 1988.

Page 230
1. Sorenson, Sugi. "Prokofiev Biography: Childhood (1891-1904)." Prokofiev. http://www.prokofiev.org/biography/childhood.html (accessed January 2010)
2. Sorenson, Sugi. "Prokofiev Biography: Enfant Terrible-The Conservatory Years (1904-1914)." Prokofiev. http://www.prokofiev.org/biography/conserv.html (accessed January 2010)
3. Allmusic.com. "Sergey Prokofiev." http://www.allmusic.com/cg/amg.dll?p=amg&sql=41:7863~T1 (accessed January 2010)

Page 235
1. Bolshoi Theatre. "Concept of artistic development for the Bolshoi Theatre of Russia: 2004-2010. http://www.bolshoi.ru/en/theatre/mission/ (accessed November 2009)

Page 236
1. Hayes, Florence. "Ottawa International Chamber Music Festival." The Canadian Encyclopedia, 2010. http://www.thecanadianencyclo-pedia.com/index.cfm?PgNm=TCE&Params=U1ARTU0004098 (accessed February 2010)
2. Littler, William. "Ottawa Chamber Music Festival hits high notes." August 1, 2009. The [Toronto] Star. http://www.thestar.com/entertainment/article/674379 (accessed February 2010)

Page 238
1. "Impressionism, in music." *The Columbia Encyclopedia* 6th ed. New York: Columbia University Press. http://www.bartleby.com/65/im/impress-mus.html. (accessed November 2009)

Page 240
1. Encyclopedia of World Biography. "Antonio Vivaldi." http://www.notablebiographies.com/Tu-We/Vivaldi-Antonio.html (accessed January 2010)
2. Baroquemusic. "Antonio Vivaldi." http://www.baroquemusic.org/bqxvivaldi.html (accessed January 2010)
3. Essentialsofmusic. "Antonio Vivaldi." http://www.essentialsofmusic.com/composer/vivaldi.html (accessed January 2010)

Page 241
1. Libbey, Ted. *The NPR Listener's Encyclopedia of Classical Music*. New York: Workman Publishing, 2006. 220.

Page 246
1. Rabin, Carol Price. *Music Festivals in America*. Massachusetts: Berkshire Traveller Press (an imprint of Berkshire House), 1990, 56-57.

Page 250
1. Biography. "Richard Strauss." http://www.biography.com/articles/Richard-Strauss-9497013?part=3 (accessed December 2009)
2. Arizona Opera. "Richard Strauss." http://www.evermore.com/azo/c_bios/rstrauss.php3 (accessed December 2009)

Page 251
1. *All Music Guide to Classical Music*. Ann Arbor, MI: All Media Guide, LLC, 2005, 1381.

Page 255
1. Opera Chic. "Patricia "Petibombs" Petibon Badly Booed at La Scala in "Alcina," Carsen Booed, Too." http://www.operachic.typepad.com/opera_chic/2009/03/breaking-news-patricia-petibombs-petibon-badly-booed-la-scala-in-alcina-carsen-booed-too.html (accessed December 2009)l

Page 256
1. Stradaviri Museum and Gli Archi Del Palazzo Comunale [Brochure]. Cremona Commune de Cremona, Ufficio Turism (Tourism Office).

Page 258
1. Dennis, Flora and Powell, Johnathon. "Futurism." *Grove Music Online*. Oxford Music Online. http://www.oxfordmusiconline.com.proxy.libraries.rutgers.edu/subscriber/article/grove/music/10420 (accessed February 2010)

Page 260
1. Allmusic.com. Jeremy Grimshaw. "Claudio Monteverdi." http://www.allmusic.com/cg/amg.dll?p=amg&sql=41:7738~T1 (accessed November 2009)
2. GoldbergWeb. "Claudio Monteverdi." Goldberg, 2003. http://www.goldbergweb.com/en/history/composers/11561.php (accessed November 2009)

Page 261
1. Libbey, Ted. *The NPR Listener's Encyclopedia of Classical Music*. New York: Workman Publishing, 2006, 15-16.

Page 264
1. Appel, Willi. *Harvard Dictionary of Music*. Cambridge, MA: Harvard University Press, 1965, 619.

Page 266
1. Salzburg Festival. http://www.salzburgerfestspiele.at/ (accessed December 2009)

Page 270
1. The Free Information Society. Dunder, Jonathan. "Dmitri Shostakovich Biography." http://www.freeinfosociety.com/site.php?postnum=786 (accessed January 2010)
2. Los Angeles Times. Pasles, Chris. "Was He or Wasn't He?" November 29, 1998. http://www.smsymphony.org/sms9899/shostakovich.html (accessed January 2010)

Page 275
1. Staatsoper under den linden. "history of the staatsoper." http://www.staatsoper-berlin.org/en_EN/content/opera_history (accessed December 2009)

Page 276
1. Boston Symphony Orchestra. http://www.bso.org/bso/index.jsp;jsessionid=O5Z30ROV5KX0ICTFQMGSFEQ?id=bcat5240070 (accessed October 2009)

Page 280
1. Sibelius Museum. "Jean Sibelius." http://web.abo.fi/fak/hf/musik/Sibelius/EN/4.htm (accessed November 2009)
2. Cummings, Robert. Allmusic.com. "Jean Sibelius." http://www.allmusic.com/cg/amg.dll?p=amg&sql=41:7975~T1 (accessed November 2009)

Page 286
1. *The New Yorker*. Ross, Alex. "The Music Mountain: The classical world's most coveted retreat." June 29, 2009.
2. Rabin, Carol Price. *Music Festivals in America*. Massachusetts: Berkshire Traveller Press (an imprint of Berkshire House), 1990, 142.
3. Ibid, *The New Yorker*.

Page 288
1. Nyman, Michael. *Experimental Music: Cage and Beyond*. Second edition. Cambridge and New York: Cambridge University Press, 1999.

Page 290
1. Baroquemusic.org. "George Frideric Handel." http://www.baroquemusic.org/bqxhandel.html (accessed November 2009)
2. Kavanaugh, Patrick. *Spiritual Lives of the Great Composers*. Zondervan Publishing House, 1996. http://www.messiahcd.com/Information/about_The_Messiah/about_the_messiah.html (accessed November 2009)
3. Ibid.

Page 295
1. LA Phil. "About Walt Disney Concert Hall." http://www.laphil.com/philpedia/wdch-overview.cfm (accessed February 2010)
2. arcspace. Goldberg, Paul. "Frank O. Gehry & Partners Walt Disney Concert Hall." http://www.arcspace.com/architects/gehry/disney2/ (accessed February 2010)
3. http://www.u-s-history.com/Pages/h3088.html (accessed February 2010)

Page 296
1. The New York Times. Loomis, Geroge. "Commanding, Time and Again." August 26, 2009. http://www.nytimes.com/2009/08/26/arts/26iht-loomis.html (accessed December 2009)

Page 299

1. 19th Century Music. Darcy, Warren. "Rotational form, teleological genesis, and fantasy-projection in the slow movement of Mahler's Sixth Symphony." July 2001, 49-74.

2. Kinderman, William and Rae Syer, Katherine (eds.) *A Companion to Wagner's Parsifal*. Camden House, 2005, 225.

Page 300

1. Essentialsofmusic.com. "Franz Joseph Haydn." http://www.essentialsofmusic.com/composer/haydn.html (accessed December 2009)

Page 304

1. Nicolas Slonimsky; Music Since 1900, 1971 New York; Charles Scribner's Sons; "Atonality," 1429.

Page 305

1. Opernhaus. http://www.opernhaus.ch/e/opernhaus/geschichtehaus.php (accessed February 2010)

2. Zurich. http://www.zuerich.com/en/Page.cfm/zurich/culture?category=&subcat=oper&id=5088 (accessed February 2010)

Page 310

1. Allmusic.com. "Edward Elgar." http://www.allmusic.com/cg/amg.dll?p=amg&sql=41:1882~T1 (accessed January 2010)

Page 311

1. *All Music Guide to Classical Music*. Ann Arbor, MI: All Media Guide, LLC, 2005, 751.

Page 315

1. Teatro Carlo Felice Fondazione. "Storia." http://www.carlofelice.it/teatro.asp?imgPath1=theatre&imgPath2=theatre&itemID=22010&level=3&ParentZ=2020&label=history (accessed February 2010)

Page 318

1. Potter, Keith. *Four Musical Minimalists: La Monte Young, Terry Riley, Steve Reich, Philip Glass*. Music in the Twentieth Century series. Cambridge and New York: Cambridge University Press, 2000.

Page 319

1. Sisman, Elaine. "Chaconne." *The New Harvard Dictionary of Music*, Don Michael Randel (ed). Cambridge, MA: Harvard University Press, 1986.

Page 320

1. Columbia Encyclopedia via Answers.com. "François Couperin." Columbia University Press, 2003. http://www.answers.com/topic/fran-ois-couperin (accessed January 2010)

2. Allmusic.com. Cummings, Robert. "François Couperin." http://www.allmusic.com/cg/amg.dll?p=amg&sql=41:1445~T1 (accessed January 2010)

Page 321

1. Libbey, Ted. *The NPR Listener's Encyclopedia of Classical Music*. New York: Workman Publishing, 2006, 498.

2. Ibid.

Page 330

1. Essentialsofmusic.com. "Robert Schumann." http://www.essentialsofmusic.com/composer/schumann_r.html (accessed January 2010)

2. Allmusic.com. Minderovic, Zoran. "Robert Schumann." http://www.allmusic.com/cg/amg.dll?p=amg&sql=41:7956~T1 (accessed January 2010)

Page 331

1. *All Music Guide to Classical Music*. Ann Arbor, MI: All Media Guide, LLC, 2005, 1221.

Page 334

1. Slonimsky, Nicolas. *Music Since 1900*, 4th Edition. New York: Charles Scribner's Sons, 1971, 1501-1502.

Page 335

1. Salzburg Festival. http://www.salzburger-festspiele.at/spielstaette/oid/129/ (accessed February 2010)

2. Osterfestspiele Salzburg. http://www.osterfestspiele-salzburg.at/en/festival/philosophy (accessed February 2010)

3. Großes Festspielhaus. http://www.salzburg.info/en/art_culture/salzburg_festival/grosses_festspielhaus.htm (accessed February 2010)

Page 338

1. Bernard, Jonathan W. 2003. "Minimalism, Post-minimalism, and the Resurgence of Tonality in Recent American Music." *American Music* 21, no. 1 (Spring): 112–33.

Page 340

1. Allmusic.com. Cummings, Robert. "Clara Wieck Schumann." http://www.allmusic.com/cg/amg.dll?p=amg&sql=41:7955~T1 (accessed November 2009)

2. Glickman, Sylvia and Scleifer, Martha. *From Convent to Concert Hall: A Guide to Women Composers*. Greenwood Press, 2003, 160.

Page 341

1. *All Music Guide to Classical Music*. Ann Arbor, MI: All Media Guide, LLC, 2005, 104.

Page 345

1. National Theater Concert Hall. http://www.ntch.edu.tw/englishAbout/showHistory (accessed February 2010)

2. National Theater Concert Hall. http://www.ntch.edu.tw/englishPlace/show?categoryName=engperformance (accessed February 2010)

3. Taiwan. http://www.taiwan.com.au/Envtra/Taipei/report08.html (accessed February 2010)

Page 350

1. Glickman, Sylvia and Scleifer, Martha Furman. *From Convent to Concert Hall: A Guide to Women Composers*. Greenwood Press, 2003, 181.

Page 351

1. *All Music Guide to Classical Music*. Ann Arbor, MI: All Media Guide, LLC, 2005, 1151

2. Ibid.

Page 355

1. Festspielhaus. "What began as a fiasco…" http://www.festspielhaus.de/en/your-visit/history-development/ (accessed February 2010)

2. MusicalCriticism.com. "Festspielhaus Baden-Baden announce 2009-10 season." 7 May 2009. http://musicalcriticism.com/news/baden-baden-0910-0509.shtml (accessed February 2010)

Page 360

1. Allmusic.com. Eddins, Stephen. "Maurice Ravel." http://www.allmusic.com/cg/amg.dll?p=amg&sql=41:7873~T1 (accessed February 2010)

2. Humanitiesweb.com. Gifford, Katya. "Maurice Ravel-Biography." http://www.humanitiesweb.org/human.php?s=c&p=a&a=i&ID=755 (accessed February 2010)

3. Allmusic.com. Eddins, Stephen. "Maurice Ravel." http://www.allmusic.com/cg/amg.dll?p=amg&sql=41:7873~T1 (accessed February 2010)

Page 361

1. Moon, Tom. *1,000 Recordings to Hear Before You Die*. New York: Workman Publishing, 2008, 38.

Page 362

1. Classical Net. Gian Carlo Menotti. http://www.classical.net/music/comp.lst/menotti.php (accessed February 2010)

2. Oxford Journals. The Opera Quarterly, The Consul. Gian Carlo Menotti http://oq.oxfordjournals.org/cgi/pdf_extract/16/4/696 (accessed February 2010)

3. G. Schirmer, Inc. Synopsis. http://www.schirmer.com/Default.aspx?TabId=2420&State_2874=2&workId_2874=30696 (accessed February 2010)

Page 365

1. The Berliner Philharmoniker Digital Concert Hall. http://dch.berliner-philharmoniker.de/ (accessed December 2009)

Page 366

1. Rabin, Carol Price. *Music Festivals in America*. Massachusetts: Berkshire Traveller Press (an imprint of Berkshire House), 1990, 136.

Page 370

1. Allmusic.com. Cummings, Robert. "Pyotr Il'yich Tchaikovsky." http://www.allmusic.com/cg/amg.dll?p=amg&sql=41:6177~T1 (accessed January 2010)

2. Encyclopedia of World Biography. "Peter Ilyich Tchaikovsky." http://www.notablebiographies.com/St-Tr/Tchaikovsky-Peter-Ilyich.html (accessed January 2010)

3. Steen, Michael. *The Life and Times of the Great Composers*. Oxford University Press, 2004, 661,669.

Page 371

1. Ould, Barry Peter. Notes for Hyperion CDA67279, *Percy Grainger: Rambles and Reflections—Piano Transcriptions*, Piers Lane, piano.

Additional Image Credits

About the Authors

Leslie Chew (LMC) is a Grammy-nominated recording engineer in Los Angeles, California. He has recorded nearly every instrument in today's symphonic orchestra, while helping artists create music for award-winning albums, films, television, and software. He enjoys music as a passion as well as a career, playing guitar and singing in the acoustic duo StuccoRainbow. Visit www.lesliechew.com.

Dwight DeReiter (DD) has worked in the music world much of his life, most recently with Capitol-EMI Music as Label Director for Western USA. As a classical music specialist, he has worked in marketing and sales, artist relations, film and television placement, public relations, and special markets. He is presently composing and producing orchestral scores for film and television projects in Los Angeles, California.

Cathy Crenshaw Doheny (CCD) holds a Bachelor of Music in vocal performance from the University of North Carolina School of the Arts and has sung mezzo-soprano roles with several regional opera companies. Equally at home creating drama in the literary world, she writes award-winning creative nonfiction and journalistic pieces in Charlotte, North Carolina, where she lives with her husband, Kevin, and daughter, Jade.

Colin Gilbert (CKG) is a freelance writer, photographer, and tutor living in Southern California. His unquenchable love of all kinds of music has manifested itself through a long history of studying, collecting, performing, and reviewing a wide variety of musical genres. Colin and his wife, Elizabeth, first bonded over a shared fondness of Rachmaninov's Piano Concerto No. 2.

Kathy Federici Greenwood (KFG) is the books and arts editor at Princeton University's alumni magazine, where she interviews musicians, composers, poets, and artists. When she isn't writing stories, she helps restore her family's 18th-century farmhouse in West Amwell Township, New Jersey. Katherine holds a Bachelor of Arts in theology from Georgetown University and a Master of Arts in journalism from New York University.

Travers Huff (TH) holds a Master of Music degree in composition from the Eastman School of Music in Rochester, New York. He is a jazz pianist and composer-arranger for film, working in Los Angeles, California. He especially enjoys film and the visual arts, as well as improvising music to literature, paintings, and comic books.